AZADI

AZADI

*Fascism, Fiction, and Freedom
in the Time of the Virus*

Arundhati Roy

Haymarket Books
Chicago, Illinois

Paperback edition published in 2022 by
Haymarket Books
P.O. Box 180165
Chicago, IL 60618
773-583-7884
www.haymarketbooks.org
info@haymarketbooks.org

ISBN: 978-1-64259-706-6

Distributed to the trade in the US through Consortium Book Sales and Distribution (www.cbsd.com) and internationally through Ingram Publisher Services International (www.ingramcontent.com).

This book was published with the generous support of Lannan Foundation and Wallace Action Fund.

Special discounts are available for bulk purchases by organizations and institutions. Please call 773-583-7884 or email info@haymarketbooks.org for more information.

Cover design by Abby Weintraub.

Printed in Canada by union labor.

Library of Congress Cataloging-in-Publication data is available.

10 9 8 7 6 5 4 3 2 1

May tomorrow be more than just another name for today.
—Eduardo Galeano

Table of Contents

Introduction   1

1. In What Language Does Rain Fall Over
    Tormented Cities? The Weather Underground
    in *The Ministry of Utmost Happiness*   7
2. Election Season in a Dangerous Democracy   47
3. Our Captured, Wounded Hearts   57
4. The Language of Literature   65
5. The Silence Is the Loudest Sound   83
6. Intimations of an Ending:
    The Rise and Rise of the Hindu Nation   97
7. The Graveyard Talks Back:
    Fiction in the Time of Fake News   135
8. There Is Fire in the Ducts, the System Is Failing   175
9. The Pandemic Is a Portal   181
10. A Battle for Love   193
11. Freedom Side: Tribunal against
    State Terror and White Supremacy   207
12. Two Conspiracies and a Cremation   215
13. India's Day of Shame   227
14. My Post-Lockdown Reverie   235
15. We Are Witnessing a Crime Against Humanity:
    The Politics of India's Covid Catastrophe   239
16. We Need a Government   257

Acknowledgments   261
Notes   263
Index   291

Introduction

While we were discussing the title of this book, my publisher in the United Kingdom, Simon Prosser, asked me what I thought of when I thought of *Azadi*. I surprised myself by answering, without a moment's hesitation, "A novel." Because a novel gives a writer the freedom to be as complicated as she wants—to move through worlds, languages, and time, through societies, communities, and politics. A novel can be endlessly complicated, layered, but that is not the same as being loose, baggy, or random. A novel, to me, is freedom with responsibility. Real, unfettered azadi—freedom. Some of the essays in this volume have been written through the eyes of a novelist and the universe of her novels. Some of them are about how fiction joins the world and *becomes* the world. All were written between 2018 and 2020, two years that in India have felt like two hundred. In this time, as the Corona pandemic burns through us, our world is passing through a portal. We have journeyed to a place from which it looks unlikely that we can return, at least not without some kind of serious rupture with the past—social, political, economic, and ideological.

The last essay in this collection is about that. Coronavirus has brought with it another, more terrible understanding of

Azadi. The Free Virus that has made nonsense of international borders, incarcerated whole populations, and brought the modern world to a halt like nothing else ever could. It casts a different light on the lives we have lived so far. It forces us to question the values we have built modern societies on—what we have chosen to worship and what to cast aside. As we pass through this portal into another kind of world, we will have to ask ourselves what we want to take with us and what we will leave behind. We may not always have a choice—but not thinking about it will not be an option. And in order to think about it, we need an even deeper understanding of the world gone by, of the devastation we have caused to our planet and the deep injustice between fellow human beings that we have come to accept. Hopefully, some of these essays, written before the pandemic came upon us, will go some small way towards helping us negotiate the rupture. Or, if nothing else, a moment in history that was recorded by a writer, like a metaphorical runway before the aircraft we're all in took off for an unknown destination. A matter of academic interest for future historians.

The first essay is the W. G. Sebald Lecture on Literary Translation, which I delivered in the British Library in London in June 2018. Much of it is about how the messy partitioning of the language we knew as Hindustani into two separate languages with two separate scripts—now sadly and somewhat arbitrarily called Hindi and Urdu (in which erroneously Hindi is associated with Hindus and Urdu with Muslims)—presaged the current project of Hindu nationalism by more than a century.

Many of us hoped that 2018 would be the last year of the reign of Narendra Modi and his Hindu nationalist party. The early essays in this collection reflect that hope. As the 2019 general election approached, polls showed Modi and his party's popularity dropping dramatically. We knew this was a dangerous moment. Many of us anticipated a false-flag attack or even a war that would be sure to change the mood of the country. One of the essays—"Election Season in a Dangerous Democracy" (September 3, 2018)—is, among other things, about this fear. We held our collective breath. In February 2019, weeks before the general election, the attack came. A suicide bomber blew himself up in Kashmir, killing forty security personnel. False flag or not, the timing was perfect. Modi and the Bharatiya Janata Party swept back to power.

And now, only a year into his second term, through a series of horrifying moves that this book deals with, Modi has changed India beyond recognition. The infrastructure of fascism is staring us in the face, the pandemic is speeding up that process in unimaginable ways, and yet we hesitate to call it by its name.

I started to write this introduction while US president Donald Trump and his family were on an official visit to India in the last week of February 2020. So it too has had to pass through the rupture, the pandemic portal. The first case of coronavirus in India had been reported on January 30. Nobody, least of all the government, paid any attention. It had been more than two hundred days since the state of Jammu and Kashmir had been stripped of its special status and placed under an information siege, and more than two months since a new anti-Muslim, unconstitutional citizenship law had brought millions of protesters onto the streets of India. In a public speech to a crowd wearing Modi and Trump masks, Donald Trump informed Indians that they play cricket, celebrate Diwali, and make Bollywood films. We were grateful to learn that about ourselves. Between the lines he sold us MH-60 helicopters worth $3 billion. Rarely has India publicly humiliated herself thus.

Not far from the Grand Presidential Suite of the Delhi hotel where Trump spent the night, and Hyderabad House, where he held trade talks with Modi, Delhi was burning. Armed Hindu vigilante mobs in northeast Delhi, backed by the police, attacked Muslims in working-class neighborhoods. Violence had been in the air for a while, with politicians belonging to the ruling party delivering open threats to Muslim women conducting peaceful sit-in protests against the new citizenship law. When the attack began, police were seen either standing aside or backing up the mob. Muslims fought back. Houses, shops, vehicles were burned. Many, including a policeman, were killed. Many more were hospitalized with gunshot wounds. Horrifying videos flew around the internet. In one of them, grievously wounded young Muslim men, laid out on the street, some piled against each other by uniformed policemen, are being forced to sing the National Anthem. (Subsequently one of them, Faizan, died from having a policeman's baton pushed down his throat.)[1]

Trump made no comment on the horror swirling around him. Instead he conferred on Narendra Modi, the most divisive, hateful political figure in modern India, the title "Father of the Nation." Until recently, this was Gandhi's title. I am no fan of Gandhi, but surely, even he did not deserve this.

After Trump left, the violence went on for days. More than fifty people lost their lives. About three hundred were admitted into hospital with grievous wounds. Thousands of people moved into refugee camps. In Parliament, the home minister praised himself and the police. Members of the ruling party gave speeches to their smirking supporters in which they more or less blamed Muslims for provoking the violence, for attacking themselves, burning their own shops and homes, and throwing their own bodies into the open sewage canals that crisscross their neighborhood. Every effort was made by the ruling party, its social media trolls, and the electronic media it controls to portray the violence as a Hindu–Muslim "riot." It was not a riot. It was an attempted pogrom against Muslims, led by an armed, fascist mob.

And while the dead bodies were still surfacing in the filth, Indian government officials held their first meeting about the virus. When Modi announced the nationwide lockdown on March 24, India spilled out her terrible secrets for all the world to see.

What lies ahead?

Reimagining the world. Only that.

April 6, 2020

CHAPTER 1

In What Language Does Rain Fall Over Tormented Cities?

The Weather Underground in
The Ministry of Utmost Happiness

A t a book reading in Kolkata, about a week after my first
novel, *The God of Small Things,* was published, a member
of the audience stood up and asked, in a tone that was
distinctly hostile: "Has any writer ever written a masterpiece in
an alien language? In a language other than his mother tongue?"

I hadn't claimed to have written a masterpiece (nor to be
a "he"), but nevertheless I understood his anger toward me,
a writer who lived in India, wrote in English, and who had
attracted an absurd amount of attention. My answer to his ques-

* The W. G. Sebald Lecture on Literary Translation, delivered at the British
Library, June 5, 2018. Previously published in *Literary Hub*, July 25, 2018,
and in *Raiot*, June 27, 2018.

tion made him even angrier. "Nabokov," I said. And he stormed out of the hall.

The correct answer to that question today would of course be "algorithms." Artificial Intelligence, we are told, can write masterpieces in any language and translate them into masterpieces in other languages. As the era that we know, and think we vaguely understand, comes to a close, perhaps we, even the most privileged among us, are just a group of redundant humans gathered here with an arcane interest in language generated by fellow redundants.

Only a few weeks after the mother tongue/masterpiece incident, I was on a live radio show in London. The other guest was an English historian, who, in reply to a question from the interviewer, composed a paean to British imperialism. "Even you," he said, turning to me imperiously, "the very fact that you write in English is a tribute to the British Empire."

Not being used to radio shows at the time, I stayed quiet for a while, as a well-behaved, recently civilized savage should. But then I sort of lost it, and said some extremely hurtful things. The historian was upset, and after the show told me that he had meant what he said as a compliment, because he loved my book. I asked him if he also felt that jazz, the blues, and all African-American writing and poetry were actually a tribute to slavery. And whether all of Latin American literature was a tribute to Spanish and Portuguese colonialism.

Notwithstanding my anger, on both occasions my responses were defensive reactions, not adequate answers. Because those incidents touched on a range of incendiary questions—regarding colonialism, nationalism, authenticity, elitism, nativism, caste, and cultural identity—all jarring pressure points on the nervous system of any writer worth her salt. However, to reify language in the way both of these men had renders language speechless. When that happens, as it usually does in debates like these, what has actually been written ceases to matter. That was what I found so hard to countenance. And yet I know—I knew—that language is that most private and yet most public of things. The challenges thrown at me were fair and square. And obviously, since I'm still talking about them, I'm still thinking about them.

The night of that reading in Kolkata, city of my estranged father and of Kali, Mother Goddess with the long red tongue and many arms, I fell to wondering what my mother tongue actually was. What was—is—the politically correct, culturally apposite, and morally appropriate language in which I ought to think and write? It occurred to me that my mother was actually an alien, with fewer arms than Kali perhaps but many more tongues. English is certainly one of them. My English has been widened and deepened by the rhythms and cadences of my alien mother's other tongues. I say *alien* because there's not much that is organic about her. Her nation-shaped body was first violently assimilated and then violently dismembered by an imperial British quill. I also say *alien* because the violence unleashed in her name on those who do not wish to belong to her (Kashmiris, for example), as well as on those who do (Indian Muslims and Dalits, for example), makes her an extremely unmotherly mother.

How many tongues does she have? Officially, approximately 780, only 22 of which are formally recognized by the Indian Constitution, while another 38 are waiting to be accorded that status. Each has its own history of colonizing or being colonized. There are few pure victims or pure perpetrators. There is no national language. Not yet. Hindi and English are designated "official languages." According to the Constitution of India (which, we must note, was written in English), the use of English by the state for official purposes was supposed to have ceased by January 26, 1965, fifteen years after the document came into effect. Hindi, written in the Devanagari script, was to take its place.[1] However, any serious move toward making Hindi the national language has been met with riots in non-Hindi-speaking regions of the country. (Imagine trying to impose a single language on all of Europe.) So, English has continued—guiltily, unofficially, and by default—to consolidate its base. Guilt in this case is an unhelpful sentiment. India as a country, a nation-state, was a British idea. So, the idea of English is as good or as bad as the idea of India itself. Writing or speaking in English is not a tribute to the British Empire, as the British imperial historian had tried to suggest; it is a practical solution to the circumstances created by it.

Fundamentally, India is in many ways still an empire, its territories held together by its armed forces and administered from Delhi, which, for most of her subjects, is as distant as any foreign metropole. If India had broken up into language republics, as countries in Europe did, then perhaps English could now be done away with. But even still, not really, not any time soon. As things stand, English, although it is spoken by a small minority (which still numbers in the tens of millions), is the language of mobility, of opportunity, of the courts, of the national press, the legal fraternity, of science, engineering, and international communication. It is the language of privilege and exclusion. It is also the language of emancipation, the language in which privilege has been eloquently denounced. *Annihilation of Caste* by Dr. B. R. Ambedkar, the most widely read, widely translated, and devastating denunciation of the Hindu caste system, was written in English. It revolutionized the debate on perhaps the most brutal system of institutionalized injustice that any society has ever dreamed up. How different things would have been had the privileged castes managed to contain Ambedkar's writing in a language that only his own caste and community could read. Inspired by him, many Dalit activists today see the denial of a quality English education to the underprivileged (in the name of nationalism or anticolonialism) as a continuation of the Brahmin tradition of denying education and literacy—or, for that matter, simply the right to pursue knowledge and accumulate wealth—to people they consider "shudras" and "outcastes." To make this point, in 2011 the Dalit scholar Chandra Bhan Prasad built a village temple to the Dalit goddess of English. "She is the symbol of Dalit Renaissance," he said. "We will use English to rise up the ladder and become free forever."[2]

As the wrecking ball of the new global economic order goes about its work, moving some people toward the light, pushing others into darkness, the "knowing" and the "not knowing" of English plays a great part in allocating light and darkness.

It is onto this mind-bending mosaic that the current Hindu nationalist ruling dispensation is trying to graft its "one nation, one religion, one language" vision. Since its inception in the 1920s, the rallying cry of the RSS (Rashtriya Swayamsevak Sangh)—Hindu nationalism's holding company and the most powerful organization in India today—has been "Hindi-Hindu-Hindustan." Ironically, all three are words derived from the Persian-Arabic *al-Hind*, and Hindustan—its suffix *-stan* (place) not to be confused with *sthan*, which also means "place," in Sanskrit—was the region that lay east of the River Indus. "Hindus" were the peoples (not the religion) that lived there. It would be too much to expect the RSS to learn from other countries' experiences, but when the Islamic Republic of Pakistan tried to impose Urdu on its Bengali-speaking citizens in East Pakistan, it ended up losing half of itself. Sri Lanka tried to impose Sinhala on its Tamil citizens, and paid with decades of bloody civil war.

All this is to say that we in India live and work (and write) in a complicated land, in which nothing is or ever will be settled. Especially not the question of language. Languages.

Susan Sontag was surely aware of some of this complexity when she delivered the W. G. Sebald lecture in 2002. Her lecture was called "The World as India: Translation as a Passport within the Community of Literature." What I'll talk about is "Translation as a Writing Strategy in a Community without Passports."

§

Twenty years after the publication of *The God of Small Things*, I finished writing my second novel, *The Ministry of Utmost Happiness*. Perhaps I shouldn't say this, but if a novel can have an enemy, then the enemy of this novel is the idea of "one nation, one religion, one language." As I composed the cover page of my manuscript, in place of the author's name, I was tempted to write: "Translated from the original(s) by Arundhati Roy." *The Ministry* is a novel written in English but imagined in several languages. Translation as a *primary* form of creation was central to the writing of it (and here I don't mean the translation of the inchoate and the pre-lingual into words). Regardless of in which language (and in whose mother tongue) *The Ministry* was written, this particular narrative about these particular people in this particular universe had to be imagined in several languages. It is a story that emerges out of an ocean of languages, in which a teeming ecosystem of living creatures—official-language fish, unofficial-dialect mollusks, and flashing shoals of word-fish— swim around, some friendly with each other, some openly hostile, and some outright carnivorous. But they are all nourished by what the ocean provides. And all of them, like the people in *The Ministry*, have no choice but to coexist, to survive, and to try to understand each other. For them, translation is not a high-end literary art performed by sophisticated polyglots. Translation is daily life, it is street activity, and it's increasingly a necessary part of ordinary folk's survival kit. And so, in this novel of many languages, it is not only the author but also the characters themselves who swim around in an ocean of exquisite imperfection, who constantly translate for and to each other, who constantly speak across languages, and who constantly realize that people who speak the same language are not necessarily the ones who understand each other best.

The Ministry of Utmost Happiness has been—is being—translated into forty-eight languages. Each of those translators has had to grapple with a language that is infused with many languages including, if I may coin a word, many kinds of Englishes (*sociolects* is perhaps the correct word, but I'll stay with *Englishes* because it is deliciously worse) and translate it into another language that is *infused* with many languages. I use the word *infused* advisedly, because I am not speaking merely of a text that contains a smattering of quotations or words in other languages as a gimmick or a trope, or one that plays the Peter Sellers game of mocking Indian English, but of an attempt to actually create a *companionship* of languages.

Of the forty-eight translations, two are Urdu and Hindi. As we will soon see, the very requirement of having to name Hindi and Urdu as separate languages, and publish them as separate books with separate scripts, contains a history that is folded into the story of *The Ministry*. Given the setting of the novel, the Hindi and Urdu translations are, in part, a sort of homecoming. I soon learned that this did nothing to ease the task of the translators. To give you an example: the human body and its organs play an important part in *The Ministry*. We found that Urdu, that most exquisite of languages, which has more words for love than perhaps any other in the world, has no word for vagina. There are words like the Arabic *furj*, which is considered to be archaic and more or less obsolete, and there are euphemisms that range in meaning from "hidden part," "breathing hole," "vent," and "path to the uterus." The most commonly used one is *aurat ki sharamgah*, "a woman's place of shame." As you can see, we had trouble on our hands. Before we rush to judgment, we must remember that *pudenda* in Latin means "that whereof one should feel shame." In Danish, I was told by my translator, the phrase is "lips of shame." So, Adam and Eve are alive and well, their fig leaves firmly in place.

Although I am tempted to say more about witnessing the pleasures and difficulties of *The Ministry of Utmost Happiness* being translated into other languages, more than the "post-writing" translations, it is the "pre-writing" translation that I want to talk about today. None of it came from an elaborate, preexisting plan. I worked purely by instinct. It is only while preparing for this lecture that I began to see just how much it mattered to me to persuade languages to shift around, to make room for each other. Before we dive into the Ocean of Imperfection and get caught up in the eddies and whirlpools of our historic blood feuds and language wars, in order to give you a rough idea of the terrain, I will quickly chart the route by which I arrived at my particular patch of the shoreline.

My mother is a Syrian Christian from Kerala—the Malayalam-speaking southernmost tip of the Indian peninsula. My father was a Bengali from Kolkata, which is where the two met. At the time, he was visiting from Assam, where he had a job as an assistant manager of a tea garden. The language they had in common was English. I was born in the Welsh Mission Hospital in the little town of Shillong, then in Assam, now the capital of the state of Meghalaya. The predominant hill tribe in Shillong is the Khasi, their language an Austroasiatic one, related to Cambodian and Mon. The Welsh missionaries of Shillong, like missionaries all over India, went to great lengths to turn oral languages into written ones, primarily in order to translate and print the Bible. As part of their own campaign to preserve the Welsh language against the tidal wave of English, they ensured that while Khasi is written in Roman script, its orthography is similar to that of Welsh.

The first two years of my life were spent in Assam. Even before I was born, my parents' relationship had broken down irretrievably. While they quarreled, I was farmed out to the tea plantation workers' quarters, where I learned my first language, which my mother informs me was a kind of Hindi. The tea workers, living on starvation wages, were (and are) among the most brutally oppressed and exploited people in India. They are descendants of indigenous tribespeople of eastern and central India, whose own languages had been broken down and subsumed into Baganiya, which literally means "garden language." It is a patois of Hindi, Axomiya, and their own languages. Baganiya was the language I first spoke. I was less than three years old when my parents separated. My mother, my brother, and I moved to South India—first to Ootacamund in Tamil Nadu and then (unwelcomed) to my grandmother's home in Ayemenem, the village in Kerala where *The God of Small Things* is set. I soon forgot my Baganiya. (Many years later, when I was in my twenties, I encountered my cheerful but distressingly alcoholic father for the first time. The very first question he asked me was, "Do you still use bad language?" I had no idea what he meant. "Oh, you were a terrible, foul-mouthed little girl," he said, and went on to tell me about how, when he had accidentally brushed a lit cigarette against my arm, I had glared at him and called him a "choo . . . ya"—an expletive in several languages, including Baganiya, whose etymology derives from the Latin word *pudenda*.)

When I was five, my utterly moneyless mother started her own school by renting, by day, a small hall that belonged to the Rotary Club in the town of Kottayam, a short bus ride away. Every evening we would pack away our tables and chairs, and put them out again in the morning. I grew up on a cultural diet that included Shakespeare, Kipling, Kathakali (a temple dance form), and *The Sound of Music*, as well as Malayalam and Tamil cinema. Before I reached my teenage years, I could recite long passages of Shakespeare, sing Christian hymns in the mournful Malayali way, and mimic a cabaret from the outlandish Tamil film called *Jesus* which Mary Magdalene performs to (literally) seduce Jesus at a party, before things began to go badly wrong for both of them.

As her little school grew successful, my mother, anxious about my career prospects, decreed that I was to speak only in English.[3] Even in my off time. Each time I was caught speaking Malayalam, I was made to write what was called an imposition—*I will speak in English, I will speak in English*—a thousand times. Many hours of many afternoons were spent doing this (until I learned to recycle my impositions). At the age of ten, I was sent to a boarding school in Tamil Nadu, founded by the British hero Sir Henry Lawrence, who died defending the British Residency during the siege of Lucknow in the 1857 "Indian Mutiny." He authored a legal code in the Punjab that forbade forced labor, infanticide, and the practice of *sati*, self-immolation by widows. Hard as it may be to accept, things aren't always as simple as they're made out to be.

The motto of our school was "Never Give In." Many of us students believed (with no real basis) that what Lawrence had actually said was, "Never Give In—to the Indian Dogs." In boarding school, in addition to Malayalam and English, I learned Hindi. My Hindi teacher was a Malayali who taught us a kind of Hindi in a kind of Malayalam. We understood nothing. We learned very little.

At sixteen, I finished school and found myself alone on a train to Delhi, which was three days and two nights away. (I didn't know then that I was leaving home for good.) I was going to join the School of Architecture. I was armed with a single sentence of Hindi that I somehow remembered. It was from a lesson called *Swamibhakt Kutiya*, about a faithful dog who saves her master's baby from a snake by getting herself bitten instead. The sentence was: *Subah uth ke dekha to kutiya mari padi thi*, "When I woke up in the morning, the bitch lay dead." For the first few months in Delhi, it was my only contribution to any conversation or question addressed to me in Hindi. Over the years, this is the slender foundation on which, as my Malayalam became rusty, I built my Hindi vocabulary.

The architecture school hostel was, obviously, populated by out-of-towners. Mostly non-Hindi speakers. Bengalis, Assamese, Nagas, Manipuris, Nepalese, Sikkimese, Goans, Tamilians, Malayalees, Afghans. My first roommate was Kashmiri. My second

Nepali. My closest friend was from Orissa. He spoke neither English nor Hindi. For most of our first year, we communicated in shared spliffs, sketches, cartoons, and maps drawn on the backs of envelopes—his extraordinary, mine mediocre. In time, we all learned to communicate with each other in standard Delhi University patois—a combination of English and Hindi—which was the language of my first screenplay, *In Which Annie Gives It Those Ones*, set in a fictional architecture school during the dope-smoking, bell-bottom-wearing era of the 1970s. Annie was the nickname of a male student, Anand Grover, repeating his final year for the fourth time. "Giving it those ones" meant "doing his or her usual thing." In Annie's case, that meant peddling his pet thesis about reviving the rural economy and reversing rural–urban migration by planting fruit trees on either side of the hundreds of thousands of miles of railway tracks in India. Why the railway tracks? Because "general *janta*" (ordinary folks) "shits near the railway tracks anyway, *hai na*? So the soil is bloody fertile, yaar." Directed by Pradip Krishen, the no-budget film was made on what must have been the cost of backup clapboards for a modest Hollywood movie.

Our publicity brochure for the film (which no one was really interested in) had the following quotes:

> "You'll have to change the title, because 'Giving It Those Ones' doesn't mean anything in English."
>
> —Derek Malcolm of *The Guardian*,
> waking up suddenly in the middle of the film

> "Obviously, Mr. Malcolm, in England you don't
> speak English anymore."
>
> —Arundhati Roy, later,
> wishing she had thought of it earlier

The film was shown just once, late at night on Doordarshan, state television. It went on to win two National Awards—one for the Best Screenplay and the other, my favorite award of all time, for Best Film in Languages Other Than Those Specified in Schedule VIII of the Indian Constitution. (I should say here that, in 2015, we returned both awards as part of a protest initiated by writers and filmmakers against what we saw as the current government's complicity in a series of assassinations of writers and rationalist thinkers, as well as the daylight lynching of Muslims and Dalits by mobs of vigilantes. It didn't help. The lynching continues, and we have run out of National Awards to return.)[4]

Writing screenplays—I wrote two—taught me to write dialogue. And it taught me how to write sparely and economically. But then I began to yearn for excess. I longed to write about the landscape of my childhood, about the people in Ayemenem, about the river that flowed through it, the trees that bent into it, the moon, the sky, the fish, the songs, the History House, and the unnamed terrors that lurked around. I could not bear the idea of writing something that began with *Scene 1. Ext. Day. River.* I wanted to write a stubbornly visual but unfilmable book. That book turned out to be *The God of Small Things*. I wrote it in English, but imagined it in English as well as Malayalam, the landscapes and languages colliding in the heads of seven-year-old twins Esthappen and Rahel, turning into a thing of its own. So, for example, when their mother, Ammu, scolds the twins and tells them that if they ever disobey her in public she will send them somewhere where they learn to "jolly well behave"—it's the "well" that jumps out at them. The deep, moss-lined well that you find in the compounds of many homes in Kerala, with a pulley and a bucket and a rope, the well children are sternly warned to stay away from until they are big enough to draw water. What could a Jolly Well possibly be? A well with happy people in it. But *people* in a well? They'd have to be dead, of course. So, in Estha's and Rahel's imagination, a Jolly Well becomes a well full of laughing dead people, into which children are sent to learn to behave. The whole novel is constructed around people, young and old, English-knowing and Malayalam-knowing, all grappling, wrestling, dancing, and rejoicing in language.

For me, or for most contemporary writers working in these parts, language can never be a given. It has to be made. It has to be cooked. Slow-cooked.

It was only after writing *The God of Small Things* that I felt the blood in my veins flow more freely. It was an unimaginable relief to have finally found a language that tasted like mine. A language in which I could write the way I think. A language that freed me. The relief didn't last long. As Estha always knew, "things can change in a day."[5]

In March 1998, less than a year after *The God of Small Things* was published, a Hindu nationalist government came to power.

The first thing it did was to conduct a series of nuclear tests. Something convulsed. Something changed. It was about language again. Not a writer's private language, but a country's public language, its public imagination of itself. Suddenly, things that would have been unthinkable to say in public became acceptable. Officially acceptable. Virile national pride, which had more to do with hate than love, flowed like noxious lava on the streets. Dismayed by the celebrations even in the most unexpected quarters, I wrote my first political essay, "The End of Imagination." My language changed, too. It wasn't slow-cooked. It wasn't secret, novel-writing language. It was quick, urgent, and public. And it was straight-up English.

Rereading "The End of Imagination" now, it is sobering to see how clear the warning signs were, to anybody, just about anybody, who cared to heed them:

> "These are not just nuclear tests, they are nationalism tests," we were repeatedly told.
>
> This has been hammered home, over and over again. The bomb is India. India is the bomb. Not just India, Hindu India. Therefore, be warned, any criticism of it is not just antinational, but anti-Hindu. (Of course, in Pakistan the bomb is Islamic. Other than that, politically, the same physics applies.) This is one of the unexpected perks of having a nuclear bomb. Not only can the government use it to threaten the Enemy, it can use it to declare war on its own people. Us . . .
>
> Why does it all seem so familiar? Is it because, even as you watch, reality dissolves and seamlessly rushes forward into the silent, black-and-white images from old films—scenes of people being hounded out of their lives, rounded up and herded

into camps? Of massacre, of mayhem, of endless columns of broken people making their way to nowhere? Why is there no soundtrack? Why is the hall so quiet? Have I been seeing too many films? Am I mad? Or am I right?[6]

The mayhem came. On October 7, 2001, three weeks after the September 11 attacks, the Bharatiya Janata Party (BJP), then in power in the state of Gujarat, removed its elected chief minister, Keshubhai Patel, and appointed Narendra Modi, a rising star in the RSS, in his place. In February 2002, in an act of arson, sixty-eight Hindu pilgrims were burned to death in a train that had stopped in Godhra, a railway station in Gujarat. Local Muslims were held responsible. As "revenge," more than two thousand people, mostly Muslim, were slaughtered by Hindu mobs in broad daylight in the cities and villages of Gujarat. A hundred and fifty thousand were hounded out of their homes and herded into refugee camps.[7] It wasn't by any means the first massacre of members of a minority community in post-independence India, but it was the first that was telecast live into our homes. And the first, that was, in some senses, proudly "owned." I was wrong about there being no soundtrack.

"The End of Imagination" was the beginning of twenty years of essay writing for me. Almost every essay was immediately translated into Hindi, Malayalam, Marathi, Urdu, and Punjabi, often without my knowledge. As we watched mesmerized, religious fundamentalism and unbridled free-market fundamentalism, which had been unleashed in the early 1990s, waltzed arm in arm, like lovers, changing the landscape around us at a speed that was exhilarating for some, devastating for others. Huge infrastructure projects were displacing hundreds of thousands of the rural poor, setting them adrift into a world that didn't seem able to—or simply did not want to—see them. It was as though the city and the countryside had stopped being able to communicate with each other. It had nothing to do with language, but everything to do with translation. For example, judges sitting in the Supreme Court seemed unable to understand that, for a person who belonged to an indigenous tribe, their relationship with land could not simply be translated into money. (I was arraigned for contempt of court for saying, among other things, that paying Adivasis, indigenous tribespeople, cash compensation for their land was like paying Supreme Court judges their salaries in fertilizer bags.) Over the years, the essays opened secret worlds for me—the best kind of royalty that any writer could ask for. As I traveled, I encountered languages, stories, and people whose ways of thinking expanded me in ways I could never have imagined.

Somewhere along the way, slow-cooking began again. Folks began to drop in on me. Their visits grew more frequent, then longer, and eventually, pretty brazenly, they moved in with me: Anjum, an Urdu speaker from Old Delhi, came with her adopted daughter, Zainab, and a laconic, cloudy dog called Biroo. A young man who called himself Saddam Hussain showed up on a white horse he introduced as Payal. He said his real name was Dayachand and that he was a Chamar, a skinner from Jhajjhar in Haryana. He told me a terrible story about what had happened to his father. He spoke in a sort of Mewati-Rajasthani that I found hard to understand. He showed me a video of the execution of Saddam Hussein, the president of Iraq, that he kept on his cell phone. It was Hussein's courage at the moment of his death, he said, even if he had been a bastard, that had made Dayachand convert to Islam and take the name Saddam Hussain. I had no idea what the connection between the video and his father was.

A rail-thin man with his right arm in a plaster cast, his shirtsleeve flapping at his side, slid in like a shadow. He refused all offers of food and drink. The man handed me a piece of paper that said:

My Full Name: Dr. Azad Bhartiya (Translation: The Free Indian)

My Home Address: Dr. Azad Bhartiya, Near Lucky Sarai Railway Station, Lucky Sarai Basti, Kokar, Bihar

My Current Address: Dr. Azad Bhartiya, Jantar Mantar, New Delhi

My Qualifications: MA Hindi, MA Urdu (First Class First), BA History, BEd, Basic Elementary Course in Punjabi, MA Punjabi ABF (Appeared But Failed), PhD (pending), Delhi University (Comparative Religions and Buddhist Studies), Lecturer, Inter College, Ghaziabad, Research Associate, Jawaharlal Nehru University, New Delhi, Founder Member *Vishwa Samajwadi Sthapana* (World People's Forum) and Indian Socialist Democratic Party (Against Price-rise).

I offered him a cigarette. He went outside to smoke it, and returned only after a few weeks. That was the beginning of Dr. Bhartiya's drifting in and out of my home. It continues to this day.

The next to come was the opposite of a drifter. Biplab Dasgupta, from the Universe of English, was an officer of the elite intelligence services currently posted in Kabul. He asked me to call him what his friends called him—Garson Hobart—the name of the character he had played in a college play. He arrived with an expensive bottle of whisky, from which he drank steadily. He seated himself at my table and, without so much as asking, used my pen to start writing something, from which he never looked up except to occasionally enunciate the Latin name of a bird, as though he were checking the spelling by saying it out loud. Later it occurred to me that he might have been doing it to trouble future translators in whose languages the scientific taxonomy of birds and trees, with their genus and species names that identified each of them as unique, did not exist. Hobart's expression changed—in fact, almost everything about him changed—when my doorbell rang, and I found a man and woman standing outside. The woman turned out to be Hobart's tenant, who had apparently gone missing. Her name was Tilotamma, and the man with her was Musa, her Kashmiri lover who seemed to know Hobart, too. They came in carrying cartons of papers and files, and towers of dusty documents. She put up a few sheets of paper on the fridge and secured them with a magnet. It was a word list, an alphabetically organized lexicon:

Kashmiri–English Alphabet

A: Azadi/army/Allah/America/Attack/AK-47/Ammunition/
Ambush/Aatankwadi/Armed Forces Special Powers Act/Area
Domination/Al Badr/Al Mansoorian/Al Jehad/Afghan/Amar-
nath Yatra

B: BSF/body/blast/bullet/battalion/barbed wire/brust (burst)/ border cross/booby trap/bunker/byte/begaar (forced labour)

C: Cross-border/Crossfire/camp/civilian/curfew/Crackdown/ Cordon-and-Search/CRPF/ Checkpost/Counter-insurgency/ Ceasefire/Counter-Intelligence/Catch and Kill/Custodial Killing/Compensation/Cylinder (surrender)/Concertina wire/ Collaborator

D: Disappeared/Defence Spokesman/Double Cross/Double Agent/Disturbed Areas Act/Dead body

It went on to cover the whole of the English alphabet, all the way to Z. When I asked what it was for, she said it was to help innocent Indian tourists in Kashmir to communicate better with the locals. She betrayed no signs of sarcasm or irony. Musa said nothing. He melted into the surroundings so quickly that I forgot he was there.

After a while Tilotamma's ex-husband, Nagaraj Hariharan, came by, looking for her but pretending not to. For some reason, he had brought his mother-in-law Maryam Ipe's fat medical file from a Cochin hospital. He showed it to me, even though I made it clear that I had no interest in the blood profiles and oxygen saturation charts of complete strangers. It was only much later that I saw the notes that contained Maryam Ipe's ICU hallucinations. I could not have imagined that, if you study people's hallucinations long enough, they tell you more than volumes of sentient conversation ever could.

Major Amrik Singh, a tall Sikh officer of the Indian Army, arrived, denying several extrajudicial killings that I hadn't even accused him of, insisting that he was being made what he called

an "escape goat." Once he picked up on the generally non-accu-
satory atmosphere of his surroundings, he began to boast about
his counterintelligence operations and how he had passed himself
off as a Hindu, a Sikh, or a Punjabi-speaking Pakistani Muslim,
depending on what the particular covert operation demanded.

A baby girl appeared on the doorstep, unaccompanied. Anjum
moved in with astonishing speed, swooped her up, and would not
let anybody else come close for at least two weeks. A hand-delivered
letter arrived from the forests of Bastar. It was written in cramped,
tiny handwriting. English, as far as I could tell. It was addressed to
Dr. Azad Bhartiya, who, for some reason, read it aloud to Anjum,
translating it into Urdu on the fly:

Dear Comrade Azad Bharathiya Garu,

I am writing this to you because in my three days time in Jantar
Mantar I observed you carefully. If anybody knows where is my
child now, I think it might be you only. I am a Telugu woman
and sorry I don't know Hindi. My English is not good also. Sorry
for that. I am Revathy, working as a fulltimer with Communist
Party of India (Maoist). When you will receive this letter I will
be already killed . . .

My home became a commune and a confederacy of languages. Over time all of us housemates learned to talk to each
other, translate each other.

The new slow-cooking recipe involved considerable risk. I
had to throw the language of *The God of Small Things* off a very
tall building. And then go down (using the stairs) to gather up the
shattered pieces. So was born *The Ministry of Utmost Happiness*.

It is not necessary for readers of *The Ministry of Utmost Happiness* to know or understand the complicated map of languages that underpins it. If it were, if readers needed a field guide in order to properly understand the book, I'd consider myself a failure. To see it in bookshops sitting side by side with pulp fiction and political thrillers gives me nothing but pleasure. The fun and games with the Language Map is just that—an extra layer of fun and games. In truth, the Map of Languages of *The Ministry*, and their intertwining histories, could become a rather large book in itself. So, all I can do right now, just as an illustration of what I mean, is to drill below the surface of the first few chapters. I'll start with the opening sentence: "She lived in the graveyard like a tree."[8]

"She" is Anjum. She's middle-aged now, and has left her home in the Khwabgah (the House of Dreams), where she lived for years with a group of others like herself. The Muslim graveyard where she now lives is close to the walled city of Delhi. The first time she gives us a hint about who she really is begins at an intersection between two languages. The traffic policeman is none other than William Shakespeare himself.

> Long ago a man who knew English told her that her name written backwards (in English) spelled Majnu. In the English version of the story of Laila and Majnu, he said, Majnu was called Romeo and Laila was Juliet. She found that hilarious. "You mean I've made a *khichdi* of their story?" she asked. "What will they do when they find that Laila may actually be Majnu and Romi was really Juli?" The next time he saw her, the Man Who Knew English said he'd made a mistake. Her name spelled backwards would be Mujna, which wasn't a name and meant nothing at all.

To this she said, "It doesn't matter. I'm all of them, I'm Romi and Juli, I'm Laila and Majnu. *And* Mujna, why not? Who says my name is Anjum? I'm not Anjum, I'm Anjuman. I'm a *mehfil*, I'm a gathering. Of everybody and nobody, of everything and nothing. Is there anyone else you would like to invite? Everyone's invited."

The Man Who Knew English said it was clever of her to come up with that one. He said he'd never have thought of it himself. She said, "How could you have, with your standard of Urdu? What d'you think? English makes you clever automatically?"[9]

Anjum is born to Shia Muslim parents in Old Delhi, in the years soon after Independence. Her father, Mulaqat Ali, who traces his family's lineage directly back to the Mongol emperor Changez Khan, is a hakim, a doctor of herbal medicine who works for the family that makes the legendary sherbet Rooh Afza, which is Persian for "elixir of the soul." Her mother, Jahanara Begum, supplements the family income by stitching white Gandhi caps that she supplies to Hindu traders in Chandni Chowk. She is already the mother of three girls when Anjum is born.

In the second chapter, "Khwabgah," we witness Anjum's birth. In addition to her mother and the midwife, her mother tongue, too, is present. And found wanting:

Ahlam Baji, the midwife who delivered her and put her in her mother's arms wrapped in two shawls, said, "It's a boy." Given the circumstances, her error was understandable. . . .

The next morning, when the sun was up and the room nice and warm, she unswaddled little Aftab. She explored his tiny body—eyes nose head neck armpits fingers toes—with sated, unhurried delight. That was when she discovered, nestling underneath his boy-parts, a small, unformed, but undoubtedly girl-part. Is it possible for a mother to be terrified of her own baby? Jahanara Begum was. . . .

In Urdu, the only language she knew, all things, not just living things but *all* things—carpets, clothes, books, pens, musical instruments—had a gender. Everything was either masculine or feminine, man or woman. Everything except her baby. Yes of course she knew there was a word for those like him—*Hijra*. Two words actually, *Hijra* and *Kinnar*. But two words do not make a language.

Was it possible to live outside language? Naturally this question did not address itself to her in words, or as a single lucid sentence. It addressed itself to her as a soundless, embryonic howl.[10]

To live outside language—for a family whose lives are intricately, obsessively, wrapped up in language—is the crisis that Anjum's birth creates. For the first few years, Jahanara Begum manages to keep her secret. But then a time comes when she has to tell her husband. Mulaqat Ali is a man whose real passion is Urdu and Persian poetry. He has a formidable repertoire of couplets, and can produce one for every occasion, every mood, every subtle shift in the political climate. He believes that poetry can cure, or at least go a long way toward curing, almost every ailment, and prescribes poems to his patients instead of medicine. When he hears the secret that his wife has kept from him for so many years, and cannot find a poem to comfort himself with, he loses his moorings. He does his best to steady himself, to come to terms with it, but eventually is unable to.

It is when we meet Mulaqat Ali that we get our first hint of the fraught history of language that mirrors the fraught history of the Indian subcontinent. The churning that eventually culminated in the bloodshed of Partition partitioned not just land and people, but a language, too, making one part "Muslim" and the other "Hindu." This is a description of how Mulaqat Ali conducts himself with the shallow young journalists who from time to time arrive to interview him for various newspapers' weekend supplements about the exotic culture and cuisine of Old Delhi:

> Mulaqat Ali always welcomed visitors into his tiny rooms with the faded grace of a nobleman. He spoke of the past with dignity but never nostalgia. He described how, in the thirteenth century, his ancestors had ruled an empire that stretched from the countries that now called themselves Vietnam and Korea all the way to Hungary and the Balkans, from Northern Siberia to the Deccan plateau in India, the largest empire the world had ever known. He often ended the interview with a recitation of an Urdu couplet by one of his favorite poets, Mir Taqi Mir:

> *Jis sar ko ghurur aaj hai yaan taj-vari ka*
> *Kal uss pe yahin shor hai phir nauhagari ka*

> The head which today proudly flaunts a crown
> Will tomorrow, right here, in lamentation drown

> Most of his visitors, brash emissaries of a new ruling class, barely aware of their own youthful hubris, did not completely grasp the layered meaning of the couplet they had been offered, like a snack to be washed down by a thimble-sized cup of thick, sweet tea. They understood of course that it was a dirge for a fallen empire whose international borders had shrunk to a grimy ghetto circum-

scribed by the ruined walls of an old city. And yes, they realized that it was also a rueful comment on Mulaqat Ali's own strait-ened circumstances. What escaped them was that the couplet was a sly snack, a perfidious samosa, a warning wrapped in mourning, being offered with faux humility by an erudite man who had abso-lute faith in his listeners' ignorance of Urdu, a language which, like most of those who spoke it, was gradually being ghettoized.[11]

The language known variously as Urdu/Hindi/Hindustani, and, in an earlier era, Hindavi, was born on the streets and in the bazaars of North India. Khari Boli, spoken in and around Delhi and what is now western Uttar Pradesh, is the base language to which the Persian lexicon came to be added. Urdu, written in the Persian-Arabic script, was spoken by Hindus and Muslims across North India and the Deccan Plateau. It was not, as it is often made out to be, the high language of the court. That, in those days, was Persian. But neither was it, as it is often made out to be, the lan-guage of ordinary people everywhere. Urdu was the language of the street, but not necessarily the language spoken in the privacy of most ordinary people's homes, particularly not by the women. It came to be the formal language of literature and poetry for Hindus and Muslims alike. Urdu varied from region to region. Each region had its own high priests staking their claim to true pedigree. In fact, it saw its brightest hour as the Mughal Empire faded.

The partitioning of Urdu began in earnest in the second half of the nineteenth century, after the failed 1857 War of Indepen-dence (known to the British as the Mutiny), when India ceased to be merely an asset of the East India Company. The titular Mughal emperor, Bahadur Shah Zafar, was formally deposed, and India was brought directly under British rule. Muslims, seen as the main instigators of the uprising, came in for severe punishment and were treated with great suspicion by the British administration. Power bases began to shift, hierarchies changed, releasing suppressed resentment and new energies that began to seep through the cracks like smoke. As the old ideas of governing by fiat and military might began to metamorphose into modern ideas of representative government, old feudal communities began to coalesce into modern "constituencies" in order to leverage power and job opportunities. Obviously, the bigger the constituency, the greater the leverage.

Demography became vitally important, so the first British census was a source of huge anxiety. "Hindu" leaders turned their attention to the millions of people who belonged to the "untouchable" castes. In the past, in order to escape the stigma of caste, millions had converted to Islam, Sikhism, or Christianity. But now their religious conversion was viewed by the privileged castes as catastrophic. Reformists rushed in to stem the hemorrhage. Hinduism became an evangelical religion. Organizations of privileged-caste Hindus, who believed deeply in caste and believed themselves to be Aryans, descended from the European race, sought to keep Untouchables and indigenous tribespeople in the "Hindu fold" by performing *ghar wapsi* (returning home) ceremonies, a farce that was meant to symbolize "spiritual cleansing." In order to clearly define itself and mark itself off from other competing constituencies, the newly emerging Hindu constituency needed cultural symbols—something to fire the imagination of its evangelists and its potential recruits.

The holy cow and the holy script became the chosen vehicles for mobilization. *Gau rakshak* (cow protection) societies proliferated, and simultaneously the demand was raised that Devanagari (Deva as in Dio/God—the script of the Gods) be officially accepted as a second script for Urdu. Devanagari, originally known as Babhni, was the script of the Brahmins,[12] and had, like Sanskrit, been jealously guarded, its purity protected from the "polluting influence" of lower castes, who had for centuries been denied the right to learn Sanskrit. But the changing times now required that it be promoted as the indigenous script of "the people." In fact, the more widely used script at the time was one called Kaithi. But Kaithi was used by non-Brahmin castes like the Kayasthas, who were seen to be partial to Muslims. Extraordinarily, in a matter of a few decades, Kaithi was not just discarded but erased from public memory.[13]

To turn a battle for a new script into a popular social movement wasn't easy when the literacy rate of the population was in single digits. How is it possible to make people passionate about something that doesn't really affect them? The solution was simple but ingenious. In his erudite tract, *Hindi Nationalism*, Alok Rai writes in some detail of how the mobilization for Devanagari came to be fused with the call for Hindu unity, cow protection, and *ghar wapsi*. The Nagari Pracharini Sabhas (Societies for the Popularization of Nagari) and the *gau rakshak* and the *ghar wapsi* evangelists shared the same offices and office-bearers. They probably still do. The campaign for Devanagari had immediate and practical goals, too, such as eligibility for jobs in government offices, for which, at the time, reading Persian was a basic qualification. The campaign gained velocity and was buoyed by the resistance to it from the Muslim elite, including Muslim leaders with a vested interest in the status quo, such as the best-known reformist and modernizer of the time, Sir Syed Ahmed Khan. Here is his defense of retaining Persian-Arabic as the only official script: "Would our aristocracy like that a man of low caste and insignificant origin, though he be a B.A. or M.A. and have the requisite ability, should be in a position above them and have power in making the laws that affect their lives and property? Never!"[14]

It's extraordinary how sworn enemies can find common ground in each other's worst prejudices. As always, it was a battle of old and new elites lobbying for opportunity, the new ones, as always, disguising their own aspirations as the will of "the people."

The Devanagari movement's first victory came in April 1900, when Sir Anthony MacDonnell, lieutenant-governor of North-Western Provinces and Oudh, issued an order allowing the use of the Devanagari script in addition to the Persian script in the courts of the province. In a matter of months, Hindi and Urdu began to be referred to as separate languages. Language mandarins on both sides stepped in to partition the waters and apportion the word-fish. On the "Hindi" side, anything seen as Persian influence, as well as the influence of languages thought to be unsophisticated vernaculars, was gradually weeded out. (Somehow the words *Hindi*, *Hindu*, and *Hindustan* escaped the dragnet.) Sanskrit began to replace Persian. But Sanskrit was the language of ritual and scripture, the language of priests and holy men. Its vocabulary was not exactly forged on the anvil of everyday human experience. It was not the language of mortal love, or toil, or weariness, or yearning.

It was not the language of song or poetry of ordinary people. That would have been Awadhi, Maithili, Braj Bhasha, Bhojpuri, or one of a myriad other dialects. Rarely if ever has there been an example in history of an effort to deplete language rather than enrich it. It was like wanting to replace an ocean with an aquarium.

As the positions on both sides hardened, even the literary canons came to be partitioned. The "Urdu" canon erased the sublime, anti-caste Bhakti poets such as Kabir, Surdas, Meera, and Raskhan, a Muslim devotee of Krishna. The "Hindi" canon erased the greatest of Urdu poets, Mir and Ghalib. (Something similar is at work in the world of Hindustani classical music, although it hasn't yet had the misfortune of being formally divided into Hindu classical music and Muslim classical music.) Fortunately, progressive writers and poets, the very best of them, resisted this pressure. They continued to produce literature and poetry that were rich and deep and fully alert to what was being done to their language. But gradually, as the older generation passes, the newer one, whose formal education comes from "new" Hindi books and textbooks that have to be approved by government committees, will find it harder and harder to reclaim an ineffably beautiful legacy that is rightfully theirs.

It is for all these reasons that when Anjum's father, Mulaqat Ali, recites his Mir couplet, his warning wrapped in mourning, he is confident that his young guests—who belong to the generation of "new" Hindi—will not grasp its true meaning. He knows that his straitened material circumstances mirror the straitened vocabulary of his visitors.

Today, many of the younger generation of Urdu speakers in India cannot read the Persian script. They can read Urdu only in the Devanagari script. Urdu is seen not just as a Muslim language but as a *Pakistani* language. Which makes it almost criminal in some people's eyes. In March 2017 two Muslim members of the legislative assembly of Uttar Pradesh were prevented from taking their oath of office in Urdu.[15] A member of the Aligarh Municipal Corporation was charged with "intent to hurt religious sentiments" for trying to do the same.[16]

Although Hindi's victory has been a resounding one, it does not seem to have entirely allayed its keepers' anxieties. Perhaps that's because their enemies are dead poets who have a habit of refusing to really die. One of the sub-themes of the 2002 Gujarat massacre was poetry. As Anjum discovers to her cost when she travels to Gujarat with Zakir Mian, who was a friend of her father, Mulaqat Ali:

> He suggested that while they were in Ahmedabad they could visit the shrine of Wali Dakhani, the seventeenth-century Urdu poet, known as the Poet of Love, whom Mulaqat Ali had been immensely fond of, and seek his blessings too. They sealed their travel plans by laughingly reciting a couplet by him—one of Mulaqat Ali's favorites:
>
> *Jisey ishq ka tiir kaari lage*
> *Usey zindagi kyuun na bhari lage*
>
> For one struck down by Cupid's bow
> Life becomes burdensome, isn't that so?[17]

A few days later they set off by train, first to Ajmer and then to Ahmedabad. And then there's no news from them.

Nobody disagreed when Saeeda (who loved Anjum and was entirely unaware of Anjum's suspicions about her) suggested that the soap operas on TV be switched off and the news be switched on and left on in case, by some small chance, they could pick up a clue about what might have happened to Anjum and Zakir Mian. When flushed, animated TV news reporters shouted out their Pieces-to-Camera from the refugee camps where tens of thousands of Gujarat's Muslims now lived, in the Khwabgah they switched off the sound and scanned the background hoping to catch a glimpse of Anjum and Zakir Mian lining up for food or blankets, or huddled in a tent. They learned in passing that Wali Dakhani's shrine had been razed to the ground and a tarred road built over it, erasing every sign that it had ever existed. (Neither the police nor the mobs nor the Chief Minister could do anything about the people who continued to leave flowers in the middle of the new tarred road where the shrine used to be. When the flowers were crushed to paste under the wheels of fast cars, new flowers would appear. And what can anybody do about the connection between flowerpaste and poetry?)[18]

Why should a twenty-first-century mob be so angry with a poet who lived more than three hundred years ago? Wali Dakhani, the Wise Man of the Dakhan (Deccan), was a seventeenth-century poet who also came to be known as Wali Aurangabadi and Wali Gujarati. He wrote in Dakhani Urdu, an idiom that was not familiar to the court poets in the north, who wrote mostly in Persian at the time. Although he wrote in Urdu, Wali Dakhani was the first poet in the subcontinent to present his poetry in the form of a *diwan*—a collection that was formally arranged in the Persian tradition in which poems were presented in alphabetical order in three mandatory sections: *masnavi* (narrative poems), *marsiya* (elegiac poems commemorating the martyrdom of Hussain), and *kasida* (the tradition of singing praise to warriors). Wali Dakhani's *diwan* took the elite circle of poets, who all wrote in Persian, by storm. He became a cultural bridge between the north and the south, and the founding father of Urdu poetry.

The modern-day mob that destroyed his shrine, so high on nativism, could have just as easily valorized Wali Dakhani for being the man who influenced poets who wrote in Persian to write in Urdu, who turned the writing of Urdu into high literature. Because Urdu is nothing if not a language born on the streets of Hindustan. But, sadly, that's not how the story goes.

The destruction of Wali Dakhani's grave during the 2002 Gujarat massacre was not the only incident of its kind.[19] During those same weeks, in the city of Baroda, a mob attacked and damaged the grave of Ustad Faiyaz Khan, one of the most accomplished singers in the Hindustani classical tradition. Many years earlier, in a riot that took place during the 1970s, a mob burned down the house of Rasoolan Bai (Garson Hobart's favorite singer).[20] The only good thing to be said of this contemporary mob tradition is that it understands the dangers posed by art. And it has impeccable taste.

§

I will end this very long lecture with a short note about slogans and mantras in *The Ministry of Utmost Happiness*.

Anjum survives the Gujarat massacre because the mob that finds her lying over the corpse of Zakir Mian, feigning death, believes that killing hijras brings bad luck. So instead of killing her, they stand over her and make her chant their slogans:

> *Bharat Mata Ki Jai! Vande Mataram!*
>
> She did. Weeping, shaking, humiliated beyond her worst nightmare.
>
> Victory to Mother India! Salute the Mother!
>
> They left her alive. Unkilled. Unhurt. Neither folded nor unfolded. She alone. So that *they* might be blessed with good fortune.
>
> Butcher's Luck.
>
> That's all she was. And the longer she lived, the more good luck she brought them.[21]

Bharat, Hindustan, and India are names that are used interchangeably for the country we live in. "Akhand Bharat"— undivided India, which contains the territories of both Pakistan and Bangladesh—is the ideal of Hindu nationalists. Chanting *Bharat Mata Ki Jai!* (Victory to Mother India!) is seen by many as being patriotic and not necessarily Hindu nationalist. In less extenuating circumstances, Anjum would surely have shouted down, perhaps even beaten up those controversialists and unimaginative literalists who ask how King Bharata, whose realm was called Bharat, came to be a Mata (mother), and why India is a motherland and not a fatherland.

The second slogan she was forced to chant, *Vande Mataram*, usually translated as "Praise Be to Thee, Mother," is the title of a poem written by the popular Bengali writer Bankim Chandra Chattopadhyay that appears in *Anandamath*, his novel, first published in the 1880s. It is a novel that is, and always has been, greatly favored by Hindu nationalists because it created a template for the ideal Hindu warrior, the fantasy Hindu warrior, who rises in rebellion against his degenerate Muslim oppressors. *Anandamath* is a wonderful example of how, in the process of its telling of the past, literature can also mold the future. In the poem, the motherland is conflated with the Hindu goddess Durga. However, the first two stanzas came to be the unofficial anthem of the National Movement because they only mention "the mother," which lent itself to being interpreted by both Hindus and Muslims as a reference to Mother India. Although it was a much-loved song during the struggle against British colonialism, in today's atmosphere of a very different kind of nationalism, a bullying, coercive nationalism, people, Muslims in particular, many of whom are not unaware of the provenance of the poem "Vande Mataram," are often forced to chant it in full as a form of ritual humiliation. Ironically, a modern version of the poem was hugely popularized in a 1990s recording by the Sufi singer A. R. Rahman. Sadly, a once loved slogan has become controversial.

It is not unusual to have a Bengali slogan being chanted in non-Bengali-speaking states. Slogans in the subcontinent—whether they are being chanted by lynch mobs or protesters, by the right wing or the left, by people in territories under military occupation or protestors against big dams—are a performance directed *outward*, for the rest of the country and the rest of the world to hear, and therefore, quite often, are not in the local people's mother tongues. In Kashmir's massive protests, you will hear chanting in Urdu and in English, rarely in Kashmiri. The chant of *Azadi! Azadi!* ("Freedom! Freedom!") is Urdu—originally, Persian—and has probably traveled east from the Iranian Revolution to become the signature slogan of the Kashmiri freedom struggle, as well as, irony of ironies, the women's movement in India. At the opposite end of the country, down south in Kerala, I grew up to the resounding roar of *Inquilab Zindabad!* (Long Live the Revolution!) in Urdu, a language that local people neither speak nor understand. The other Communist Party slogan was *Swadandriyam, Janadhipathyam, Socialism, Zindabad!* (Freedom, Democracy, Socialism, Long Live!). That's Sanskrit, Malayalam, English, and Urdu in a single slogan.

I'll end with the journey of a mantra through *The Ministry of Utmost Happiness*.

Two months after Anjum and Zakir Mian go missing, and the murdering in Gujarat has begun to tail off, Zakir Mian's son, Mansoor, goes to Ahmedabad to look for his father. As a precaution, he shaves off his beard, hoping to pass as Hindu. He does not find his father, but finds a terrified Anjum, who has been enrolled in the men's section of a refugee camp, dressed in men's clothes, her hair cut short, and brings her back to the Khwabgah. She refuses to tell anybody what happened to her, but—haunted by memories of "how the men were folded and the women unfolded"—she takes a wailing young Zainab, her adopted daughter, to a barber, has her hair cut off, and dresses her in boy's clothes, "in case Gujarat comes to Delhi." The other precaution she takes is to teach Zainab to chant the Sanskrit Gayatri Mantra that she says she learned while she was in the camp in Gujarat. She says that many of the other refugees had learned it because they believed that, in mob situations, they could recite it to try to pass as Hindu. Neither Anjum nor Zainab has any idea what it means, but Zainab takes to it happily, chanting as she dresses for school and feeds her pet goat.

Om bhur bhuvah svaha
Tat savitur varenyam
Bhargo devasya dhimahi
Dhiyo yo nah pracodayat

O God, thou art the giver of life,
Remover of pain and sorrow,
Bestower of happiness,
O Creator of the Universe,
May we receive thy supreme sin-destroying light,
May thou guide our intellect in the right direction.[22]

The Gayatri Mantra appears three times in *The Ministry of Utmost Happiness*. The first time as a talisman against mob violence. The second time as promotional material in a British Airways commercial to attract customers from India's new and exponentially expanding middle class. And the third time in a fast food restaurant in a shopping mall. Zainab has grown up now, and is betrothed to a man named Saddam Hussain. Saddam tells them the story of how, years ago, his father was beaten to death by a mob outside a police station. The mall they were in, Saddam says, was exactly where that police station used to be. Zainab says she knows a Hindu prayer, and recites the Gayatri Mantra as a gesture of love for her future (as well as late) father-in-law.

Such are the ways in which Sanskrit has been finally been indigenized.

A few months after Anjum returns from Gujarat, ravaged and broken, unable to continue living her old life, she moves into the old graveyard, where she sets up home. Over the years, as she gradually recovers, she builds the Jannat (Paradise) Guest House. When Saddam Hussain joins her, they expand their business to include funeral services. The graveyard becomes a place where anybody—any *body*—that has been denied the grace of a funeral by the Duniya (the outside world) is given a dignified burial. Under the auspices of the Jannat Guest House and Funeral Services, depending on what the occasion calls for, prayers for the dead include the Fateha, singing "The Internationale" in Hindi, and reciting from Shakespeare's *Henry V*. In English.

So, how shall we answer Pablo Neruda's question that is the title of this lecture?

In what language does rain fall
over tormented cities?[23]

I'd say, without hesitation, in the Language of Translation.

CHAPTER 2

Election Season in a Dangerous Democracy

L ast Thursday's morning papers in India settled something that we have been debating for a while. A front-page report about the arrests of five political activists in the *Indian Express* was headlined, "Those Held Part of Anti-Fascist Plot to Overthrow Govt, Pune Police Tell Court."[1] We should know by now that we are up against a regime that its own police force calls fascist. In the India of today, to belong to a minority is a crime. To be murdered is a crime. To be lynched is a crime. To be poor is a crime. To defend the poor is to plot to overthrow the government.

When the Maharashtra state police conducted simultaneous raids on the homes of several well-known activists, poets, lawyers, and priests across the country, and arrested five people—three

*Delivered at a press conference in New Delhi on August 29, 2018. First published on August 29, 2018, as "#MeTooUrbanNaxal," in *The Wire*, *Scroll*, and other publications, and then published under this title in *New York Review of Books*, September 3, 2018.

high-profile civil rights defenders and two lawyers—on ludicrous charges, with little or no paperwork, the government would have known that it was stirring up outrage. It would have already taken all our reactions into account, including all the protests that have taken place across the country, before it made this move. So why has this happened?

Recent analyses of actual voter data, as well the most recent Lokniti-CSDS-ABP Mood of the Nation survey, have shown that the ruling Bharatiya Janata Party (BJP) and prime minister Narendra Modi are losing popularity at an alarming (for them) pace.[2] This means that we are entering dangerous times. There will be ruthless and continuous attempts to divert attention away from the reasons for this loss of popularity, and to fracture the growing solidarity of the opposition. It will be a constant circus from now until the elections in 2019—arrests, assassinations, lynchings, bomb attacks, false-flag attacks, riots, pogroms. We have learned to connect the season of elections with the onset of all kinds of violence. Divide and rule, yes. But add to that—divert and rule. From now until the elections, we will not know when, where, or how the fireball will fall on us, or what the nature of that fireball will be.

So, before I speak about the arrests of the lawyers and activists, let me reiterate a few points that we must not allow our attention to stray from, even while it rains fire and strange events befall us.

1. It has been a year and almost ten months since November 8, 2016, when Prime Minister Modi appeared on TV and announced his policy of demonetization of 80 percent of the

currency in circulation. His own cabinet seemed to have been taken by surprise. Now the Reserve Bank of India has announced that more than 99 percent of the currency was returned to the banking system. *The Guardian* reported that the policy has likely wiped 1 percent from the country's GDP and cost approximately 1.5 million jobs.[3] Meanwhile, just the printing of new currency has cost the country several thousand crores (a crore is 10 million rupees, equivalent to about $140,000). After demonetization came the Goods and Services Tax—a tax that is structured in ways that have dealt a further body blow to small and medium-sized businesses that were already reeling under demonetization.

While small businesses, traders, and, most of all, the poor have suffered enormously, several corporations close to the BJP have multiplied their wealth many times over. Businessmen like the Kingfisher Airlines and Beer magnate Vijay Mallya and the diamond merchant Nirav Modi have been permitted to decamp with thousands of crores of public money while the government looked away. What kind of accountability can we expect for all of this? None? Zero?

Throughout, as it prepares for the 2019 election, the BJP has emerged as the wealthiest political party in India by far. Outrageously, the recently introduced electoral bonds—promissory notes that donors can buy and donate anonymously to the political party of their choice—ensure that the sources of the wealth of political parties can remain hidden from public scrutiny.

2. We all remember the farce in Mumbai at the "Make in India" event inaugurated by Modi in 2016, at which a huge fire

burned down the main stage at the cultural festival. Well, the real bonfire of "Make in India" turned out to be the Rafale fighter plane deal with the French government, which was announced by the Indian prime minister in Paris in April 2015 seemingly without the knowledge of his own defense minister. This is against all known protocol. We know the bare bones: a deal had already been put in place in 2012 under the Congress-led United Progressive Alliance government to buy planes that would be assembled by the public-sector company Hindustan Aeronautics Limited. That deal was scrapped by Modi and reconfigured. Hindustan Aeronautics was surgically excised. The Congress Party, as well as several others who have studied the new deal, has alleged corruption on an unimaginable scale and accused the government of negotiating an "offset contract" for Reliance Defence Limited, a private-sector company in India that is deep in debt and has never built a plane in its life.[4]

The opposition has demanded a joint parliamentary committee probe. Can we expect one? Or must we swallow this whole fleet of planes along with everything else and not even gulp?

3. The investigation by the Karnataka state police into the assassination of the journalist and activist Gauri Lankesh has led to several arrests, which have, in turn, led to the unveiling of the activities of several right-wing Hindutva organizations, such as the extremist Sanatan Sanstha group. What has emerged is the existence of a shadowy, full-blown terrorist network, with hit lists, hideouts, and safe houses, flush with arms, ammunition, and plans to bomb, kill, and poison people.

How many of these groups do we know about? How many are continuing to work in secret? With the assurance that they have the blessings of the powerful, and possibly even the police, what plans do they have in store for us? What false-flag attacks? And what real ones? Where will they occur? Will it be in Kashmir? In Ayodhya? (Where the BJP has promised to build a temple in place of the Babri Masjid mosque, which was demolished in 1992 by a mob backed by senior leaders of the BJP.)[5] In Assam? (Where four million people have been excluded by the recently published National Register of Citizens.)[6] At the Kumbh Mela? (A Hindu festival at which up to ten million pilgrims gather.) How easily they could derail everything—*everything*—with some major, or even minor, attacks that are amplified by the government's pet media houses. To divert attention from this, the real threat, we have the hue and cry over the recent arrests.

4. The speed at which educational institutions are being dismantled. The destruction of universities with fine track records, the elevation of phantom universities that exist only on paper. This is arguably the saddest thing of all. It is happening in several ways. We are watching Jawaharlal Nehru University (JNU) being taken down before our very eyes. The students as well as the staff are under continuous attack. Several television channels have actively participated in spreading lies and fake videos that have endangered the lives of students, and these have led to an assassination attempt on the young scholar Umar Khalid, who has been mercilessly defamed.

Then you have the falsification of history and the "dunceification" of the syllabus, which will, just in a few years' time, lead to a kind of foolishness from which we will be unable to recover. Finally, the privatization of education is undoing even the very small good that the policy of reservation (the equivalent of what in the United States is called affirmative action) did. We are witnessing the re-Brahminization of education, this time fitted out in corporate clothes. Students from Dalit, Adivasi, and "Other Backward Caste" (OBC; the official government term) backgrounds are once again being pushed out from institutions of learning because they cannot afford the fees. This has begun to happen already. It is completely unacceptable.

5. Some other things we must not look away from: enormous distress in the agricultural sector, increasing numbers of farmers' suicides, the lynching of Muslims and the relentless attack on Dalits, the public floggings, the arrest of Chandrashekhar Azad, the leader of the Bhim Army (a Bahujan-rights organization), who dared to stand up to attacks by upper castes. The dilution of the legal protections for minority groups enacted in the 1989 Scheduled Caste and Scheduled Tribe (Prevention of Atrocities) Act.

Having said this much, I come to the recent arrests.

None of the five people who were arrested last week—Vernon Gonsalves, Arun Ferreira, Sudha Bharadwaj, Varavara Rao, and Gautam Navlakha—were present at the Elgar Parishad rally in Pune that took place on December 31, 2017, and was organized by two eminent retired judges, Justice Sawant and Justice Kolse-Patil, or at the rally the following day, when approximately three hundred thousand people, mostly Dalit, gathered to commemorate the two hundredth anniversary of the Bhima–Koregaon victory.

(Dalits joined the British to defeat an oppressive Peshwa regime—one of the few victories that Dalits can celebrate with pride.)

This second rally was attacked by Hindutva fanatics, which led to days of unrest. The two main people accused of fomenting this violence are Milind Ekbote and a Hindutva ideologue, Sambhaji Bhide. Both are still at large. Instead, following a FIR (First Information Report) registered by one of their supporters, in June 2018 the Pune police arrested five people: Rona Wilson, a political activist from Delhi; Sudhir Dhawale, a Dalit activist from Mumbai; Shoma Sen, a professor from Nagpur; Mahesh Raut, an activist and former prime minister's Rural Development program fellow; and the lawyer Surendra Gadling. They are accused of plotting violence at the January 1 rally, and also of plotting to kill Prime Minister Modi. They remain in custody, charged under the draconian Unlawful Activities Prevention Act. Fortunately, they are still alive, unlike the nineteen-year-old woman Ishrat Jahan, and Sohrabuddin Sheikh and his wife Kauser Bi, who were accused of the same crime but did not live to see a trial because they were shot dead in what the police called "encounters," claiming self-defense in what are suspected cases of extrajudicial executions (Ishrat Jahan in 2004; the other two in 2006).

The Maharashtra state police say that this recent round of arrests is based on information, gleaned from the documents seized from those arrested in June, that implicates all the accused in a plot to fund and foment violence at the Elgar Parishad and the Bhima–Koregaon anniversary rallies, as well as in a plot to kill Narendra Modi. Justice Sawant and Justice Kolse-Patil have made public statements that they were the main organizers and sole funders of the Elgar Parishad, with the aim of rallying people against divisive Hindutva forces. Both have taken full responsibility for the event. Yet the police and the government have ignored them completely. The police and government have their reasons.

It has been important for recent governments, both the Congress-led UPA and the BJP, to disguise their attacks on Adivasis, and now, in the case of the BJP, their attack on Dalits, as attacks on "Maoists" or "Naxalites." This is because all the main political parties have an eye on those Adivasi and Dalit constituencies as potential vote banks—unlike the Muslim constituency, which has almost been erased from electoral arithmetic. By arresting activists and calling them Maoist or Naxalite militants, the government manages to undermine and insult Dalit aspiration by giving it another name while, at the same time, appearing to be sensitive to "Dalit issues." Today, there are thousands of people in jail across the country, poor and disadvantaged people, fighting for their homes, for their lands, for their dignity—people accused of sedition and worse, languishing without trial in crowded prisons.

The arrests of these ten people—now including three lawyers, and seven well-known activists—also serve to cut off whole populations of vulnerable people from any hope of justice or representation. Because these were their representatives. Years ago, when paramilitary forces and the government-sponsored Adivasi vigilante army known as the Salwa Judum went on a rampage in the mineral-rich forests of Bastar, killing people, raping women, and burning down whole villages, Dr. Binayak Sen, then the general secretary of the People's Union for Civil Liberties in the state of Chhattisgarh, spoke up for its victims. When Binayak Sen was jailed, Sudha Bharadwaj, a lawyer and labor union leader who had worked in the area for years, took his place. Professor Saibaba, who campaigned relentlessly against the paramilitary operations in Bastar, stood up for Binayak Sen. When they arrested Saibaba, Rona Wilson stood up for him. Surendra Gadling was Saibaba's lawyer. When they arrested Rona Wilson and Surendra Gadling, Sudha Bharadwaj, Gautam Navlakha, and the others stood up for them . . . and so it goes.

The vulnerable are being cordoned off and silenced. The vociferous are being incarcerated. God help us to get our country back.

CHAPTER 3

Our Captured, Wounded Hearts

With his reckless "preemptive" airstrike on Balakot in Pakistan, prime minister Narendra Modi has inadvertently undone what previous Indian governments almost miraculously succeeded in doing for decades. Since 1947 the Indian government has bristled at any suggestion that the conflict in Kashmir could be resolved by international arbitration, insisting that it is an "internal matter." By goading Pakistan into a counterstrike, and so making India and Pakistan the only two nuclear powers in history to have launched airstrikes on each other, Modi has internationalized the Kashmir dispute. He has demonstrated to the world that Kashmir is potentially the most dangerous place on earth, the flashpoint for nuclear war. Every person, country, and organization that worries about the prospect of nuclear war has the right to intervene and do everything in its power to prevent it.

On February 14, 2019, a convoy of 2,500 paramilitary soldiers was attacked in Pulwama (Kashmir) by Adil Ahmad Dar,

---

* First published in *HuffPost India*, March 1, 2019.

a twenty-year-old Kashmiri suicide bomber who, it has been declared, belonged to the Pakistan-based Jaish-e-Mohammad.[1] The attack, which killed at least forty men, was yet another hideous chapter in the unfolding tragedy of Kashmir.[2] Since 1990, more than seventy thousand people have been killed in the conflict, thousands have "disappeared," tens of thousands have been tortured and hundreds of young people maimed and blinded by pellet guns. The death toll over the last twelve months has been the highest since 2009.[3] The Associated Press reports that almost 570 people have lost their lives, 260 of them militants, 160 civilians, and 150 Indian armed personnel who died in the line of duty.[4]

Depending on the lens through which this conflict is viewed, the rebel combatants are called "terrorists," "militants," "freedom fighters," or "mujahids." Most Kashmiris call them "mujahids," and when they are killed, hundreds of thousands of people— whether they agree with their methods or not—turn out for their funerals, to mourn for them and bid them farewell. Indeed, most of the civilians who were killed this past year are those who put their bodies in the way of harm to allow militants cornered by soldiers to escape.

In this long-drawn-out, blood-drenched saga, the Pulwama bombing is the deadliest, most gruesome attack of all. There are hundreds, if not thousands, of young men in the Kashmir Valley like Adil Ahmad Dar who have been born into war, who have seen such horror that they have become inured to fear and are willing to sacrifice their lives for freedom. Any day, there could be another attack, worse or less worse than the Pulwama atrocity. Is the government of India willing to allow the actions of these young men to control the fate of this country and the whole subcontinent? By reacting in the empty, theatrical way that he did, this is exactly what Narendra Modi has done. He has actually bestowed upon them the power to direct our future. The young Pulwama bomber could not have asked for more.

Indians who valorize their own struggle for independence from British rule and virtually worship those who led it are for the most part strangely opaque to Kashmiris who are fighting for the same thing. The armed struggle in Kashmir against what people think of as "Indian Rule" is almost thirty years old. That Pakistan has (at one time officially and now mostly through non-government actors) supported the struggle with arms, men, and logistics is hardly a secret. Nor is it a secret that no militant can operate in the war zone that is Kashmir if they do not have the overt support of local people. Who in their right mind could imagine that this hellishly complicated, hellishly cruel war would be solved or even mitigated in any way by a one-off, hastily executed, theatrical "surgical strike," which turns out to have been not-so-surgical after all? A similar "strike" that took place after the 2016 attack on an Indian Army camp in Uri achieved little more than inspiring a Bollywood action film. The Balakot strikes in turn seem to have been inspired by the film. And now the media reports that Bollywood producers are already lining up to copyright "Balakot" as the name of their next film project.[5] On the whole, it has to be said, this absurd waltz looks and smells more like "pre-election" than "preemptive."

For the prime minister of this country to press its formidable air force into performing dangerous theatrics is deeply disrespectful. And what an irony it is, that while this irresponsible nuclear brinkmanship is being played out in our subcontinent, the mighty United States of America is in talks with the Taliban forces, whom it has not managed to defeat or dislodge even after seventeen years of straight-out war.

The spiraling conflict in the subcontinent is certainly as deadly as it appears to be. But is it as straightforward?

Kashmir is the most densely militarized zone in the world, with an estimated half a million Indian soldiers posted there. In addition to the Intelligence Bureau, the Research and Analysis Wing, and the National Intelligence Agency, the uniformed forces—the Army, the Border Security Force, the Central Reserve Police Force, and, of course, the Jammu and Kashmir Police—each does its own intelligence gathering. People live in terror of informers, double agents, and triple agents, who could be anybody from old classmates to family members. Under these circumstances, an attack on the scale of what happened in Pulwama is more than just shocking. As one pithy Twitter commentator put it (she was referring to the increasingly popular Hindu vigilante practice in North India of tracking down and lynching Muslims accused of killing cows), how is it that the BJP "can trace 3 kg of beef but cannot trace 350 kg of RDX"?[6]

Who knows?

After the attack, the governor of Jammu and Kashmir called it the result of "an intelligence failure."[7] A few intrepid media portals reported the fact that the Jammu and Kashmir Police *had* indeed raised an urgent alert about a possible attack.[8] Nobody in the media seems overly worried about why the warning was ignored, and where, in the chain of command, the breach took place.

Tragic as it was, the Pulwama attack came as a perfect political opportunity for Narendra Modi to do what he does best—grandstand. Many of us had predicted months ago that a BJP that was losing its political footing would call down a fireball from the skies just before elections, and we watched with horror as our prediction came true.[9] And we watched the Ruling Party adroitly parley the Pulwama tragedy into petty, political advantage.

In the immediate aftermath of the Pulwama attack, as enraged mobs attacked Kashmiris who worked and studied in mainland India, Modi kept dead quiet and reacted only after the Supreme Court said it was the government's duty to protect them. But after the airstrikes he was quick to appear on TV to take credit, sounding for all the world as though he had personally flown the planes and dropped the bombs. Immediately, India's roughly four hundred round-the-clock news channels, most of them unapologetically partisan, set about amplifying this performance with their own personal "inputs." Using old videos and fake facts, their screaming anchors masquerading as frontline commandos, orchestrated an orgy of crazed, triumphalist nationalism, in which they claimed the air strikes had destroyed a Jaish-e-Mohammad "terror factory" and killed more than three hundred "terrorists." The next morning, even the most sober national newspapers followed suit with ridiculous, embarrassing headlines. The *Indian Express* said:

"India Strikes Terror, Deep in Pakistan."[10] Meanwhile, Reuters, which sent a journalist to the site in Pakistan where the bombs had actually fallen, reported only damage to trees and rocks and injuries sustained by one villager.[11] The Associated Press reported something similar.[12] The *New York Times* said, "Analysts and diplomats in New Delhi said the targets of the Indian airstrikes were unclear, as any terrorist groups operating along the border would have cleared out in recent days after Prime Minister Narendra Modi of India vowed retaliation over the Kashmir attack."[13]

The mainstream Indian media did not carry the Reuters report. So, for the bulk of India's voting people who don't read the *New York Times*, their prime minister—with his famous fifty-six-inch chest—had dismantled terrorism forever.

For the moment at least, it looked as though Modi had completely outmaneuvered his political opponents, who were reduced to tweeting in praise of India's brave pilots. Meanwhile, he and his men were out electioneering. Doubters and dissenters were terrorized by Hindutva trolls, charged with being anti-national, or just debilitated by the fear of the on-call lynch mob that seems to lurk at every street corner in North India.

But things can change in a day. The sheen of false victory faded quickly after Pakistan struck back, shot down a fighter plane, and captured a pilot of the Indian Air Force—Wing Commander Abhinandan Varthaman.[14] Once again, the BJP's see-sawing electoral prospects have begun to look distinctly less rosy.

Leaving aside the business of electoral politics and the question of who will win the next elections, Modi's actions are unforgivable. He has jeopardized the lives of more than a billion people and brought the war in Kashmir to the doorsteps of ordinary Indians. The madness on television, fed to people like an IV drip morning, noon, and night, asks people to lay aside their woes, their joblessness, their hunger, the closing down of their small businesses, the looming threat of eviction from their homes, their demands that there be an inquiry into the mysterious deaths of judges, as well as into what looks like the biggest, most corrupt Ministry of Defense deal in the history of India, their worries that if they are Muslim, Dalit, or Christian they could be attacked or killed—and instead vote, in the name of national pride, for the very people who have brought about this devastation.

This government has wounded India's soul so very deeply. It will take years for us to heal. For that process to even begin, we must vote to remove these dangerous, spectacle-hungry charlatans from office.

We cannot afford to have a prime minister who, on a whim, has broken the back of the economy of a country of a billion people by declaring overnight, without consulting anybody, that 80 percent of a country's currency is no longer legal tender. Who in history has ever done this? We cannot have a prime minister of a nuclear power who continues to shoot a movie about himself in a national park while a huge crisis befalls the country, and then airily declares that he has left the decision of what to do next to the *Sena*—the Army. Which democratically elected leader in history has ever done this?

Modi has to go. The quarrelsome, divided, unstable coalition government that might come in his place is not a problem. It is the very essence of democracy. It will be far more intelligent and far less foolhardy.

There remains the matter of the captured wing commander. Whatever anybody's opinion of him, and whatever Pakistan's role has been in the Kashmir conflict, Imran Khan, the prime minister of Pakistan, has acted with dignity and rectitude throughout this crisis. The Indian government was right to demand that Varthaman be accorded all the rights that the Geneva Convention accords a prisoner of war. It was right to demand that the International Committee of the Red Cross (ICRC) be given access to him while he was in Pakistan's custody. Today Prime Minister Khan has announced that, as a gesture of good will, the wing commander will be released.

Perhaps India can offer the same courtesy to its political prisoners in Kashmir and the rest of the country: protection of their rights under the Geneva Convention, and access to the ICRC?

The war that we are in the middle of is not a war between India and Pakistan. It is a war that is being fought in Kashmir, which expanded into the beginnings of yet another war between India and Pakistan. Kashmir is the real theater of unspeakable violence and moral corrosion that can spin us into violence and nuclear war at any moment. To prevent that from happening, the conflict in Kashmir has to be addressed and resolved. That can only be done if Kashmiris are given a chance to freely and fearlessly tell the world what they are fighting for and what they really want.

Dear World, find a way.

CHAPTER 4

The Language of Literature

I am truly honored to have been invited by PEN America to deliver this year's Arthur Miller Freedom to Write Lecture. Had Arthur Miller and I belonged to the same generation, and had I been a US citizen, I suspect we'd have bumped into each other while we answered summons to the House Un-American Activities Committee. In India, my credentials are impeccable. My name is high up on the A-List of "Anti-Nationals"—and that's not because it begins with an *A*. These days the list has become so long, there's a good chance that it might soon overtake the list of Patriots. Of late, the criterion for being considered anti-national has been made pretty simple: if you don't vote for Narendra Modi (the prime minister) you're a Pakistani. I don't know how Pakistan feels about its growing population.

Sadly, I won't be able to vote for anybody this time around,

* The PEN Arthur Miller Freedom to Write Lecture, delivered at the Apollo Theater, New York, May 12, 2019. First published in *The Guardian*, May 13, 2019. This lecture has been lightly edited to avoid repetition.

because today, May 12, is the day that Delhi, my city, votes. My friends and comrades (excluding those who are in prison) have been queuing up outside election booths, with their hearts in their mouths, hoping the fate of Turkey and Brazil does not await us too. I don't believe it will. For the record, I accepted the invitation to speak here before the dates of the Indian election were announced. So, if Mr. Modi wins by just one vote, remember that all of you share the blame.

Anyway, here we are in legendary Harlem, in the Apollo Theater, whose walls have heard, and perhaps secretly archived, the heart-stopping music that has been made here. They probably hum to themselves when nobody's listening. A little Aretha Franklin, some James Brown, a riff by Stevie Wonder or Little Richard. What better venue than this hall full of history to think together about a place for literature, at this moment in time, when an era that we think we understand—at least vaguely, if not well—is coming to a close.

While many of us dreamt that "another world is possible," some other folks were dreaming that, too. And it is their dream—our nightmare—that is perilously close to being realized.

Capitalism's gratuitous wars and sanctioned greed have jeopardized the planet and filled it with refugees. Much of the blame for this rests squarely on the shoulders of the government of the United States. Seventeen years after invading Afghanistan, after bombing it "into the Stone Age" with the sole aim of toppling the Taliban, the US government is back in talks with the very same Taliban. In the interim it has destroyed Iraq, Libya, and Syria.

Hundreds of thousands have lost their lives to war and sanctions, a whole region has descended into chaos—ancient cities, pounded into dust. Amid the desolation and the rubble, a monstrosity called Daesh (ISIS) has been spawned. It has spread across the world, indiscriminately murdering ordinary people who had absolutely nothing to do with America's wars. Over these last few years, given the wars it has waged, and the international treaties it has arbitrarily reneged on, the US government perfectly fits its own definition of a rogue state. And now, resorting to the same old scare tactics, the same tired falsehoods, and the same old fake news about nuclear weapons, it is gearing up to bomb Iran. That will be the biggest mistake it has ever made.

So, as we lurch into the future, in this blitzkrieg of idiocy, Facebook "likes," fascist marches, fake-news coups, and what looks like a race toward extinction—what is literature's place? What counts as literature? Who decides? Obviously, there is no single, edifying answer to these questions. So, if you will forgive me, I'm going to talk about my own experience of being a writer during these times—of grappling with the question of *how* to be a writer during these times, in particular in a country like India, a country that lives in several centuries simultaneously.

A few years ago, I was in a railway station, reading the papers while I waited for my train. On an inside page I spotted a small news report about two men who had been arrested and charged with being couriers for the banned, underground Communist Party of India (Maoist). Among the "items" recovered from the men, the report said, were "some books by Arundhati Roy." Not long after that, I met a college lecturer who spent much of her time organizing the legal defense of jailed activists, many of them young students and villagers in prison for "anti-national activities." For the most part this meant protesting corporate mining and infrastructure projects that were displacing tens of thousands from their lands and homes. She told me that in several of the prisoners' "confessions"—usually extracted under coercion—my writing often merited a reference as a factor that led them down what the police call "the wrong path."

"They're laying a trail—building a case against you," she said.

The books in question were not my novels (at that point I had written only one—*The God of Small Things*). These were books of nonfiction, although in a sense they were stories, too—different kinds of stories, but stories, nevertheless. Stories about the massive corporate attack on forests, rivers, crops, seeds, on land, on farmers, labor laws, on policy-making itself. And yes, on the post-9/11 US and NATO attacks on country after country. Most were stories about people who have fought against these attacks—specific stories, about specific rivers, specific mountains, specific corporations, specific people's movements, all of them being specifically crushed in specific ways. These were the real climate warriors, local people with a global message, who had understood the crisis before it was recognized as one. And yet, they were consistently portrayed as villains—the anti-national impediments to progress and development. The former prime minister of India Manmohan Singh, a free-market evangelist, called the guerrillas—mostly indigenous people, Adivasis—fighting corporate mining projects in the forests of central India the "single largest internal security challenge." A war called "Operation Green Hunt" was declared on them. The forests were flooded with soldiers whose enemies were the poorest people in the world. It's been no different elsewhere— in Africa, Australia, Latin America.

And now, irony of ironies, a consensus is building that climate change is the world's single largest security challenge. Increasingly the vocabulary around it is being militarized. And no doubt very soon its victims will become the "enemies" in the new war without end. Calls for a climate "emergency," although well meaning, could hasten the process that has already begun. The pressure is already on to move the debate from the UNFCC (United Nations Framework Convention on Climate Change) to the United Nations Security Council, in other words, to exclude most of the world and place decision making straight back into the den of the same old suspects. Once again, the Global North, the creators of the problem, will see to it that they profit from the solution that they propose. A solution whose genius will, no doubt, lie deep in the heart of the "market" and involve more selling and buying, more consuming, and more profiteering by fewer and fewer people. In other words, more capitalism.

When the essays were first published (first in mass-circulation magazines, then on the internet, and finally as books), they were viewed with baleful suspicion, at least in some quarters, often by those who didn't necessarily even disagree with the politics. The writing sat at an angle to what is conventionally thought of as literature. Balefulness was an understandable reaction, particularly among the taxonomy-inclined, because they couldn't decide exactly what this was—pamphlet or polemic, academic or journalistic writing, travelogue, or just plain literary adventurism? To some, it simply did not count as writing: "Oh, why have you stopped writing? We're waiting for your next book." Others imagined that I was just a pen for hire. All manner of offers came my way: "Darling, I loved that piece you wrote on the dams, could you do one for me on child abuse?" (This actually happened.) I was sternly lectured (mostly by upper-caste men) about how to write, the subjects I should write about, and the tone I should take.

But in other places—let's call them places off the highway—the essays were quickly translated into other Indian languages, printed as pamphlets, distributed for free in forests and river valleys, in villages that were under attack, on university campuses where students were fed up of being lied to. Because these readers, out there on the front lines, already being singed by the spreading fire, had an entirely different idea of what literature is or should be.

I mention this because it taught me that the place for literature is built by writers and readers. It's a fragile place in some ways, but an indestructible one. When it's broken, we rebuild it. Because we need shelter. I very much like the idea of literature that is needed. Literature that provides shelter. Shelter of all kinds.

Over time, an unspoken compromise was arrived at. I began to be called a "writer-activist." Implicit in this categorization was that the fiction was not political and the essays were not literary.

I remember sitting in a lecture hall in a college in Hyderabad in front of an audience of five or six hundred students. On my left, chairing the event, was the vice-chancellor of the university. On my right, a professor of poetry. The vice-chancellor whispered in my ear, "You shouldn't spend any more time on fiction. Your political writing is the thing to concentrate on." The professor of poetry whispered, "When will you get back to writing fiction? That is your true calling. This other stuff you do is just ephemeral."

I have never felt that my fiction and nonfiction were warring factions battling for suzerainty. They aren't the same certainly, but trying to pin down the difference between them is actually harder than I imagined. Fact and fiction are not converse. One is not necessarily truer than the other, more factual than the other, or more real than the other. Or even, in my case, more widely read than the other. All I can say is that I feel the difference in my body when I'm writing.

Sitting between the two professors, I enjoyed their contradictory advice. I sat there smiling, thinking of the first message I received from John Berger. It was a beautiful handwritten letter, from a writer who had been my hero for years: "Your fiction and nonfiction—they walk you around the world like your two legs." That settled it for me.

Whatever the case that was being built against me was, it didn't—or at least hasn't yet—come to fruition. I'm still here, standing on my two writing legs, speaking to you. But my lecturer friend is in jail, charged with participating in anti-national activity. India's prisons are packed tight with political prisoners—most of them accused of being either Maoist or Islamist terrorists. These terms have been defined so broadly that they have come to include almost anyone who disagrees with government policy. In the latest batch of pre-election arrests, teachers, lawyers, activists, and writers have been jailed, charged with plotting to assassinate Prime Minister Modi. The plot is so ludicrous that a six-year-old could have improved on it. The fascists need to take some good fiction-writing courses.

Reporters Without Borders say that India is the fifth most dangerous place for journalists in the world, ranked just below Afghanistan, Syria, Yemen, and Mexico. Here I must pause to thank PEN for the work it does to protect writers and journalists who are or have been imprisoned, prosecuted, censored, and worse. From one day to the next, it could be any one of us that is in the line of fire. To know that there is an organization looking out for us is a consolation.

In India, those who've been jailed are the lucky ones. The less fortunate are dead. Gauri Lankesh, Narendra Dabholkar, M. M. Kalburgi, and Govind Pansare, all critics of the Hindu far right, have been assassinated. Theirs were the high-profile killings. Scores of other activists using the Right to Information Act to uncover massive corruption scandals have been killed or found dead in suspicious circumstances. Over the last five years, India has distinguished itself as a lynching nation. Muslims and Dalits have been publicly flogged and beaten to death by vigilante Hindu mobs in broad daylight, and the "lynch videos" then gleefully uploaded to YouTube. The violence is flagrant, open, and certainly not spontaneous. Although the violence against Muslims is not new and the violence against Dalits is ancient, these lynchings have a clear ideological underpinning.

The lynchers know that they have protection in the highest places. Protection not just from the government and the prime minister but from the organization that controls them both—the far-right, proto-fascist Rashtriya Swayamsevak Sangh (RSS), the most secretive and most powerful organization in India. It was founded in 1925. Its founding ideologues were greatly influenced by European fascism—they openly praised Hitler and Mussolini, and compared Indian Muslims to the "Jews of Germany." The RSS has worked ceaselessly for ninety-five years toward having India formally declared a Hindu nation. Its declared enemies are Muslims, Christians, and Communists.

The RSS runs a shadow government that functions through tens of thousands of *shakhas* (branches) and other ideologically affiliated organizations with different names—some of them astonishingly violent—spread across the country. Traditionally controlled by a sect of west coast Brahmins known as Chitpavan Brahmins, the RSS today has white supremacists and racists from the United States and Europe circling around it, writing in praise of Hinduism's age-old practice of caste. It's more accurately known as Brahminism—a brutal system of social hierarchy they envy for its elaborate, institutionalized cruelty, which has survived more or less intact from ancient times. Brahminism also has admirers in the most unexpected places. One of them, you will be saddened to know, was Mohandas Gandhi—who considered caste to be the "genius" of Hindu society. I have written at length about Gandhi's attitude toward caste and race in a book called *The Doctor and the Saint*, so I will not dwell on it now.

Let me just leave you with this: at a speech at a missionary conference in Madras in 1916, he said:

> The vast organization of caste answered not only the religious wants of the community, but it answered too its political needs. The villagers managed their internal affairs through the caste system, and through it they dealt with any oppression from the ruling power or powers. It is not possible to deny the organizing capability of a nation that was capable of producing the caste system its wonderful power of organization.[1]

India is fighting for her soul. Even if the Bharatiya Janata Party (BJP) loses the elections—which, despite having more money than all the other political parties put together, despite its more or less complete control of the mainstream media, it well might—it will not mean that we are out of danger. The RSS is chameleon-like, and millipede-like, too, for it moves on a million legs. Capturing power with an absolute majority, as it did five years ago, put motors on those legs. But merely losing an election will not prevent it from continuing its long walk to hell. It can change color when it has to, wear a mask of reason and inclusiveness when it needs to. It has proved its ability to function as an underground organization as well as an overground one. It is a patient, hardworking beast that has burrowed its way into every institution in the country—courts, universities, media outlets, security forces, intelligence services.

If a new, non-BJP government is sworn in—most likely a fragile coalition—it is likely to be met by a ferocious onslaught of manufactured communal violence and false-flag attacks to which we have become accustomed. There will be cow carcasses discovered on highways, beef found in temples, and pigs thrown into mosques. When the country burns, the far right will once again ·present themselves to us as the only ones capable of running a "hard state" and handling the problem. Will a polity that has been deeply polarized be able to see through these games? It's hard to say.

Much of this has been the subject of my writing, fiction as well as nonfiction, for several years.

§

The God of Small Things, published in the summer of 1997, was the result of a search for a language and a form to describe the world I had grown up in, to myself and to people I loved, some of whom were entirely unfamiliar with Kerala. I had studied architecture, written screenplays, and now I wanted to write a novel. A novel that could only be a novel—not a novel that really wanted to be a film, or a manifesto, or sociological treatise of some kind. I was astonished when some critics described it as a work of magical realism—how could that be? The setting of the book—the old house on the hill in Ayemenem, my grandmother's pickle factory that I grew up in (I still have some of the jars and labels), the Meenachal River—all of it gritty reality to me, was exotic and magical to many Western critics. Fair enough. But I reserve the right to think that way about New York and London.

Back home in Kerala, the reception was pretty unmagical. The Communist Party of India (Marxist), which had ruled Kerala on and off since 1959, was upset with what it considered a critique of the party in *The God of Small Things*. I was quickly labeled anti-communist, a crying-talking-sleeping-walking Imperialist Plot. I *had* been critical, it is true, and the sharp end of my critique was that the Left, by which I mean the various communist parties in India, has been not just opaque to caste, but, more often than not, overtly casteist. The transgressive relationship in the novel between Ammu (a Syrian Christian woman) and Velutha (a Dalit man) was viewed with consternation. The consternation had as much to do with the novel's politics of caste as it did with gender. The portrayal of one of the main characters, Comrade K. N. M. Pillai, and his relationship with his wife, Kalyani, and of Ammu, a divorced woman who "combined the infinite tenderness of motherhood and the reckless rage of a suicide bomber," "who loved by night the man who her children loved by day," was not received with applause and hallelujahs. Five male lawyers got together and filed a criminal case against me, accusing me of obscenity and "corrupting public morality."

There were factors outside of the novel that were swirling around too. My mother, Mary Roy, had won a case in the Supreme Court that struck down the archaic 1916 Travancore Christian Succession Act that cut women out of their fathers' property. Women could now inherit an equal share. This caused a great deal of anger. There was a palpable sense that mother and daughter needed to be taught a lesson. By the time the case came up for its third or fourth hearing, *The God of Small Things* had won the Booker Prize. That divided public opinion. A local Malayali woman, winning a prestigious international literary prize, was not something that could be easily dismissed—should she be shunned or embraced? I was present in court with my lawyer, who had told me in confidence that he thought that parts of my book were "quite obscene." But, he said, according to the law, a work of art should be seen as a whole and since the *whole* book was not obscene, we stood a fighting chance. The judge took his seat and said, "Every time this case comes before me, I get chest pains." He postponed the hearing. The judges who came after him did the same. Meanwhile people celebrated the non-transgressive aspects of the book—the language, the evocation of childhood. It's still hard for many to look at the relationship between Ammu and Velutha without flinching a little. It took almost ten years before the case was dismissed.

In March 1998, less than a year after the publication of *The God of Small Things*, for the first time in India's history, a BJP-led coalition formed the government at the center. The prime minister at the time, Atal Bihari Vajpayee, was a member of the RSS. Within weeks of taking office, he fulfilled a longstanding dream of the RSS by conducting a series of nuclear tests. Pakistan responded immediately with tests of its own. The nuclear tests were the beginning of the journey toward the crazed rhetoric of nationalism that has become a normal form of public speech in India today. I was taken aback by the orgy of celebration that greeted the nuclear tests—including from the most unexpected quarters. That was when I wrote my first essay, "The End of Imagination," condemning the tests. I said that entering the nuclear race would colonize our imagination: "If protesting against having a nuclear bomb implanted in my brain is anti-Hindu and anti-national," I wrote, "then I secede. I hereby declare myself a mobile republic."

I will leave you to imagine the reaction that followed.

"The End of Imagination" was the first of what would turn out to be twenty years' worth of nonfiction essays. They were years during which India was changing at lightning speed. For each essay, I searched for a form, for language, for structure and narrative. Could I write as compellingly about irrigation as I could about love and loss and childhood? About the salinization of soil? About drainage? Dams? Crops? About structural adjustment and privatization? About the per unit cost of electricity? About things that affect ordinary people's lives? Not as reportage, but as a form of storytelling? Was it possible to turn these topics into literature? Literature for everybody—including for people who couldn't read and write, but who had taught me how to think, and could be read to?

I tried. And as the essays kept appearing, so did the five male lawyers (not the same ones, different ones, but they seemed to hunt in packs). And so did the criminal cases, mostly for contempt of court. One of them ended in a very short jail sentence; another is still pending. The debates were often acrimonious. Sometimes violent. But always important.

Almost every essay got me into enough trouble to make me promise myself that I wouldn't write another. But inevitably, situations arose in which the effort of keeping quiet set up such a noise in my head, such an ache in my blood, that I succumbed, and wrote. Last year when my publishers suggested they be collected into a single volume, I was shocked to see that the collection, *My Seditious Heart,* is more than a thousand pages long.

After twenty years of writing, traveling into the heart of rebellions, meeting most extraordinary as well as exquisitely ordinary people, fiction returned to me. It became clear that only a novel would be able to contain the universe that was building in me, spinning up from the landscapes I had wandered through, and composing itself into a story-universe. I knew it would be unapologetically complicated, unapologetically political, and unapologetically intimate. I knew that if *The God of Small Things* was about home, about a family with a broken heart in its midst, *The Ministry of Utmost Happiness* would begin after the roof had blown off the home, and the broken heart had shattered and distributed its shards in war-torn valleys and city streets. It would be a novel, but the story-universe would refuse all forms of domestication and conventions about what a novel could and could not be. It would be like a great city in my part of the world in which the reader arrives as a new immigrant. A little frightened, a little intimidated, plenty excited. The only way to know it would be to walk through it, get lost, and learn to live in it. Learn to meet people, small and big. Learn to love the crowd. It would be a novel that would say what cannot otherwise be said. Particularly about Kashmir, where only fiction can be true because the truth cannot be told. In India, it is not possible to speak of Kashmir with any degree of honesty without risking bodily harm.

About the story of Kashmir and India, and India and Kashmir, I can do no better than to quote James Baldwin: "And they would not believe me, precisely because they would know that what I said was true." The story of Kashmir is not the sum of its human rights reports. It's not only about massacres, torture, disappearance, and mass graves, or about victims and their oppressors. Some of the most terrifying things that happen in Kashmir would not necessarily qualify as human rights violations. For a writer, Kashmir holds great lessons about the human substance. About power, powerlessness, treachery, loyalty, love, humor, faith. What happens to people who live under a military occupation for decades? What are the negotiations that take place when the very air is seeded with terror? What happens to language?

What happens to people who administer, digest, and justify the horror? What happens to people who allow it to go on and on—in their name? The narrative of Kashmir is a jigsaw puzzle whose jagged parts do not fit together. There is no final picture.

Strange people made their way onto my pages. Foremost among them, Biplab Dasgupta, an intelligence officer. I was unnerved when he arrived, speaking in the first person. I thought I was in his head, and realized later that perhaps he was in mine. What was chilling about him was not his villainy but his reasonableness, his intelligence, his wit, his self-deprecation, his vulnerability.

Even still, none of Dasgupta's sophistication and erudite political analysis can see what the building contractor, Mr. D. D. Gupta, one of the minor characters in *The Ministry of Utmost Happiness*, easily can. Mr. Gupta has returned to India from Iraq, after several years of earning his living building blast walls—pictures of which he proudly stores in his mobile phone. Sickened by what he has seen and lived through in Iraq, he looks around at the place he used to think of as home. His considered assessment of what is happening in his own country is that all of it in the long run will only end up creating a market for blast walls.

Novels can bring their authors to the brink of madness. Novels can shelter their authors, too.

As a writer, I protected the characters in *The God of Small Things*, because they were vulnerable. Many of the characters in *The Ministry of Utmost Happiness* are, for the most part, even more vulnerable. But they protect me. Especially Anjum, who was born as Aftab, who ends up as the proprietor and manager of the Jannat Guest House, located in a derelict Muslim graveyard just outside the walls of Old Delhi. Anjum softens the borders between men and women, between animals and humans, and between life and death. I go to her when I need shelter from the tyranny of hard borders in this increasingly hardening world.

CHAPTER 5

The Silence
Is the Loudest Sound

As India celebrates her seventy-third year of independence from British rule, ragged children thread their way through traffic in Delhi, selling outsized national flags and souvenirs that say, *Mera Bharat Mahan*, My India Is Great. Quite honestly, it's hard to feel that way right now, because it looks very much as though our government has gone rogue.

Last week it unilaterally breached the fundamental conditions of the Instrument of Accession, by which the former princely state of Jammu and Kashmir acceded to India in 1947.[1] In preparation for this, at midnight on August 4, it turned all of Kashmir into a giant prison camp. Seven million Kashmiris were barricaded in their homes, internet connections were cut, and their phones went dead.[2]

On August 5, India's home minister proposed in Parliament that Article 370 of the Indian Constitution (the article that outlines

* First published in the *New York Times*, August 15, 2019.

the legal obligations that arise from the Instrument of Accession) be overturned.[3] The opposition parties rolled over. By the next evening the Jammu and Kashmir Reorganization Act, 2019 had been passed by the upper as well as the lower house.

The act strips the state of Jammu and Kashmir of its special status—which includes its right to have its own constitution and its own flag. It also strips it of statehood and partitions it into two union territories. The first, Jammu and Kashmir, will be administered directly by the central government in New Delhi, although it will continue to have a locally elected legislative assembly but one with drastically reduced powers. The second, Ladakh, will be administered directly from New Delhi and will not have a legislative assembly.[4]

The passing of the act was welcomed in Parliament by the very British tradition of desk-thumping. There was a distinct whiff of colonialism in the air. The masters were pleased that a recalcitrant colony had finally, formally, been brought under the crown. For its own good. Of course.

Indian citizens can now buy land and settle in their new domain. The new territories are open for business. Already India's richest industrialist, Mukesh Ambani, of Reliance Industries, has promised several "announcements." What this might mean to the fragile Himalayan ecology of Ladakh and Kashmir, the land of vast glaciers, high-altitude lakes, and five major rivers, barely bears consideration.[5]

The dissolution of the legal entity of the state also means the dissolution of Article 35A, which granted residents rights and privileges that made them stewards of their own territory.[6] So, "being open for business," it must be clarified, can also include Israeli-style settlements and Tibetan-style population transfers.

For Kashmiris, in particular, this has been an old, primal fear. Their recurring nightmare (an inversion of the one being peddled by Donald Trump) of being swept away by a tidal wave of triumphant Indians wanting a little home in their sylvan valley could easily come true.

As news of the new act spread, Indian nationalists of all stripes cheered. The mainstream media, for the most part, made a low, sweeping bow. There was dancing in the streets and horrifying misogyny on the internet. Manohar Lal Khattar, chief minister of the state of Haryana, bordering Delhi, while speaking about the improvement he had brought about in the skewed gender ratio in his state, joked: "Our minister Dhankharji used to say that we will have to bring daughters-in-law from Bihar. . . . Now people say that since Kashmir is open, we can bring girls from there."[7]

Amid these vulgar celebrations the loudest sound, however, is the deathly silence from Kashmir's patrolled, barricaded streets and its approximately seven million caged, humiliated people, stitched down by razor wire, spied on by drones, living under a complete communications blackout. That in this age of information a government can so easily cut off a whole population from the rest of the world for days on end says something serious about the times we are heading toward.

Kashmir, they often say, is the unfinished business of the "Partition." That word suggests that in 1947, when the British drew their famously careless border through the subcontinent, there was a "whole" that was then partitioned. In truth, there was no "whole." Apart from the territory of British India, there were hundreds of sovereign principalities, each of which individually negotiated the terms on which it would merge with either India or Pakistan. Many that did not wish to merge were forced to.[8]

While Partition and the horrifying violence that it caused is a deep, unhealed wound in the memory of the subcontinent, the violence of those times, as well as in the years since, in India and Pakistan, has as much to do with assimilation as it does with partition. In India the project of assimilation, which goes under the banner of nation-building, has meant that there has not been a single year since 1947 when the Indian Army has not been deployed within India's borders against its "own people." The list is long—Kashmir, Mizoram, Nagaland, Manipur, Hyderabad, Assam.

The business of assimilation has been complicated and painful and has cost tens of thousands of lives. What is unfolding today on both sides of the border of the erstwhile state of Jammu and Kashmir is the unfinished business of assimilation.

What happened in the Indian Parliament last week was tantamount to cremating the Instrument of Accession. It was a document with a complicated provenance that had been signed by a discredited monarch, the Dogra Hindu king, Maharaja Hari Singh. His unstable, tattered kingdom of Jammu and Kashmir lay on the fault lines of the new border between India and Pakistan.

The rebellions that had broken out against him in 1945 had been aggravated and subsumed by the spreading bush fires of

Partition. In the western mountain district of Poonch, Muslims, who were the majority, turned on the Maharaja's forces and on Hindu civilians. In Jammu, to the south, the Maharaja's forces, assisted by troops borrowed from other princely states, massacred Muslims. Historians and news reports of the time estimated that somewhere between seventy thousand and two hundred thousand were murdered in the streets of the city, and in its neighboring districts.[9]

Inflamed by the news of the Jammu massacre, Pakistani "irregulars" swooped down from the mountains of the North-Western Frontier Province, burning and pillaging their way across the Kashmir Valley. Hari Singh fled from Kashmir to Jammu, from where he appealed to Jawaharlal Nehru, the Indian prime minister, for help. The document that provided legal cover for the Indian Army to enter Kashmir was the Instrument of Accession.

The Indian Army, with some help from local people, pushed back the Pakistani "irregulars," but only as far as the ring of mountains on the edge of the valley. The former Dogra kingdom now lay divided between India and Pakistan. The Instrument of Accession was meant to be ratified by a referendum to ascertain the will of the people of Jammu and Kashmir.[10] That promised referendum never took place. So was born the subcontinent's most intractable and dangerous political problem.

In the seventy-two years since then, successive Indian governments have undermined the terms of the Instrument of Accession until all that was left of it was its skeletal structure. Now even that has been shot to hell.

It would be foolhardy to try to summarize the twists and turns of how things have come to this. Let's just say that it's as complicated and as dangerous as the games the United States played with its puppet regimes in South Vietnam all through the 1950s and 1960s.

After a long history of electoral manipulation, the watershed moment came in 1987 when New Delhi flagrantly rigged the state elections. By 1989, the thus far mostly nonviolent demand for self-determination grew into a full-throated freedom struggle.[11] Hundreds of thousands of people poured onto the streets only to be cut down in massacre after massacre.

The Kashmir Valley soon thronged with militants, Kashmiri men from both sides of the border, as well as foreign fighters, trained and armed by Pakistan and embraced, for the most part, by the Kashmiri people. Once again, Kashmir was caught up in the political winds that were blowing across the subcontinent— an increasingly radicalized Islam from Pakistan and Afghanistan, quite foreign to Kashmiri culture, and the fanatical Hindu nationalism that was on the rise in India.

The first casualty of the uprising was the age-old bond between Kashmir's Muslims and its tiny minority of Hindus, known locally as Pandits. When the violence began, according to the Kashmiri Pandit Sangharsh Samiti, or the KPSS, an organization run by Kashmiri Pandits, about four hundred Pandits were targeted and murdered by militants. By the end of 1990, according to a government estimate, twenty-five thousand Pandit families had left the valley.[12]

They lost their homes, their homeland and everything they had. Over the years thousands more left—almost the entire Pandit population.[13] As the conflict continued, in addition to tens of thousands of Muslims, the KPSS says 650 Pandits have been killed.[14]

Since then, great numbers of Pandits have lived in miserable refugee camps in Jammu city. Thirty years have gone by, yet successive governments in New Delhi have not tried to help them return home. They have preferred instead to keep them in limbo, and stir their anger and understandable bitterness into a mephitic brew with which to fuel India's dangerous and extremely effective nationalistic narrative about Kashmir. In this version, a single aspect of an epic tragedy is cannily and noisily used to draw a curtain across the rest of the horror.

Today Kashmir is one of the most, or perhaps *the* most, densely militarized zone in the world. More than a half-million soldiers have been deployed to counter what the army itself admits is now just a handful of "terrorists." If there were any doubt earlier, it should be abundantly clear by now that their real enemy is the Kashmiri people. What India has done in Kashmir over the last thirty years is unforgivable. An estimated seventy thousand people—civilians, militants, and security forces—have been killed in the conflict. Thousands have been "disappeared," and tens of thousands have passed through torture chambers that dot the valley like a network of small-scale Abu Ghraibs.[15]

Over the last few years, hundreds of teenagers have been blinded by the use of pellet-firing shotguns, the security establishment's new weapon of choice for crowd control.[16] Most militants operating in the valley today are young Kashmiris, armed and trained locally. They do what they do knowing full well that the minute they pick up a gun, their "shelf life" is unlikely to be more than six months. Each time a "terrorist" is killed, Kashmiris turn up in their tens of thousands to bury a young man whom they revere as a *shaheed*, a martyr.

These are only the rough coordinates of a thirty-year-old military occupation. The most cruel effects of an occupation that has lasted decades are impossible to describe in an account as short as this.

In Narendra Modi's first term as India's prime minister, his hardline approach exacerbated the violence in Kashmir. In February [2019], after a Kashmiri suicide bomber killed forty Indian security personnel, India launched an airstrike against Pakistan.[17] Pakistan retaliated. They became the first two nuclear powers in history to actually launch airstrikes against each other. Now two months into Narendra Modi's second term, his government has played its most dangerous card of all. It has tossed a lit match into a powder keg.

If that were not bad enough, the cheap, deceitful way in which it was done is disgraceful. In the last week of July, forty-five thousand extra troops were rushed into Kashmir on various pretexts.[18] The one that got the most traction was that there was a Pakistani "terror" threat to the Amarnath Yatra—the annual pilgrimage in which hundreds of thousands of Hindu devotees trek (or are carried by Kashmiri porters) through high mountains to visit the Amarnath cave and pay their respects to a natural ice formation that they believe is an avatar of Shiva.[19]

On August 1, some Indian television networks announced that a land mine with Pakistani Army markings on it had been found on the pilgrimage route.[20] On August 2, the government published a notice asking all pilgrims (and even tourists who were miles from the pilgrimage route) to leave the valley immediately.[21] That set off a panicky exodus. The approximately two hundred thousand Indian migrant day laborers in Kashmir were clearly not a concern to those supervising the evacuation. Too poor to matter, I'm guessing. By Saturday, August 3, tourists and pilgrims had left and the security forces had taken up position across the valley.

By midnight Sunday, Kashmiris were barricaded in their homes, and all communication networks went down. The next morning, we learned that, along with several hundred others, three former chief ministers—Farooq Abdullah, his son, Omar Abdullah of the National Conference, and Mehbooba Mufti of the People's Democratic Party—had been arrested.[22] Those are the mainstream pro-India politicians who have carried India's water through the years of insurrection.

Newspapers report that the Jammu and Kashmir police force has been disarmed.[23] More than anybody else, these local policemen have put their bodies on the front line, have done the groundwork, provided the apparatus of the occupation with the intelligence that it needs, done the brutal bidding of their masters and, for their pains, earned the contempt of their own people. All to keep the Indian flag flying in Kashmir. And now, when the situation is nothing short of explosive, they are going to be fed to the furious mob like so much cannon fodder.

The betrayal and public humiliation of India's allies by Narendra Modi's government comes from a kind of hubris and ignorance that has gutted the sly, elaborate structures painstakingly cultivated over decades by cunning, but consummate, Indian statecraft. Now that that's done, it is down to the Street vs. the Soldier. Apart from what it does to the young Kashmiris on the street, it is also a preposterous thing to do to soldiers.

The more militant sections of the Kashmiri population, who have been demanding the right to self-determination or merger with Pakistan, have little regard for India's laws or constitution. They will no doubt be pleased that those they see as collaborators have been sold down the river and that the game of smoke and mirrors is finally over. It might be too soon for them to rejoice. Because as sure as eggs are eggs and fish are fish, there will be new smoke and new mirrors. And new political parties. And a new game in town.

On August 8, four days into the lockdown, Narendra Modi appeared on television to address an ostensibly celebrating India and an incarcerated Kashmir. He sounded like a changed man. Gone was his customary aggression and his jarring, accusatory tone. Instead he spoke with the tenderness of a young mother. It's his most chilling avatar to date.

His voice quivered and his eyes shone with unspilled tears as he listed the slew of benefits that would rain down on the people of the former state of Jammu and Kashmir, now that it was rid of its old, corrupt leaders and was going to be ruled directly from New Delhi. He evoked the marvels of Indian modernity as though he were educating a bunch of feudal peasants who had emerged from a time capsule. He spoke of how Bollywood films would once again be shot in their verdant valley.

He didn't explain why Kashmiris needed to be locked down and put under a communications blockade while he delivered his stirring speech. He didn't explain why the decision that supposedly benefited them so hugely was taken without consulting them. He didn't say how the great gifts of Indian democracy could be enjoyed by a people who live under a military occupation. He remembered to greet them in advance for Eid, a few days away. But he didn't promise that the lockdown would be lifted for the festival. It wasn't.

The next morning, the Indian newspapers and several liberal commentators, including some of Narendra Modi's most trenchant critics, gushed over his moving speech. Like true colonials, many in India who are so alert to infringements of their own rights and liberties have a completely different standard for Kashmiris.

On August 15, in his Independence Day speech, Narendra Modi boasted from the ramparts of Delhi's Red Fort that his government finally had achieved India's dream of "One Nation, One Constitution" with his Kashmir move.[24] But just the previous evening, rebel groups in several troubled states in the northeast of India, many of which have special status like the erstwhile state of Jammu and Kashmir, announced a boycott of Independence Day.[25] While Narendra Modi's Red Fort audience cheered, about seven million Kashmiris remained locked down.

The communication shutdown, we now hear, could be extended for some time to come.

When it ends, as it must, the violence that will spiral out of Kashmir will inevitably spill into India. It will be used to further inflame the hostility against Indian Muslims who are already being demonized, ghettoized, pushed down the economic ladder, and, with terrifying regularity, lynched.[26] The state will use it as an opportunity to also close in on others—the activists, lawyers, artists, students, intellectuals, journalists—who have protested courageously and openly.

The danger will come from many directions. The most powerful organization in India, the far-right Hindu nationalist Rashtriya Swayamsevak Sangh, or the RSS, with more than six hundred thousand members including Narendra Modi and many of his ministers, has a trained "volunteer" militia, inspired by Mussolini's Black Shirts.[27] With each passing day, the RSS tightens its grip on every institution of the Indian state. In truth, it has reached a point when it more or less *is* the state.

In the benevolent shadow of such a state, numerous smaller Hindu vigilante organizations, the storm troopers of the Hindu nation, have mushroomed across the country, and are conscientiously going about their deadly business.

Intellectuals and academics are a major preoccupation.[28] In May, the morning after the Bharatiya Janata Party won the general elections, Ram Madhav, a general secretary of the party and a former spokesman for the RSS, wrote that the "remnants" of the "pseudo-secular/liberal cartels that held a disproportionate sway and stranglehold over the intellectual and policy establishment of the country . . . need to be discarded from the country's academic, cultural and intellectual landscape."[29]

On August 1, in preparation for that "discarding," the already draconian Unlawful Activities Prevention Act was amended to expand the definition of "terrorist" to include individuals, not just organizations.[30] The amendment allows the government to designate any individual as a terrorist without following the due process of a First Information Report, charge sheet, trial, and conviction. Just who—just what kind of individuals it means—was made clear when in Parliament, Amit Shah, our chilling home minister, said: "Sir, guns do not give rise to terrorism, the root of terrorism is the propaganda that is done to spread it. . . . And if all such individuals are designated as terrorists, I don't think any member of Parliament should have any objection."[31]

Several of us felt his cold eyes staring straight at us. It didn't help to know that he has done time as a defendant, as the main accused in a series of murders in his home state, Gujarat. His trial judge, Justice Brijgopal Harkishan Loya, died mysteriously during the trial and was replaced by another, who acquitted him speedily. Emboldened by all this, far-right television anchors on hundreds of India's news networks now openly denounce dissidents, make wild allegations about them and call for their arrest, or worse. "Lynched by TV" is likely to be the new political phenomenon in India.

As the world looks on, the architecture of Indian fascism is quickly being put into place.

I was booked to fly to Kashmir to see some friends on July 28. The whispers about trouble, and troops being flown in, had already begun. I was of two minds about going. A friend of mine and I were chatting about it at my home. He is a senior doctor at a government hospital who has dedicated his life to public service, and happens to be Muslim. We started talking about the new phenomenon of mobs surrounding people, Muslims in particular, and forcing them to chant, "Jai Shri Ram!" (Victory to Lord Ram!)[32]

If Kashmir is occupied by security forces, India is occupied by the mob.

He said he had been thinking about that, too, because he often drove on the highways out of Delhi to visit his family who live some hours away.

"I could easily be stopped," he said.

"You must say it then," I said. "You must survive."

"I won't," he said, "because they'll kill me either way. That's what they did to Tabrez Ansari."[33]

These are the conversations we are having in India while we wait for Kashmir to speak. And speak it surely will.

CHAPTER 6

Intimations of an Ending

The Rise and Rise of the Hindu Nation

While protest reverberates on the streets of Chile, Catalonia, Britain, France, Iraq, Lebanon, and Hong Kong, and a new generation rages against what has been done to its planet, I hope you will forgive me for speaking about a place where the street has been taken over by something quite different. There was a time when dissent was India's best export. But now, even as protest swells in the West, our great anti-capitalist and anti-imperialist movements for social and environmental justice—the marches against big dams, against the privatization and plunder of our rivers and forests, against mass displacement and the alienation of indigenous peoples' homelands—have largely fallen silent. On September 17 this year, prime minister Narendra Modi gifted

* The Jonathan Schell Memorial Lecture Series on the Fate of the Earth, delivered at Cooper Union Great Hall, New York, November 19, 2019. First published in *The Nation*, November 22, 2019.

himself the filled-to-the-brim reservoir of the Sardar Sarovar Dam on the Narmada River for his sixty-ninth birthday, while thousands of villagers who had fought that dam for more than thirty years watched their homes disappear under the rising water. It was a moment of great symbolism.

In India today, a shadow world is creeping up on us in broad daylight. It is becoming more and more difficult to communicate the scale of the crisis even to ourselves—its size and changing shape, its depth and diversity. An accurate description runs the risk of sounding like hyperbole. And so, for the sake of credibility and good manners, we groom the creature that has sunk its teeth into us—we comb out its hair and wipe its dripping jaw to make it more personable in polite company. India isn't by any means the worst, or most dangerous, place in the world, at least not yet, but perhaps the divergence between what it could have been and what it has become makes it the most tragic.

Right now, seven million people in the valley of Kashmir, overwhelming numbers of whom do not wish to be citizens of India and have fought for decades for their right to self-determination, are locked down under a digital siege and the densest military occupation in the world. Simultaneously, in the eastern state of Assam, almost two million people who long to belong to India have found their names missing from the National Register of Citizens, and risk being declared stateless.[1] The Indian government has announced its intention of extending the NRC to the rest of India.[2] Legislation is on its way. This could the lead to the manufacture of statelessness on a scale previously unknown.

The rich in Western countries are making their own arrangements for the coming climate calamity. They're building bunkers and stocking reservoirs of food and clean water. In poor countries—India, despite being the fifth largest economy in the world, is, shamefully, still a poor and hungry country—different kinds of arrangements are being made. The Indian government's August 5, 2019, annexation of Kashmir has as much to do with the Indian government's urgency to secure access to the rivers that run through the state of Jammu and Kashmir as it does with anything else.[3] And the NRC, which will create a system of tiered citizenship in which some citizens have more rights than others, is also a preparation for a time when resources become scarce. Citizenship, as Hannah Arendt famously said, is the right to have rights.[4]

The dismantling of the idea of liberty, fraternity, and equality will be—in fact already is—the first casualty of the climate crisis. I'm going to try to explain in some detail how this is happening. And how, in India, the modern management system that emerged to handle this very modern crisis has its roots in an odious, dangerous filament of our history.

The violence of inclusion and the violence of exclusion are precursors of a convulsion that could alter the foundations of India, and rearrange its meaning and its place in the world. The Constitution calls India a secular, socialist republic. We use the word *secular* in a slightly different sense from the rest of the world—for us, it's code for a society in which all religions have equal standing in the eyes of the law. In practice, India has been neither secular nor socialist. In effect, it has always functioned as an upper-caste Hindu state. But the conceit of secularism, hypocritical though it may be, is the only shard of coherence that makes India *possible*. That hypocrisy was the best thing we had. Without it, India will end.

In his May 2019 victory speech, after his party won a second term, Modi boasted that no politicians from any political party had dared to use the word *secularism* in their campaigns.[5] The tank of secularism, Modi said, was now empty. So, it's official. India is running on empty. And we are learning, too late, to cherish hypocrisy. Because with it comes a vestige, a pretense at least, of remembered decency.

India is not really a country. It is a continent. More complex and diverse, with more languages—780 at last count, excluding dialects—more nationalities and sub-nationalities, more indigenous tribes and religions than all of Europe. Imagine this vast ocean, this fragile, fractious, social ecosystem, suddenly being commandeered by a Hindu supremacist organization that believes in a doctrine of One Nation, One Language, One Religion, One Constitution.

I am speaking here of the RSS, the Rashtriya Swayamsevak Sangh, founded in 1925—the mother ship of the ruling Bharatiya Janata Party. Its founding fathers were greatly influenced by German and Italian fascism. They likened the Muslims of India to the Jews of Germany, and believed that Muslims have no place in Hindu India. The RSS today, in typical RSS chameleon-speak, distances itself from this view. But its underlying ideology, in which Muslims are cast as permanent, treacherous "outsiders," is a constant refrain in the public speeches of BJP politicians, and finds utterance in chilling slogans raised by rampaging mobs. For example: *Mussalman ka ek hi sthan—Kabristan ya Pakistan.* Only one place for the Mussalman—the graveyard or Pakistan. In October this year, Mohan Bhagwat, the supreme leader of the RSS, said, "India is a Hindu rashtra"—a Hindu nation. "This is non-negotiable."

That idea turns everything that is beautiful about India into acid.

For the RSS to portray what it is engineering today as an epochal revolution, in which Hindus are finally wiping away centuries of oppression at the hands of India's earlier Muslim rulers, is a part of its fake-history project. In truth, millions of India's Muslims are the descendants of people who converted to Islam to escape Hinduism's cruel practice of caste.

If Nazi Germany was a country seeking to impose its imagination onto a continent (and beyond), the impetus of an RSS-ruled India is, in a sense, the opposite. Here is a continent seeking to shrink itself into a country. Not even a country, but a province. A primitive, ethno-religious province. This is turning out to be an unimaginably violent process—a kind of slow-motion political fission, triggering a radioactivity that has begun to contaminate everything around it. That it will self-destruct is not in doubt. The question is what else, who else, and how much else will go down with it.

None of the white-supremacist, neo-Nazi groups that are on the rise in the world today can boast of the infrastructure and manpower that the RSS commands. It says that it has fifty-seven thousand *shakhas*—branches—across the country, and an armed, dedicated militia of more than six hundred thousand "volunteers."[6] It runs schools in which millions of students are enrolled, and has its own medical missions, trade unions, farmers' organizations, media outlets, and women's groups. Recently, it announced that it was opening a training school for those who wish to join the Indian Army. Under its *bhagwa dhwaj*—its saffron pennant—a whole host of far-right organizations, known as the Sangh Parivar—the RSS's "family"—have prospered and multiplied. These organizations, the political equivalents of shell companies, are responsible for shockingly violent attacks on minorities in which, over the years, uncounted thousands have been murdered. Violence, communal conflagration, and false-flag attacks are their principal strategies, and have been at the very core of the saffron campaign.

Prime minister Narendra Modi has been a member of the RSS all his life. He is a creation of the RSS. Although not Brahmin, he, more than anyone else in its history, has been responsible for turning it into the most powerful organization in India, and for writing its most glorious chapter yet. It is exasperating to have to constantly repeat the story of Modi's ascent to power, but the officially sanctioned amnesia around it makes reiteration almost a duty.

Modi's political career .was jump-started in October 2001, just weeks after the 9/11 attacks in the United States, when the BJP removed its elected chief minister in the state of Gujarat, and installed Modi in his place. He was not, at the time, even an elected member of the state's legislative assembly. Five months into his first term there was a heinous but mysterious act of arson in which fifty-nine Hindu pilgrims were burned to death in a train coach. As "revenge," Hindu vigilante mobs went on a well-planned rampage across the state. An estimated twenty-five hundred people, almost all of them Muslim, were murdered in broad daylight. Women were gang-raped on city streets, and tens of thousands were driven from their homes. Immediately after the pogrom, Modi called for elections. He won, not despite the massacre but because of it. He became known as Hindu Hriday Samrat—the Emperor of the Hindu Heart—and was re-elected as chief minister for three consecutive terms. During Modi's 2014 campaign as the prime ministerial candidate of the BJP—which also featured the massacre of Muslims, this time in the district of Muzaffarnagar in the state of Uttar Pradesh—a Reuters journalist asked him whether he regretted the 2002 pogrom in Gujarat under his watch.[7] He replied, in all sincerity, that he would regret even the death of a dog if it accidentally came under the wheels of his car.[8] This was pure, well-trained RSS-speak.

When Modi was sworn in as India's fourteenth prime minister, he was celebrated not just by his support base of Hindu nationalists, but also by India's major industrialists and businessmen, by many Indian liberals and by the international media, as the epitome of hope and progress, a savior in a saffron business suit, whose very person represented the confluence of the ancient and the modern—of Hindu nationalism and no-holds-barred free-market capitalism.

While Modi has delivered on Hindu nationalism, he has stumbled badly on the free-market front. Through a series of blunders, he has brought India's economy to its knees. In 2016, a little over a year into his first term, he appeared one night on television to announce that, from that moment on, all Rs 500 and Rs 1,000 banknotes—more than 80 percent of the currency in circulation—had ceased to be legal tender.[9] Nothing like it had ever been done on such a scale in the history of any country. Neither the finance minister nor the chief economic adviser seemed to have been taken into confidence.[10] This "demonetization," Modi said, was a "surgical strike" on corruption and terror funding. This was pure quack economics, a home remedy being laid on a nation of more than a billion people. It turned out to be nothing short of devastating. But there were no riots. No protests. People stood meekly in line outside banks for hours on end to deposit their old currency notes—the only way left to redeem them. No Chile, Catalonia, Lebanon, Hong Kong. Almost overnight, jobs disappeared, the construction industry ground to a halt, small businesses simply shut down.

Some of us foolishly believed that this act of unimaginable hubris would be the end of Modi. How wrong we were. People rejoiced. They suffered, but rejoiced. It was as though pain had been spun into pleasure. As though their suffering was the labor pain that would soon birth a glorious, prosperous, Hindu India.

Most economists agree that demonetization, along with the new Goods and Services Tax Modi announced soon after—promising "one nation, one tax"—was the policy equivalent of shooting out the tires of a speeding car. Many argue that the official figures the government has since put out about economic growth, depressing as they already are, are experiments with the truth. They argue that the Indian economy is now in recession, and that demonetization was the catalyst. Even the government admits that unemployment is at a forty-five-year high.[11] The 2019 Global Hunger Index ranks India almost at the bottom—a shameful 102nd out of 117 countries. (Nepal comes in at seventy-third, Bangladesh eighty-eighth, and Pakistan ninety-fourth.)[12]

But demonetization was never about economics alone. It was a loyalty test, a love exam that the Great Leader was putting us through. Would we follow him, would we always love him, no matter what? We emerged with flying colors. The moment we as a people accepted demonetization, we infantilized ourselves and surrendered to tin-pot authoritarianism.

But what was bad for the country turned out to be excellent for the BJP. Between 2016 and 2017, even as the economy tanked, it became one of the richest political parties in the world.[13] Its income increased by 81 percent, making it nearly five times richer than its main rival, the Congress Party, whose income declined by 14 percent. Smaller political parties were virtually bankrupted. This war chest won the BJP the crucial state elections in Uttar Pradesh, and turned the 2019 general election into a race between a Ferrari and a few old bicycles. And since elections are increasingly about money—and the accumulation of power and the accumulation of capital seem to be convergent—the chances of a free and fair election in the near future seem remote. So maybe demonetization was not a blunder after all.

In Modi's second term, the RSS has stepped up its game like never before. It is no longer a shadow state or a parallel state. It *is* the state. Day by day, we see examples of its control over the media, the police, the intelligence agencies. Worryingly, it appears to exercise considerable influence over the armed forces, too. Foreign diplomats have been hobnobbing with the RSS leadership.[14] The German ambassador (of all ambassadors) trooped all the way to the RSS's headquarters in Nagpur.[15]

In truth, things have reached a stage where overt control is no longer even necessary. More than four hundred round-the-clock television news channels and millions of WhatsApp groups and TikTok videos keep the population on a drip feed of frenzied bigotry.

On November 9, the Supreme Court of India ruled on what some have called one of the most important cases in the world.[16] On December 6, 1992, in the town of Ayodhya, a Hindu vigilante mob, organized by the BJP and the Vishwa Hindu Parishad (VHP)—the World Hindu Council—literally hammered a four-century-old mosque into dust. They claimed that this mosque, the Babri Masjid, was built on the ruins of a Hindu temple that had marked the birthplace of Lord Ram. More than two thousand people, mostly Muslims, were killed in the communal violence that followed. In its recent judgment, the court held that Muslims could not prove their exclusive and continuous possession of the site. It turned the site over to a trust—to be constituted by the BJP government—tasked with building a temple on it. There have been mass arrests of people who have criticized the judgment. The VHP has refused to back down on its past statements that it will turn its attention to other mosques. Theirs can be an endless campaign—after all, everybody came from some-where, and everything is built over something.

With the influence that immense wealth generates, the BJP has managed to co-opt, buy out, or simply crush its political rivals. The hardest blow has fallen on the parties with bases among the Dalit and other disadvantaged castes in the northern states of Uttar Pradesh and Bihar. A major section of their traditional voters has deserted these parties—the Bahujan Samaj Party, Rashtriya Janata Dal, and Samajwadi Party—and migrated to the BJP. To achieve this feat—and it is nothing short of a feat—the BJP worked hard to exploit and expose the caste hierarchies within the Dalit and disadvantaged castes, which have their own internal universe of hegemony and marginalization. The BJP's overflowing coffers and its deep, cunning understanding of caste have completely altered the conventional electoral math of caste politics.

Having secured Dalit and disadvantaged-caste votes, the BJP's policies of privatizing education and the public sector are rapidly reversing the gains made by affirmative action—known in India as "reservation"—and are pushing those who belong to disadvantaged castes out of jobs and educational institutions. Meanwhile, the National Crime Records Bureau shows a sharp increase in atrocities against Dalits, including lynchings and public floggings.[17] In September 2019, while Modi was being honored by the Gates Foundation for making India open-defecation-free, two Dalit children, whose home was just the shelter of a plastic sheet, were beaten to death for shitting in the open.[18] To honor a prime minister for his work on sanitation while tens of thousands of

Dalits continue to work as manual scavengers—carrying human excreta on their heads—is grotesque.

What we are living through now, in addition to the overt attack on religious minorities, is an aggravated class and caste war.

In order to consolidate their political gains, the RSS and BJP's main strategy is to generate long-lasting chaos on an industrial scale. They have stocked their kitchen with a set of simmering cauldrons that can, whenever necessary, be quickly brought to the boil.

On August 5, 2019, the Indian government unilaterally breached the fundamental conditions of the Instrument of Accession by which the former princely state of Jammu and Kashmir agreed to become part of India in 1947. It stripped Jammu and Kashmir of statehood and its special status—which included its right to have its own constitution and its own flag. The dissolution of the legal entity of the state also meant the dissolution of Article 35A of the Indian Constitution, which secured the erstwhile state's residents the rights and privileges that made them stewards of their own territory. In preparation for the move, the government flew in tens of thousand more troops to supplement the hundreds of thousands already stationed there.[19] By the night of August 4, tourists and pilgrims had been evacuated from the Kashmir Valley. By midnight, the internet was cut and phones went dead. Schools and markets were shut down. More than four thousand people were soon arrested.[20] That included politicians, businessmen, lawyers, rights activists, local leaders, students, and three former chief ministers. Kashmir's entire political class, including those who have been loyal to India, was incarcerated.

The abrogation of Kashmir's special status, the promise of an all-India National Register of Citizens, the building of the Ram temple in Ayodhya—are all on the front burners of the RSS and BJP kitchen. To reignite flagging passions, all they need to do is to pick a villain from their gallery and unleash the dogs of war. There are several categories of villains—Pakistani jihadis, Kashmiri terrorists, Bangladeshi "infiltrators," or any one of a population of nearly two hundred million Indian Muslims who can always be accused of being Pakistan-lovers or anti-national traitors. Each of these "cards" is held hostage to the other, and often made to stand in for the other. They have little to do with each other, and are often hostile to each other because their needs, desires, ideologies, and situations are not just inimical but end up posing an existential threat to one another. Simply because they are all Muslim, they have to suffer the consequences of each other's actions.

In two consecutive national elections now, the BJP has shown that it can win a brute majority in Parliament without the "Muslim vote." As a result, Indian Muslims have been effectively disenfranchised, and are becoming that most vulnerable of people—a community without political representation, without a voice. Various forms of undeclared social boycott are pushing them down the economic ladder, and, for reasons of physical security, into ghettos. Indian Muslims have also lost their place in the mainstream media—the only Muslim voices we hear on television shows are the absurd ones of those few who are constantly and deliberately invited to play the part of the primitive, Islamist *mau-*

lana (preacher), to make things worse than they already are. Other than that, the only acceptable public speech for the Muslim community is to constantly reiterate and demonstrate its loyalty to the Indian flag. So, while Kashmiris, brutalized as they are because of their history and, more importantly, their geography, still have a lifeboat—the dream of *azadi*, of freedom—Indian Muslims have to stay on deck to help fix the broken ship.

(There is another category of "anti-national" villains—human rights activists, lawyers, students, academics, "urban Maoists"— who have been defamed, jailed, embroiled in legal cases, snooped on by Israeli spyware, and, in several instances, assassinated. But that's a whole other deck of cards.)

The lynching of Tabrez Ansari illustrates just how deep the rot is. Lynching is a public performance of ritualized murder, in which a man or woman is killed to remind their community that it lives at the mercy of the mob. And that the police, the law, the government, as well as the good people in their homes—who wouldn't hurt a fly, who go to work and take care of their families—are friends of the mob. Tabrez was lynched in June 2019.[21] He was an orphan, raised by his uncles in the state of Jharkhand. As a teenager, he went away to the city of Pune, where he found a job as a welder. When he turned twenty-two, he returned home to get married. Soon after his wedding to eighteen-year-old Shahista, Tabrez was caught by a mob, tied to a lamppost, beaten for hours, and forced to chant the new Hindu war cry, "Jai Shri Ram!"—Victory to Lord Ram! The police eventually took Tabrez into custody but refused to allow his distraught family and young bride to take him to the hospital.

Instead they accused him of being a thief, and produced him before a magistrate, who sent him back to custody. He died four days later.

In its latest report, released in October, the National Crime Records Bureau has carefully left out data on mob lynchings. According to the Indian news site The Quint, there have been 113 deaths by mob violence since 2015.[22] Lynchers, and others accused in hate crimes, including mass murder, have been rewarded with public office and honored by ministers in Modi's cabinet. Modi himself, usually garrulous on Twitter, generous with condolences and birthday greetings, goes very quiet each time a person is lynched. Perhaps it's unreasonable to expect a prime minister to comment every time a dog comes under the wheels of someone's car. Particularly since it happens so often. Mohan Bhagwat, the supreme leader of the RSS, has said that lynching is a Western concept imported from the Bible, and that Hindus have no such tradition. He has declared that all the talk of a "lynching epidemic" is a conspiracy to defame India.

We know what happened in Europe when an organization with a similar ideology imposed itself first on a country and then sought *Lebensraum* (living space). We know that it happened because the rest of the world did not pay heed to the early warnings from those who saw and heard enough to know what was coming. Perhaps those warnings did not sound sufficiently balanced and moderate to a masculine, Anglo-Saxon world, suspicious of any overt display of distress or emotion.

A certain kind of over-the-top emotion, however, is still clearly acceptable. There was plenty on display in the United States on

September 22, 2019—five days after Modi's birthday party at the Narmada dam site—when fifty thousand Indian Americans gathered in the NRG Stadium in Houston for the "Howdy, Modi!" extravaganza.[23] It has already become the stuff of urban legend. President Donald Trump was gracious enough to allow a visiting prime minister to introduce him as a special guest in his own country, to his own citizens. Several members of the US Congress spoke, their smiles too wide, their bodies arranged in attitudes of ingratiation. Over a crescendo of drumrolls and wild cheering, the adoring crowd chanted, "Modi! Modi! Modi!" At the end of the show, Trump and Modi linked hands and did a victory lap. The stadium exploded. In India, the noise was amplified a thousand times over by carpet coverage on television channels. "Howdy" became a Hindi word. Meanwhile, news organizations ignored the thousands of people protesting outside the stadium.

Back home, some of us frightened ourselves by flipping between "Howdy, Modi!" and Marshall Curry's short documentary about the 1939 Nazi rally that filled Madison Square Garden.[24]

Not all the roaring of the fifty thousand in the Houston stadium could mask the deafening silence from Kashmir. That day, September 22, marked the forty-eighth day of curfew and communication blockade in the valley.

Once again, Modi has managed to unleash his unique brand of cruelty on a scale unheard of in modern times. And, once again, it has endeared him further to his loyal public. When the Jammu and Kashmir Reorganisation Bill was passed in India's Parliament on August 6, there were celebrations across the political spectrum.

Sweets were distributed in offices, and there was dancing in the streets. A conquest—a colonial annexation, another triumph for the Hindu nation—was being celebrated. Once again, the conquerors' eyes fell on the two primeval trophies of conquest—women and land. Statements by senior BJP politicians, and patriotic pop videos that notched up millions of views, legitimized this indecency.[25] Google Trends showed a surge in searches for the phrases "marry a Kashmiri girl" and "buy land in Kashmir."

It was not all limited to loutish searches on Google. Within weeks of the siege, the Forest Advisory Committee cleared 125 projects that involve the diversion of forest land in Kashmir for other uses.[26]

In the early days of the lockdown, little news came out of the valley. The Indian media told us what the government wanted us to hear. Kashmiri newspapers were completely censored. They carried pages and pages of news about canceled weddings, the effects of climate change, the conservation of lakes and wildlife sanctuaries, tips on how to live with diabetes, and front-page government advertisements about the benefits that Kashmir's new, downgraded legal status would bring to the Kashmiri people.[27] Those "benefits" are likely to include the building of projects that control and commandeer the water from the rivers that flow through Kashmir. They will certainly include the erosion that results from deforestation, the destruction of the fragile Himalayan ecosystem, and the plunder of Kashmir's bountiful natural wealth by Indian corporations.

Real reporting about ordinary people's lives came mostly from the journalists and photographers working for the international media—Agence France-Presse, the Associated Press, Al Jazeera, *The Guardian*, the BBC, the *New York Times,* and the *Washington Post.* The reporters, mostly Kashmiris, working in an information vacuum, with none of the tools usually available to modern-day reporters, traveled through their homeland at great risk to themselves, to bring us the news. And the news was of nighttime raids, of young men being rounded up and beaten for hours, their screams broadcast on public address systems for their neighbors and families to hear, of soldiers entering villagers' homes and mixing fertilizer and kerosene into their winter food stocks.[28] The news was of teenagers, their bodies peppered with shotgun pellets, having to be treated at home because they would be arrested if they went to a hospital.[29] The news was of hundreds of children being whisked away in the dead of night, of parents debilitated by desperation and anxiety.[30] The news was of fear and anger, depression, confusion, steely resolve, and incandescent resistance.

But the home minister, Amit Shah, said that the siege only existed in people's imaginations; the governor of Jammu and Kashmir, Satya Pal Malik, said phone lines were not important for Kashmiris and were only used by terrorists; and the army chief, Bipin Rawat, said, "Normal life in Jammu and Kashmir has not been affected. People are doing their necessary work. . . . Those who feel that life has been affected are the ones whose survival depends on terrorism."[31] It isn't hard to work out who exactly the government of India sees as terrorists.

Imagine if all of New York City was put under an information lockdown and a curfew managed by hundreds of thousands of soldiers. Imagine the streets of your city remapped by razor wire and torture centers. Imagine if mini Abu Ghraibs appeared in your neighborhoods. Imagine thousands of you being arrested and your families not knowing where you have been taken. Imagine not being able to communicate with anybody, not your neighbor, not your loved ones outside the city, no one in the outside world, for weeks together. Imagine banks and schools being closed, children locked into their homes. Imagine your parent, sibling, partner, or child dying and you not knowing about it for weeks. Imagine the medical emergencies, the mental-health emergencies, the legal emergencies, the shortages of food, money, gasoline. Imagine, being a day laborer or a contract worker, earning nothing for weeks on end. And then imagine being told that all of this was for your own good.

The horror that Kashmiris have endured over the last few months comes on top of the trauma of a thirty-year-old armed conflict that has already taken seventy thousand lives and covered their valley with graves. They have held out while everything was thrown at them—war, money, torture, mass disappearance, an army of more than half a million soldiers, and a smear campaign in which an entire population has been portrayed as murderous fundamentalists.

The siege has lasted for more than three months as I speak. Kashmiri leaders are still in jail. The only condition under which they are offered release is if they sign a document affirming that they will not make public statements for a whole year. Most have refused.

Now, the curfew has been eased, schools have been reopened, and some phone lines have been restored. "Normalcy" has been declared. In Kashmir, normalcy is always a declaration—a fiat issued by the government or the army. It has little to do with people's daily lives.

So far, Kashmiris have refused to accept this new normalcy. Classrooms are empty, streets are deserted, and the valley's bumper apple crop is rotting in the orchards. What could be harder for a parent or a farmer to endure? The imminent annihilation of their very identity, perhaps.

The new phase of the Kashmir conflict has already begun. Militants have warned that, from now on, all Indians will be considered legitimate targets. More than ten people, mostly poor, non-Kashmiri migrant workers, have been shot already. (Yes, it's the poor, almost always the poor, who get caught in the line of fire.) It is going to get ugly. Very ugly.

Soon all this recent history will be forgotten, and once again there will be debates in television studios that create an equivalence between atrocities by Indian security forces and Kashmiri militants. Speak of Kashmir, and the Indian government and its media will immediately tell you about Pakistan, deliberately conflating the misdeeds of a hostile foreign state with the democratic aspirations of ordinary people living under a military occupation. The Indian government has made it clear that the only option for Kashmiris is complete capitulation, that no form of resistance is acceptable—violent, nonviolent; spoken, written, or sung. Yet Kashmiris know that to exist, they must resist.

Why should they want to be a part of India? For what earthly reason? If freedom is what they want, freedom is what they should have.

It's what Indians should want, too. Not on behalf of Kashmiris, but for their own sake. The atrocity being committed in their name involves a form of corrosion that India will not survive. Kashmir may not defeat India, but it will consume India. In many ways, it already has.

This may not have mattered all that much to the fifty thousand cheering in the Houston stadium, living out the ultimate Indian dream of having made it to America. For them, Kashmir may just be a tired old conundrum, for which they foolishly believe the BJP has found a lasting solution. Surely, however, as migrants themselves, their understanding of what is happening in Assam could be more nuanced. Or maybe it's too much to ask of those who, in a world riven by refugee and migrant crises, are the most fortunate of migrants. Many of those in the Houston stadium, like people with an extra holiday home, probably hold US citizenship as well as Overseas Citizenship of India certificates.

The "Howdy, Modi!" event marked the twenty-second day since almost two million people in Assam found their names missing from the National Register of Citizens.

Like Kashmir, Assam is a border state with a history of multiple sovereignties, with centuries of migration, wars, invasion, continuously shifting borders, British colonialism, and more than seventy years of electoral democracy that has only deepened the fault lines in a dangerously combustible society.

That an exercise like the NRC even took place has to do with Assam's very particular cultural history. Assam was among the territories ceded to the British by the Burmese in the peace treaty signed after the First Anglo-Burmese War in 1826. At the time, it was a densely forested, scantily populated province, home to hundreds of communities—among them Bodos, Cachar, Mishing, Lalung, Ahomiya Hindus, and Ahomiya Muslims—each with its own language or speech practice, each with an organic, though often undocumented, relationship to the land. Like a microcosm of India, Assam has always been a collection of minorities jockeying to make alliances in order to manufacture a majority—ethnic as well as linguistic. Anything that altered or threatened the prevailing balance became a potential catalyst for violence.

The seeds for just such an alteration were sowed in 1837, when the British, the new masters of Assam, made Bengali the official language of the province. It meant that almost all administrative and government jobs were taken by an educated, Hindu, Bengali-speaking elite. Although the policy was reversed in the early 1870s, and Assamese was given official status along with Bengali, it shifted the balance of power in serious ways and marked the beginning of what has become an almost two-century-long antagonism between speakers of Assamese and Bengali.

Toward the middle of the nineteenth century, the British discovered that the climate and soil of the region were conducive to tea cultivation. Local people were unwilling to work as serfs in the tea gardens, so a large population of indigenous tribespeople were transported from central India. They were no different from the shiploads of indentured laborers the British transported to their colonies all over the world. Today, the plantation workers in Assam make up 15 to 20 percent of the state's population. But unlike, say, the Indian-origin population in South Africa, in India, shamefully, these workers are looked down upon by local people, and continue to live on the plantations, at the mercy of plantation owners and earning slave wages.

By the late 1890s, as the tea industry grew and as the plains of neighboring East Bengal reached the limits of their cultivation potential, the British encouraged Bengali Muslim peasants—masters of the art of farming on the rich, silty, riverine plains and shifting islands of the Brahmaputra, known as *chars*—to migrate to Assam. To the British, the forests and plains of Assam were, if not terra nullius, then terra *almost*-nullius. They hardly registered the presence of Assam's many tribes, and freely allocated what were tribal commons to "productive" peasants whose produce would contribute to British revenue collection. The migrants came in the thousands, felled forests and turned marshes into farmland, where they cultivated food as well as jute. By 1930, migration had drastically changed both the economy and the demography of Assam.

At first, the migrants were welcomed by Assamese nationalist groups, but soon tensions arose—ethnic, religious, and linguistic. They were temporarily mitigated when, in the 1941 census, as a gesture of solidarity with their new homeland, the entire population of Bengali-speaking Muslims—whose local dialects are together known as the Miya language—designated Assamese as their mother tongue, thereby ensuring that it retained the status of an official language. Even today, Miya dialects are written in the Assamese script.

Over the years, the borders of Assam were redrawn continuously, almost dizzyingly. When the British partitioned Bengal in 1905, they attached the province of Assam to Muslim-majority East Bengal, with Dhaka as its capital. Suddenly, what was a migrant population in Assam was no longer migrant, but part of a majority. Six years later, when Bengal was reunified and Assam became a province of its own, its Bengali population became migrants once again. After the 1947 Partition, when East Bengal became part of Pakistan, the Bengal-origin Muslim settlers in Assam chose to stay on. But Partition also led to a massive influx of Bengali refugees into Assam, Hindus as well as Muslims. This was followed in 1971 by yet another incursion of refugees fleeing from the Pakistan Army's genocidal attack on East Pakistan and the liberation war that birthed the new nation of Bangladesh, which together took millions of lives.

So, Assam was a part of East Bengal, and then it wasn't. East Bengal became East Pakistan and East Pakistan became Bangladesh. Countries changed, flags changed, anthems changed. Cities grew, forests were felled, marshes were reclaimed, tribal commons swallowed by modern "development." And the fissures between people grew old and hard and intractable.

The Indian government is so proud of the part it played in Bangladesh's liberation from Pakistan. Indira Gandhi, the prime minister at the time, ignored the threats of China and the United States, who were Pakistan's allies, and sent in the Indian Army to stop the genocide. That pride in having fought a "just war" did not translate into justice or real concern, or any kind of thought-out state policy for either the refugees or the people of Assam and its neighboring states.

The demand for a National Register of Citizens in Assam arose out of this unique, vexed, and complex history. Ironically, the word *national* here refers not so much to India as it does to the nation of Assam. The demand to update the first NRC, conducted in 1951, grew out of a student-led Assamese nationalist move-ment that peaked between 1979 and 1985, alongside a militant separatist movement in which tens of thousands lost their lives. The Assamese nationalists called for a boycott of elections unless "foreigners" were deleted from the electoral rolls—the clarion call was for "3D," which stood for Detect, Delete, Deport. The number of so-called foreigners, based on pure speculation, was estimated to be between five and eight million. The movement quickly turned violent. Killings, arson, bomb blasts, and mass demonstrations generated an atmosphere of hostility and almost uncontrollable rage toward "outsiders." By 1979, the state was up in flames. Though the movement was primarily directed against Bengalis and Bengali-speakers, Hindu communal forces within the movement also gave it an anti-Muslim character. In 1983 this culminated in the horrifying Nellie massacre, in which more than two thousand Bengal-origin Muslim settlers were murdered over six hours. (Unofficial estimates put the death toll at more than double that.) According to police records, the killers belonged to a neighboring hill tribe. The tribe was not Hindu, nor known to be virulently ethno-Assamese. The motivation for that sudden, brutal spasm of violence remains something of a mystery. Unsubstantiated whispers attribute it to manipulation by RSS workers present in Assam at the time.

In *What the Fields Remember*, a documentary about the massacre, an elderly Muslim who lost all his children to the violence tells of how one of his daughters had, not long before the massacre, been part of a march asking for "foreigners" to be expelled.[32] Her dying words, he said, were, "Baba, are we also foreigners?"

In 1985, the student leaders of the Assam agitation signed the Assam Accord with the central government. That same year, they won the state's assembly elections and formed the state government. A date was agreed upon: those who had arrived in Assam after midnight of March 24, 1971—the day the Pakistan Army began its attack on civilians in East Pakistan—would be expelled. The updating of the NRC was meant to sift the "genuine citizens" of Assam from post-1971 "infiltrators."

Over the next several years, "infiltrators" detected by the border police, or those declared "Doubtful Voters"—D-Voters—by election officials, were tried under the Illegal Migrants (Determination by Tribunal) Act, passed in 1983 by a Congress government under Indira Gandhi. In order to protect minorities from harassment, the IMDT Act put the onus of disproving a person's citizenship on the police or the accusing party—instead of burdening the accused with proving their citizenship. Since 1997, more than four hundred thousand D-voters and Declared Foreigners (D-Voters who are unable to prove their citizenship) have been tried in Foreigners

Tribunals.[33] More than a thousand are still locked up in detention centers, jails within jails where detainees don't even have the rights that ordinary criminals do.[34]

In 2005, the Supreme Court adjudicated a case that asked for the IMDT Act to be struck down on the grounds that it made the "detection and deportation of illegal immigrants nearly impossible."[35] In its judgment annulling the act, the court noted, "There can be no manner of doubt that the state of Assam is facing external aggression and internal disturbance on account of large scale illegal migration of Bangladeshi nationals."[36] Now, it put the onus of proving citizenship on the citizen. This completely changed the paradigm and set the stage for the new, updated NRC. The case had been filed by Sarbananda Sonowal, a former president of the All Assam Students' Union who is now with the BJP, and is currently the chief minister of Assam.[37]

In 2013 the Supreme Court took up a case filed by an NGO called Assam Public Works that asked for illegal migrants' names to be struck off electoral rolls.[38] Eventually, the case for finalizing the modalities of the NRC was assigned to the court of Justice Ranjan Gogoi, who happens to be Assamese.

In December 2014 a two-judge bench of the Justices Gogoi and Rohinton Fali Nariman ordered that an updated list of the NRC be produced before the Supreme Court within a year.[39] Nobody had any clue about what could or would be done to the five million "infiltrators" that it was hoped would be detected. There was no question of them being deported to Bangladesh. Could that many people be locked up in detention camps? For how long? Would they be stripped of citizenship? And was India's highest constitutional court going to oversee and micromanage a colossal bureaucratic exercise involving more than thirty million people, nearly fifty-two thousand bureaucrats, and a massive outlay of funds?

Millions of villagers living in far-flung areas were expected to produce a specified set of documents—"legacy papers"—which prove direct and unbroken paternal lineage dating back to before 1971. The Supreme Court's deadline turned the exercise into a nightmare. Impoverished, illiterate villagers were delivered into a labyrinth of bureaucracy, legalese, documentation, court hearings, and all the ruthless skullduggery that goes with them.

The only way to reach the remote, semi-nomadic settlements on the shifting, silty char islands of the Brahmaputra is by often perilously overcrowded boats run by local people. The roughly two and a half thousand char islands are impermanent offerings, likely to be snatched back at any moment by the legendarily moody Brahmaputra and reoffered at some other location, in some other shape or form. The settlements on them are temporary, and the dwellings are just shacks. Yet some of the islands are so fertile, and the farmers on them so skilled, that they raise three crops a year. Their impermanence, however, has meant the absence of land deeds, of development, of schools and hospitals.

In the less fertile chars that I visited early last month, the poverty washes over you like the dark, silt-rich waters of the Brahmaputra. The only signs of modernity were the bright plastic bags containing documents which their owners—who quickly gather around visiting strangers—cannot read but kept looking at anxiously, as though trying to decrypt the faded shapes on the pages and work out whether they would save them and their children from the massive new detention camp they had heard is being constructed deep in the forests of Goalpara, in Assam. Imagine a whole population of millions of people like this, debilitated, rigid with fear and worry about their documentation. It's not a military occupation, but it's an occupation by documentation. These documents are people's most prized possessions, cared for more lovingly than any child or parent. They have survived floods and storms and every kind of emergency. Grizzled, sunbaked farmers, men and women, scholars of the land and the many moods of the river, use English words like "legacy document," "link paper," "certified copy," "re-verification," "reference case," "D-voter," "declared foreigner," "voter list," "refugee certificate"—as though they were words in their own language. They are. The NRC has spawned a vocabulary of its own. The saddest phrase in it is "genuine citizen."

In village after village, people told stories about being served notices late at night that ordered them to appear in a court two or three hundred kilometers away by the next morning. They described the scramble to assemble family members and their documents, the treacherous rides in small rowboats across the rushing river in pitch darkness, the negotiations with canny transporters on the shore who had smelled their desperation and tripled their rates, the reckless drives through the night on dangerous highways. The most chilling story I heard was about a family traveling in a pickup truck that collided with a roadworks truck carrying barrels of tar. The barrels overturned, and the injured family was covered in tar. "When I went to visit them in hospital," the young activist I was traveling with said, "their young son was trying to pick off the tar on his skin and the tiny stones embedded in it. He looked at his mother and asked, 'Will we ever get rid of the *kala daag* [stigma] of being foreigners?'"

And yet, despite all this, despite reservations about the process and its implementation, the updating of the NRC was welcomed by almost everybody in Assam, each for reasons of their own. Assamese nationalists hoped that millions of Bengali infiltrators, Hindu as well as Muslim, would finally be detected and formally declared "foreigners." Indigenous tribal communities hoped for some recompense for the historical wrong they had suffered. Hindus as well as Muslims of Bengal origin wanted to see their names on the NRC to prove they were "genuine" Indians, so that the *kala daag* of being "foreign" could be laid to rest once and for all. And the Hindu nationalists—now in government in Assam, too—wanted to see millions of Muslim names deleted from the NRC. Everybody hoped for some form of closure.

After a series of postponements, the final updated list was published on August 31, 2019. The names of 1.9 million people were missing.[40] That number could yet expand because of a provision that permits people—neighbors, enemies, strangers—to raise "objections." At last count, more than two hundred thousand objections had been raised. A great number of those who have found their names missing from the list are women and children, most of whom belong to communities where women are married in their early teenage years, and by custom have their names changed. They have no "link documents" to prove their legacy. A great number are illiterate people whose names or parents' names have been wrongly transcribed over the years: a H-a-s-a-n who became a H-a-s-s-a-n, a Joynul who became Zainul, a Mohammad whose name has been spelled in several ways. A single slip, and you're out. If your father died, or was estranged from your mother, if he didn't vote, wasn't educated, and didn't have land, you're out. Because, in practice, mothers' legacies don't count. Among all the prejudices at play in updating the NRC, perhaps the greatest of all is the built-in, structural prejudice against women and against the poor. And the poor in India today are made up mostly of Muslims, Dalits, and tribals.

All the 1.9 million people whose names are missing will now have to appeal to a Foreigners Tribunal. There are, at the moment, a hundred Foreigners Tribunals in Assam, and another thousand are in the pipeline.[41] The men and women who preside over them, known as "members" of the tribunals, hold the fates of millions in their hands, but have no experience as judges. They are bureaucrats or junior lawyers, hired by the government and paid generous salaries. Once again, prejudice is built into the system. Government documents accessed by activists show that the sole criterion for rehiring members whose contracts have expired is the number of appeals they have rejected. All those who have to go in appeal to the Foreigners Tribunals will also have to hire lawyers, perhaps take loans to pay their fees or sell their land or their homes, and surrender to a life of debt and penury. Many of course have no land or home to sell. Several people faced with this have committed suicide.[42]

After the whole elaborate exercise and the millions of rupees spent on it, all the stakeholders in the NRC are bitterly disappointed with the list. Bengal-origin migrants are disappointed because they know that rightful citizens have been arbitrarily left out. Assamese nationalists are disappointed because the list has fallen well short of excluding the five million speculated "infiltrators" they expected it to detect, and because they feel too many illegal foreigners have made it onto the list. And India's ruling Hindu nationalists are disappointed because it is estimated that more than half of the 1.9 million are non-Muslims. (The reason for this is ironic. Bengali Muslim migrants, having faced hostility for so long, have spent years gathering their "legacy papers." Hindus, being less insecure, have not.)

Justice Gogoi ordered the transfer of Prateek Hajela, the chief coordinator of the NRC, giving him seven days to leave Assam. Justice Gogoi did not offer a reason for this order.

Demands for a fresh NRC have already begun.

How can one even try to understand this craziness, except by turning to poetry? A group of young Muslim poets, known as the Miya poets, began writing of their pain and humiliation in the language that felt most intimate to them, in the language that until then they had used only in their homes—the Miya dialects of Dhakaiya, Maimansingia, and Pabnaiya. One of them, Rehna Sultana, in a poem called "Mother," wrote:

Ma, ami tumar kachchey aamar porisoi diti diti biakul oya dzai.

Mother, I'm so tired, tired of introducing myself to you.[43]

When these poems were posted and circulated widely on Facebook, a private language suddenly became public. And the old specter of linguistic politics reared its head again. Police cases were filed against several Miya poets, accusing them of defaming Assamese society. Rehna Sultana had to go into hiding.

That there is a problem in Assam cannot be denied. But how is it to be solved? The trouble is that once the torch of ethno-nationalism has been lit, it is impossible to know in which direction the wind will take the fire. In the new union territory of Ladakh—granted this status by the abrogation of Jammu and Kashmir's special status—tensions simmer between Buddhists and Shia Muslims. In the states of India's northeast alone, sparks have already begun to ignite old antagonisms. In Arunachal Pradesh, it is the Assamese who are unwanted immigrants. Meghalaya has closed its borders with Assam, and now requires all "outsiders" staying more than twenty-four hours to register with the government under the new Meghalaya Residents Safety and Security Act. In Nagaland, twenty-two-year-long peace talks between the central government and Naga rebels have stalled over demands for a separate Naga flag and constitution. In Manipur, dissidents worried about a possible settlement between the Nagas and the central government have announced a government-in-exile in London. Indigenous tribes in Tripura are demanding their own NRC in order to expel the Hindu Bengali population that has turned them into a tiny minority in their own homeland.

Far from being deterred by the chaos and distress created by Assam's NRC, the Modi government is making arrangements to import it to the rest of India. To take care of the possibility of Hindus and its other supporters being caught up in the NRC's complexities, as has happened in Assam, it drafted a new Citizenship Amendment Bill. (After being passed in Parliament, it is now the Citizenship Amendment Act.)[44] It says that all non-Muslim "persecuted minorities" from Pakistan, Bangladesh, and Afghanistan—meaning Hindus, Sikhs, Buddhists, and Christians—will be given asylum in India. By default, the CAA will ensure that those deprived of citizenship will only be Muslims.

Before the process of the NRC begins, the plan is to draw up a National Population Register.[45] This will involve a door-to-door survey in which, in addition to basic census data, the government plans to collect iris scans and other biometric data. It will be the mother of all data banks.

The groundwork has already begun. On his very first day as home minister, Amit Shah issued a notification permitting state governments across India to set up Foreigners Tribunals and detention centers manned by non-judicial officers with draconian powers. The governments of Karnataka, Uttar Pradesh, and Haryana have already begun work. As we have seen, the NRC in Assam grew out of a very particular history. To apply it to the rest of India is pure malevolence. The demand for an updated NRC in Assam is more than forty years old. There, people have been collecting and holding on to their documents for fifty years. How many people in India can produce "legacy documents"? Perhaps not even our prime minister, whose date of birth, college degree, and marital status have all been the subject of national controversies.

We are being told that the India-wide NRC is an exercise to detect several million Bangladeshi "infiltrators"—"termites," as our home minister likes to call them. What does he imagine language like this will do to India's relationship with Bangladesh? Once again, phantom figures that run into the tens of millions are being thrown around. There is no doubt that there are a great many undocumented workers from Bangladesh in India. There is also no doubt that they make up one of the poorest, most marginalized populations in the country. Anybody who claims to believe in the free market should know that they are only filling a vacant economic slot by doing work that others will not do, for wages that nobody else will accept. They do an honest day's work for an honest day's pay. They are not the ones destroying the country, stealing public money or bankrupting the banks. They're only a decoy, a Trojan horse for the RSS's real objective, its historic mission.

The real purpose of an all-India NRC, coupled with the CAA, is to threaten, destabilize, and stigmatize the Indian Muslim community, particularly the poorest among them. It is meant to create a tiered citizenship, in which one set of citizens has no rights and lives at the mercy, or on the good will, of another—a modern caste system, which will exist alongside the ancient one, in which Muslims are the new Dalits. Not notionally, but actually. Legally. In places like West Bengal, where the BJP is on an aggressive takeover drive, suicides have already begun.

Here is M. S. Golwalkar, the supreme leader of the RSS in 1940, writing in his book *We or Our Nationhood Defined*:

Ever since that evil day, when Moslems first landed in Hindustan, right up to the present moment the Hindu Nation has been gallantly fighting on to take on these despoilers. . . . The Race Spirit has been awakening. . . .

[I]n Hindustan, the land of the Hindus, lives and should live the Hindu Nation. . . .

All others are either traitors and enemies to the National Cause, or, to take a charitable view, idiots. . . .

[T]he foreign races in Hindusthan . . . may stay in the country, wholly subordinated to the Hindu Nation, claiming nothing, deserving no privileges, far less any preferential treatment—not even citizen's rights.[46]

He continues:

To keep up the purity of the Race and its culture, Germany shocked the world by her purging the country of the Semitic Races—the Jews. Race pride at its highest has been manifested here. . . . a good lesson for us in Hindusthan to learn and profit by.[47]

How do you translate this in modern terms if not as the National Register of Citizens coupled with the Citizenship Amendment Bill? This is the RSS's version of Germany's 1935 Nuremberg Laws, by which German citizens were only those who had been granted citizenship papers—legacy papers—by the government of the Third Reich. The amendment against Muslims is the first such amendment. Others will no doubt follow, against Christians, Dalits, communists—all enemies of the RSS.

The Foreigners Tribunals and detention centers that have already started springing up across India may not, at the moment, be intended to accommodate hundreds of millions of Muslims.

But they are meant to remind us that India's Muslims truly deserve such treatment if they cannot produce legacy papers. Because only Hindus are considered India's real aboriginals, who don't need those papers. Even the four-century-old Babri Masjid didn't have the right legacy papers. What chance would a poor farmer or a street vendor have?

This is the wickedness that the fifty thousand people in the Houston stadium were cheering. This is what the president of the United States linked hands with Modi to support. It's what the Israelis want to partner with, the Germans want to trade with, the French want to sell fighter jets to, and the Saudis want to fund.

Perhaps the whole process of the all-India NRC can be privatized, including the data bank with our iris scans. The employment opportunities and accompanying profits might revive our dying economy. The detention centers could be built by the Indian equivalents of Siemens, Bayer, and IG Farben. It isn't hard to guess what corporations those will be. Even if we don't get to the Zyklon B stage, there's plenty of money to be made.

We can only hope that, someday soon, the streets in India will throng with people who realize that unless they make their move, the end is close.

If that doesn't happen, consider these words to be intimations of an ending from one who lived through these times.

CHAPTER 7

The Graveyard Talks Back

Fiction in the Time of Fake News

T hank you for inviting me to deliver this, the Clark Lecture, now in its 132nd year. When I received the invitation, I scrolled down the list of previous speakers, the many "Sirs" and Sir-sounding names who have spoken on topics as varied as "Literary Criticism of the Age of Queen Anne," "Shakespeare as Criticised in France from the Time of Voltaire," "The Crowning Privilege: Professional Standards in English Poetry" and "Makers and Materials: The Poetry of Spenser, Shakespeare, Milton, Yeats, and Eliot." In the cartoon version of this story, at this point the character playing me would furrow her brow and her speech

* The 2020 Clark Lecture in English Literature instituted by Trinity College, University of Cambridge. Due to an ongoing dispute between the Trinity College Board of Trustees and the University of Cambridge's University and College Union, and in defense of a request by the Union, this lecture, meant to be given on February 13, 2020, was not delivered in person.

balloon would say, "Huh?" I was reassured when my eye fell on "Studies in American Africanism" by Toni Morrison, but only momentarily. I asked Dr. John Marenbon, who invited me, if I could look at the texts of some previous lectures, since I couldn't find them on the internet. He most helpfully replied that speakers were never asked to deposit their lectures with Trinity, but that T. S. Eliot's *The Varieties of Metaphysical Poetry* had evolved from his Clark lecture, as had E. M. Forster's *Aspects of the Novel.*

In other words—no pressure.

This lecture has evolved from a series of recent talks I have given about the place for literature in the times in which we live, and about the politics of language, both public and private. This makes my task a little slippery. It might occasionally involve the presumption that many of you are familiar with my work, which may not be the case and for which I apologize.

Graveyards in India are, for the most part, Muslim graveyards, because Christians make up a minuscule part of the population, and, as you know, Hindus and most other communities cremate their dead. The Muslim graveyard, the *kabristan*, has always loomed large in the imagination and rhetoric of Hindu nationalists. *Mussalman ka ek hi sthan, Kabristan ya Pakistan!* Only one place for the Mussalman, the graveyard or Pakistan—is among the more frequent war cries of the murderous, sword-wielding militias and vigilante mobs that have overrun India's streets.

As the Hindu right has taken almost complete control of the state, as well as non-state apparatuses, the increasingly blatant social and economic boycott of Muslims has pushed them further down the societal ladder and made them even more unwelcome in "secular" public spaces and housing colonies. For reasons of safety as well as necessity, in urban areas many Muslims, including the elite, are retreating into enclaves that are often hatefully referred to as "mini-Pakistans." Now in life, as in death, segregation is becoming the rule. In cities like Delhi, meanwhile, the homeless and destitute congregate in shrines and around graveyards, which have become resting places not just for the dead, but for the living, too. I will speak today about the Muslim graveyard, the kabristan, as the new ghetto—literally as well as metaphorically—of the new Hindu India. And about writing fiction in these times.*

In some sense, *The Ministry of Utmost Happiness*, my novel published in 2017, can be read as a conversation between two graveyards. One is a graveyard where a hijra, Anjum—raised as a boy by a Muslim family in the walled city of Delhi—makes her home and gradually builds a guest house, the Jannat (Paradise) Guest House, and where a range of people come to seek shelter. The other is the ethereally beautiful valley of Kashmir, which is now, after thirty years of war, covered with graveyards, and in this way has become, literally, almost a graveyard itself. So,

---

* Ten days after this lecture was first published, violence engulfed northeast Delhi. Organized fascist mobs, armed and backed up by the police, went on a killing spree against working-class Muslims. Their homes, shops, mosques, and neighborhoods were burnt down. Many have been killed. Many have gone missing. Thousands of Muslim refugees are crowded into the local Muslim graveyards. (See chapter 8, "There Is Fire in the Ducts, the System Is Failing.")

a graveyard covered by the Jannat Guest House, and a Jannat covered with graveyards.

This conversation, this chatter between two graveyards, is and always has been strictly prohibited in India. In the real world, all conversation about Kashmir with the exception of Indian Government propaganda, is considered a high crime—treasonous even. Fortunately, in fiction, different rules apply.

Before we get to the forbidden conversation, let me describe for you the view from my writing desk. Some writers may wish to shut the window or move to another room. But I cannot. So you will have to bear with me, because it is in this landscape that I heat my stove and store my pots and pans. It is here that I make my literature.

Today, February 13, 2020, marks the 193rd day of the Indian government's shut down of the internet in Kashmir. After months of having no access to mobile data or broadband, now seven million Kashmiris, who live under the densest military occupation in the world, have been allowed to view what is known as a white list—a handful of government-approved websites. These include a few selected news portals, but not the social media that Kashmiris so depend on, given the Indian media's hostility toward them, to put out their versions of their lives. In other words, Kashmir now has a formally firewalled internet, which could well be the future for many of us in the world. It's the equivalent of giving a thirsty person water from an eyedropper.

The internet shutdown has crippled almost every aspect of daily life in Kashmir. The full extent of the hardship it has caused has not even been studied yet. It's a pioneering experiment in the mass violation of human rights. The information siege aside, thousands of Kashmiris, including children, civil society activists, and political figures, are imprisoned—some under the draconian Public Safety Act. These are just the bare bones of an epic and continuously unfolding tragedy. While the world looks away, business has ground to a halt, tourism has slowed to a trickle, Kashmir has been silenced and is slowly falling off the map. None of us needs to be reminded of what happens when places fall off the map. When the blowback comes, I, for one, will not be among those feigning surprise.

Meanwhile, the Indian government has passed a new citizenship law that, even if intricately constructed, is blatantly discriminatory against Muslims. I have written about this at length in a lecture I delivered last November, so I will not elaborate on the law now—except to say that it could create a crisis of statelessness on a scale hitherto unknown.[1] It is for the Rashtriya Swayamsevak Sangh—the wellspring of Hindu nationalism, and the parent of Narendra Modi's Bharatiya Janata Party—what Germany's 1935 Nuremberg Laws were for the Third Reich, conferring upon it the power to decide who is a rightful citizen and who isn't, based on specific documents that people are expected to produce to prove their heredity. That lecture is one of the bleakest texts I have written.

Three months on, the bleakness has turned into cautious hope. The Citizenship Amendment Bill was passed in Parliament on December 11, 2019, becoming the Citizenship Amendment Act. Within days, students rose. The first to react were the students of Aligarh Muslim University, and Jamia Millia Islamia University in Delhi. In response, riot police attacked the campuses with tear gas and stun guns. Students were ruthlessly beaten, some were maimed, and one was blinded in one eye. Anger has now spread to campuses across the country and spilled over into the streets. Outraged citizens, led from the front by students and Muslim women, have occupied public squares and blocked roads for weeks together. The Hindu right—which lavishes enormous energy on stigmatizing the Muslim man as a woman-hating, terrorist jihadi, and even offers itself up as the savior of Muslim women—is a little confounded by this brilliant, articulate, and very female anger. In Delhi's now iconic Shaheen Bagh protest, thousands, tens of thousands, and sometimes a hundred thousand people, have blocked a major road for almost two months. This has spawned mini Shaheen Baghs across the country. Millions are on the street, taking back their country, waving the Indian flag, pledging to uphold the Indian Constitution and reading out its preamble, which says India is a secular, socialist republic.

The anthem of this new uprising, the slogan that is reverberating through towns and college campuses and crossroads across the country, is a variation of the iconic chant of the Kashmiri freedom struggle, *Hum kya chahtey? Azadi!*—What do we want? Freedom! That slogan is the refrain within a set of lyrics that describes people's anger, their dream, and the battle ahead. This is not to suggest that any one group can claim ownership of the Azadi slogan—it has a long and varied history. It was the slogan of the Iranian Revolution, which recently celebrated its fortieth anniversary, and of a section of the feminist movement in our subcontinent in the seventies and eighties. But over the last three decades, it has, more than anything else, become known as the anthem of the Kashmiri street. And now, while Kashmir's streets have been silenced, the irony is that its people's refrain, with similar lyrics, rhythm, and cadence, echoes on the streets of the country that most Kashmiris view as their colonizer. What lies between the silence of one street and the sound of the other? Is it a chasm, or could it become a bridge?

Let me read you a short elucidation of the Kashmiri chant of "Azadi!" from *The Ministry of Utmost Happiness*. The "I" in the text is Biplab Dasgupta, known to his friends—for reasons we need not go into here—as Garson Hobart. He is a suave, even brilliant, Indian intelligence officer serving in Kashmir. Hobart is no friend of the Kashmiri struggle. It's 1996—one of the darkest periods of the armed uprising that raged in the valley through the 1990s. Hobart is trapped with the governor's entourage in a national park on the outskirts of Srinagar. They are unable to return home because the city has been taken over by hundreds of thousands of mourners carrying their most recent batch of martyrs to the graveyard. Hobart's secretary is on the phone, advising him not to return until the streets are taken back:

> Sitting on the verandah of the Dachigam Forest Guest House, over birdsong and the sounds of crickets, I heard the reverberating boom of a hundred thousand or more voices raised together calling for freedom: *Azadi! Azadi! Azadi!* On and on and on. Even on the phone it was unnerving. . . . It was as though the city was breathing through a single pair of lungs, swelling like a throat

with that urgent, keening cry. I had seen my share of demonstrations by then, and heard more than my share of slogan-shouting in other parts of the country. This was different, this Kashmiri chant. It was more than a political demand. It was an anthem, a hymn, a prayer. . . .

During those (fortunately short-lived) occasions when it was in full cry, it had the power to cut through the edifice of history and geography, of reason and politics. It had the power to make even the most hardened of us wonder, even if momentarily, what the hell we were doing in Kashmir, governing a people who hated us so viscerally.[2]

To be sure, protesters in India are calling for an entirely different kind of azadi—azadi from poverty, from hunger, from caste, from patriarchy, and from repression. "It is not azadi from India, it is azadi in India," says Kanhaiya Kumar, the charismatic young politician credited with customizing and retooling the chant for the uprising in India today.[3] On the streets, every one of us is painfully aware that even an atom of sympathy for the Kashmiri cause expressed even by a single person, even accidentally, will be met by nationalist hellfire that will incinerate not just the protests, but every last person standing. And if that person happens to be Muslim, it would be something exponentially worse than even hellfire. Because when it comes to Muslims, for everything—from parking tickets to petty crime—different rules apply. Not on paper, but effectively. That is how deeply unwell India has become.

At the heart of these massive, democratic protests over the anti-Muslim citizenship laws, therefore, inside this borrowed song from Kashmir, is an enforced, pin-drop silence over crimes committed in the Kashmir Valley. That silence is decades old, and the shame of it is corrosive. The shame must be shared not just by Hindu nationalists, not just by India's entire political spectrum, but also by the majority of the Indian people, including many who are bravely out on the streets today. It's a hard thing to have to hold in one's heart.

But perhaps it's only a matter of time before the cry for justice by the young on India's streets will come to include a demand for justice for Kashmiris too. Perhaps this is why in the BJP-ruled state of Uttar Pradesh, the chief minister, Yogi Adityanath, seen by many as a Modi in the making, has declared the "Azadi!" slogan to be treasonous.

The government's response to the protests has been ferocious. Prime Minister Modi fired the starting gun with his trademark toxic innuendo. At an election rally, he said the protesters could easily be "identified by their clothes"—implying that they were all Muslim. This is untrue. But it serves to clearly mark off the population that must be punished. In Uttar Pradesh, Yogi Adityanath has, like some kind of gangster, openly vowed "revenge."[4] More than twenty people have been killed so far. At a public tribunal a few weeks ago, I heard testimonies of how police in the state are entering people's homes in the dead of night, terrorizing and looting them. People spoke of being kept naked and beaten for days in police lockups. They described how hospitals had turned away critically injured people, how Hindu doctors had refused to treat them. In videos of the police attacking protesters, the slurs they use against Muslims are unspeakable, their muttered prejudice is almost more frightening than the injuries they inflict. When a government openly turns on a section of its own population with all the power at its disposal, the terror it generates is not easy for those outside that community to comprehend, or even believe.

Needless to say, political support for Yogi Adityanath has been forthright and unflinching. The president of the BJP in the state of West Bengal, who seems to be simultaneously envious and proud of the Uttar Pradesh model, boasted, "Our government shot them like dogs." A union minister in Modi's cabinet addressed a rally in Delhi with shouts of *Desh ke gaddaron ko,* and the crowd screamed back, *Goli maaro saalon ko*—What's to be done with the traitors to the nation? Shoot the bastards![5] A member of Parliament said that unless the protesters of Shaheen Bagh were dealt with, they would enter homes and "rape your sisters and daughters"—which is an interesting idea, considering that the protesters of Shaheen Bagh are predominantly women. The home minister, Amit Shah, has asked people to choose between Modi, "who conducted airstrikes and surgical strikes on Pakistan," and the "people who back Shaheen Bagh."[6]

Modi, for his part, has declared that it would take India only ten days to defeat Pakistan in a military confrontation.[7] It might sound like a non sequitur at a time like this, but it's not. It's his sly way of conflating the protesters with Pakistan. The whole country is holding its breath, waiting for more bloodshed, and perhaps even war.

As India embraces majoritarian Hindu nationalism, which is a polite term for fascism, many liberals and even communists continue to be squeamish about using that term. This, notwithstanding the fact that RSS ideologues are openly worshipful of Hitler and Mussolini, and that Hitler has found his way onto the cover of an Indian school textbook about great world leaders, alongside Gandhi and Modi.[8] The division in opinions on the use of the term comes down to whether you believe that fascism became fascism only after a continent was destroyed and millions of people were exterminated in gas chambers, or whether you believe that fascism is an ideology that led to those high crimes—that *can* lead to those crimes—and that those who subscribe to it are fascists.

Let me spend a moment on the subtitle of my talk—"Fiction in the Time of Fake News." Fake news is at least as old as fiction is—and, of course, both can often be the same thing. Fake news is the skeletal structure, the scaffolding over which the specious wrath that fuels fascism drapes itself. The foundation on which that scaffolding rests is fake history—possibly the oldest form of fake news. The history being peddled by Hindu nationalists, that hackneyed tale of spurious valor and exaggerated victimhood in which history is turned into mythology and mythology into history, has been very ably perforated and demolished by serious scholars. But the tale was never meant for serious scholars. It is meant for an audience that few serious scholars can hope to reach. While we laugh in derision, it is spreading like an epidemic and blossoming in the popular imagination like a brain-deadening malignancy. There is also something deeper, more disturbing, at work here, which I cannot dwell on, though I will gesture toward it. If any of my assertions startle you, please know that I have elaborated on them at length in a book called *The Doctor and the Saint*.[9]

At the heart of Hindu nationalism and the cult of Hindu supremacy is the principle of *varnashrama dharma*, the caste system, or what the anti-caste tradition calls *Brahmanvaad*—Brahminism. Brahminism organizes society in a vertical hierarchy based on a supposedly celestially ordained, graded scale of purity and pollution, entitlements and duties, and hereditary occupations. Right on top of the ladder are Brahmins, the embodiment of purity, the resting place of all entitlement. At the bottom are the "outcastes"—Dalits, once known as Untouchables, who have been dehumanized, ghettoized, and violated in unimaginable ways for centuries. None of these categories is homogeneous, each is divided into its own elaborate universe of hierarchies. The principles of equality, fraternity, or sorority are anathema to the caste system. It's not hard to see how the idea that some human beings are inherently superior or inferior to others by divine mandate slides easily into the fascist idea of a "master race." To escape the tyranny of Brahminism over the centuries, millions of Dalits and people from other subjugated castes converted to Islam, Sikhism, or Christianity. So, the politics of Hindu majoritarianism and its persecution of minorities are also intricately intertwined with the question of caste. Even today, caste is the engine and the organizing principle that runs almost every aspect of modern Indian society. And yet so many celebrated writers, historians, philosophers, sociologists, and filmmakers have collectively managed to produce a formidable body of work on India—work that is domestically as well as internationally applauded and handsomely rewarded—that either turns caste into a footnote or completely elides the issue. I would call that fake history, too. The great Project of Unseeing.

A fine example of this is Sir Richard Attenborough's Oscar-winning film *Gandhi*, which was co-funded by the government of India. The film is inaccurate to the point of being false about Gandhi's time in South Africa and his attitude toward Black Africans. Almost more disturbing is the complete absence of Dr. Bhimrao Ambedkar, who is easily as much or more of an icon in India as Gandhi is. Ambedkar, a Dalit from Maharashtra, was the man who challenged Gandhi morally, politically, and intellectually. He denounced Hinduism and the caste discrimination it entailed, and showed Dalits a path out by renouncing the Hindu religion in favor of Buddhism. Both were extraordinary men, and the conflict between them has contributed greatly to our thinking today. While Gandhi's views on caste were not inimical to those of the Hindu right, his views on the place of Muslims in India were. That is what eventually led to his assassination by a former member (some say a member) of the RSS.[10] Still, what does it mean, this exalted, seriously falsified mythification of Gandhi and the erasure of Ambedkar in a government co-funded—a *Congress* government co-funded—multimillion-dollar movie extravaganza that still forms the basis of most of the world's idea of Gandhi and India's freedom struggle? Yes, the film was made a long time ago, but where is the corrective—the other extravaganza that at least tries to tell the truth? Where are the big films about Kabir, Ravidas, Ambedkar, Periyar, Ayyankali, Pandita Ramabai, Jotiba, Savitribai Phule, and all those who fought against caste through the ages? There are Indian liberals who sternly castigate the British for leaving British colonialism out of their history books, but are guilty of the exactly the same wrongdoing when it comes to the practice of caste.

In South Africa, Gandhi tried to distance dominant-caste Passenger Indians from oppressed-caste indentured laborers and Black Africans, whom he often called "kaffirs" and "savages"—a campaign that he sustained for years. In 1894, he wrote in an open letter to the Natal Legislative Assembly that Indians and the English both "spring from a common stock, called the Indo-Aryan."[11] This is the conceit of many dominant-caste Hindus even today. They like to think of themselves as a conquering race of Aryan descent. (This goes some way towards explaining their obsession with white skin and horror of dark skin.) And yet, when it comes to the Muslim question, they suddenly transform themselves into the aboriginal sons of the soil of the Hindu homeland, and mark Muslims and Christians off as "foreigners."

To our paid-up Hindu fascists, known affectionately as the Sangh Parivar—the Family Collective—Muslims are the "internal enemy" whose real loyalties lie outside India. For many good-hearted liberals, Muslims are welcome guests, but guests nevertheless—burdened with the expectation of good behavior, which is a terrible thing to thrust onto fellow citizens. It's like giving women rights as long as they promise to be good—good mothers, sisters, wives, and daughters. Even the most well-intentioned, progressive people often counter anti-Muslim slander by talking up Muslim patriotism. Many liberals, including some Muslims themselves, have described Muslims as Indians "by choice" and not by chance—suggesting that they *chose* to stay in India and not to move to Pakistan after Partition in 1947. Many did, many didn't, and for many the choice simply did not exist. But to frame Indian Muslims as a people who are in India "by choice" draws a dangerous ring, a false bloodline, around a whole population, suggesting it has a less elemental relationship with the land—and could just as well live elsewhere. This plays straight into the binary of the Good Muslim–Bad Muslim, or the Muslim Patriot–Muslim Jihadi, and could inadvertently trap a whole population into having to redeem itself with a lifetime of regular flag-waving and constitution-reading. It also inadvertently shores up the appalling logic of Hindu nationalists: Muslims have so many homelands, but Hindus only have India. The corollary to this, of course, is the well-known taunt thrown at Muslims as well as anyone else who challenges the Hindu nationalist view: "Go to Pakistan."[12]

Pakistan, Bangladesh, and India are organically connected, socially, culturally, and geographically. Reverse the Hindu nationalists' logic, and imagine how it plays out for the tens of millions of Hindus living in Bangladesh and Pakistan. Hindu nationalism and Muslim alienation in India make these minorities extremely vulnerable. The new Citizenship Amendment Act, which pretends to welcome persecuted non-Muslim minorities from Pakistan, Afghanistan, and Bangladesh—a pretense that suggests, ridiculously, that no Muslims are persecuted in those countries—will most likely endanger those minorities further. Across the border, "Go to India!" is likely to be the reaction to "Go to Pakistan!" The consequence of destabilizing whole populations in this way can be genocide. We know this. We've been here before. We've gone through the bloodshed of 1947. It is a great misconception to believe that this current regime in India, with its bottomless ability to be ruthless, is remotely concerned about the persecution of anybody by anybody, Hindus included. In fact, persecution appears to animate it.

All of this is to say that the foundation of today's fascism, the unacceptable fake history of Hindu nationalism, rests on a deeper foundation of another, apparently more acceptable, more sophisticated set of fake histories that elide the stories of caste, of women, and a range of other genders—and of how those stories intersect below the surface of the grand narrative of class and capital. To challenge fascism means to challenge all of this.

Sometimes I feel—self-servingly perhaps, the way a surgeon has faith in surgery—that fiction is uniquely positioned to do this, because fiction has the capaciousness, the freedom and latitude, to hold out a universe of infinite complexity. Because every human is really a walking sheaf of identities—a Russian doll that contains identities within identities, each of which can be shuffled around, each of which may, in entirely inconsistent ways, defy or comply with other "normal" conventions by which people are crudely and often cruelly defined, identified, and organized. Particularly so in this feudal, medieval society of ours in India, one that is pretending to be modern yet continues to practice one of the most brutal forms of social hierarchy in the world.

I'm not talking here of fiction as exposé, or as the righter of social wrongs (pardon the pun). Nor do I mean fiction that is a disguised manifesto or is written to address a particular issue or subject. I mean fiction that attempts to recreate the universe of the familiar, but then makes visible what the Project of Unseeing seeks to conceal.

The Project of Unseeing works in mysterious ways. It can even appear in the seductive avatar of high praise. For example, in my first novel, *The God of Small Things*, published more than twenty years ago, sexual and emotional transgression across caste lines and the complicated relationship between caste and communism are central themes. Much has been said about the novel's lyricism, its metaphors, its structure, its understanding of children's minds. But except in Kerala, where the novel was very well understood and therefore ran into some hostility, the caste question tends to be glossed over, or treated as a class issue. As though Ammu and Velutha were Lady Chatterley and Oliver Mellors. This is to understand absolutely nothing about Indian society. Certainly, caste and class overlap, but they aren't identical. As India's many Communist parties are discovering to their peril.

By the time I began to write *The Ministry of Utmost Happiness*, the direction things were heading in the subcontinent had become truly alarming. India and Pakistan had become nuclear powers, turning Kashmir into a possible nuclear flashpoint. (I fear that just as fascism will not be called fascism unless millions have been gassed in concentration camps, the nuclear threat will not be taken seriously until it is too late.) In India, the previously protected market had been opened to international capital. Neoliberal economic evangelists and Hindu nationalists had ridden into town on the same horse—a flaming saffron steed whose dapples were really dollar signs. The upshot of this is that while all our energies are spent trying to douse the bushfire of hatred, of human pitted against human, our forests and rivers are dying, our mountains are eroding, our ice caps are melting, and even as the Indian economy is entering freefall the combined wealth of the country's sixty-three richest people outstrips the annual budget outlay for a nation of 1.3 billion. By far.[13]

Under these circumstances, how does one write? *What* does one write?

More often than not, the folks in my novels teach me how to think and what to write. I leave it to them.

Here is a section from the second chapter of *The Ministry of Utmost Happiness*: Anjum and Saddam Hussain, her friend and business partner, are on the roof of the Jannat Guest House. They're having a lazy day, drinking tea and gazing at kites circling in the sky. Anjum, who is in her fifties and has lived in the graveyard for years, has just confronted young Saddam with the fact that she has always known he isn't really Muslim. Saddam begins to tell her his story. He was born into a family of Dalit chamars—skinners—in a village in Haryana. His parents named him Dayachand. A terrible experience—which I based on an actual incident in which five Dalits were lynched by a Hindu mob—caused him to run away from home. Rage and humiliation made him renounce Hinduism and convert to Islam. Enthralled by a video of Saddam Hussein of Iraq facing his executioners with complete equanimity—which he watches for inspiration on his cell phone from time to time—Dayachand changed his name to Saddam Hussain.

Saddam's conversion to Islam is uncommon for our times. But only late last year, three thousand Dalits in a village in Tamil Nadu announced their intention to embrace Islam. In June, the village was rocked by the "honor killing" of a young couple, a Dalit girl and non-Dalit boy, by the boy's brother. One night in December, a wall that the dominant castes had earlier built into the hillside—a caste wall, separating the Dalit settlement at the bottom of the hill from the rest of the village—collapsed onto the huts below and killed seventeen people. It was unstable and structurally unsound, and people had protested against it, but to no avail. Ravichandran, the founder of a Dalit blog and YouTube channel—Dalit Camera: Through Un-Touchable Eyes—reported this story, and has also converted to Islam. He is now Abdul Raees.[14]

For three thousand Dalits to convert to Islam now, when the political commentariat is abuzz with somewhat gleeful talk of the "Hinduization" of Dalits, and right when the Modi government is moving to disempower and disenfranchise Muslims, is pure political dynamite. Even on the evidence of just this one example, how can we argue with Ambedkar's call to his people to renounce Hinduism?

But here is young Saddam Hussain from *The Ministry of Utmost Happiness,* who, for reasons of his own, had made that move several years before. He is just beginning to tell Anjum his story. The saffron parakeets in the text are a euphemism for Hindu vigilantes, who often wear saffron headbands when they swarm:

"So we would go and collect the carcasses, skin them, and turn the hides into leather . . . I'm talking about the year 2002. I was still in school. You know better than me what was going on then . . . what it was like . . . Yours happened in February, mine in November. It was the day of Dussehra. On our way to pick up the cow we passed a Ramlila maidan where they had built huge effigies of the demons . . . Ravan, Meghnad and Kumbhakaran, as high as three-storeyed buildings—all ready be to blown up in the evening."

No Old Delhi Muslim needed a lesson about the Hindu festival of Dussehra. It was celebrated every year in the Ramlila grounds, just outside Turkman Gate. Every year the effigies of Ravan, the ten-headed "demon" King of Lanka, his brother Kumbhakaran and his son Meghnad grew taller and were packed with more and more explosives. Every year the Ramlila, the story of how Lord Ram, King of Ayodhya, vanquished Ravan in the battle of Lanka, which Hindus believed was the story of the triumph of Good over Evil, was enacted with greater aggression and ever-more generous sponsorship. A few audacious scholars had begun to suggest that the Ramlila was really history turned into mythology, and that the evil demons were really dark-skinned Dravidians—indigenous rulers—and the Hindu gods who vanquished them (and turned them into Untouchables and other oppressed castes who would spend their lives in service of the new rulers) were the Aryan invaders. They pointed to village rituals in which people worshiped deities, including Ravan, that in Hinduism were considered to be demons. In the new dispensation however, ordinary people did not need to be scholars to know, even if they could not openly say so, that in the rise and rise of the Parakeet Reich, regardless of what may or may not have been meant in the scriptures, in saffron parakeetspeak, the evil demons had come to mean not just indigenous people, but everybody who was not Hindu. Which included of course the citizenry of Shahjahanabad.

When the giant effigies were blown up, the sound of the explosions would boom through the narrow lanes of the old city. And few were in doubt about what that was meant to mean.[15]

One of today's most prominent faces in the protests against the Citizenship Amendment Act is a young Dalit politician who heads the Bhim Army—named after Bhimrao Ambedkar. He calls himself Chandrashekhar Aazad "Ravan." He has chosen to not just honor but personify Ravan, Ram's vanquished "demon" foe. What does that signify? It is an audacious declaration that at least some people view Hinduism—not just Hindutva, the Hindu nationalist political ideology, but Hinduism, the religion—as a form of colonialism and cruel subjugation. Ravan is seen frequently on the front pages of the papers, infuriating the government by making common cause with the Muslim community. He appeared late one night on the crowded steps of Delhi's Jama Masjid, a night filled with shouts of *Jai Bhim!* and *Inquilab Zindabad!*—Long live Bhimrao Ambedkar! and Long live the Revolution!

A precarious solidarity is evolving between Muslims and Ambedkarites and followers of other anti-caste leaders like Jotiba and Savitribai Phule, Sant Ravidas and Birsa Munda, as well as a new generation of young leftists who, unlike the older generation, place caste alongside class at the center of their worldview. It's still brittle, still full of material and ideological contradictions, still full of suspicion and resentment, but it's the only hope we have.

The trouble is that this fragile coalition is being slaughtered even as it is being born. The fake-news project—its history department as well as its current-affairs desk—has been corporatized, Bollywoodized, televised, Twitterized, atomized, weaponized, WhatsAppized, and is disseminating its product at the speed of light. It's all around us. It's the weather we endure and the air we breathe. It's the smell of spring and the winter chill. It's what we see and hear and swim in. It's the threat. It's the promise. It's the grey pillar that presses down on our hearts in our dreams and our waking hours. It's what we react to and what we write against. And it's what makes writing that most perilous of activities, whose consequences are not literary prizes or good or bad reviews. For some of us, every sentence, spoken or written, real or fake, every word, every punctuation mark can be torn from the body of a text, mangled and turned into a court notice, a police case, a mob attack, a television lynching by crazed news anchors—or, as in the case of the journalist Gauri Lankesh and so many less-well-known others, an assassination. Gauri was shot dead outside her home in Bangalore in September 2017. The last message she sent me was a photograph of her holding *The Ministry of Utmost Happiness*.

Assassination is the extreme end of the spectrum. Elsewhere on it are threats, arrests, beatings and, if you are a woman, fake videos and character assassination—"she's a whore, she's a drunk!"[16] (Neither of which do I, personally, consider an insult.) And not to forget, the all-time favorite—"she should be gang-raped!" Attacks on people with a profile, like me—whether they are wildly defamatory (or absolutely true—"she's not a Hindu"), or physical assaults on meetings and stages, or legal harassment with false cases—are usually appeals for the attention of the BJP high command by political workers aspiring to a promotion. A kind of job application. Because it is well known that those who show this kind of initiative are often rewarded—lynchers are feted, those accused of murder become cabinet ministers. In keeping with this spirit, days before *The Ministry* was published, a reasonably well-known Bollywood actor who is also a BJP member of Parliament suggested that the Indian Army tie me to a jeep and use me as a human shield in Kashmir, as it had recently done with a Kashmiri civilian.[17] Mainstream television channels spent hours debating the pros and cons of his proposal. You can imagine how this kind of thing plays out in the minds of aspiring job-seekers. But we must remember to be kind, because the Indian economy being what it is, these are increasingly becoming the only jobs available.

All this is nothing compared to what millions of people in India are having to live through. I mention it only in order to think aloud about how this continuous, unceasing threat affects writers and their writing. Each one of us reacts differently, of course. Speaking for myself, as the pressure mounts and the windows are shut one by one, every cell of my writing brain seems to want to force them open again. Does that shrink or expand writers? Sharpen or blunt them? Most people, I imagine, believe it would restrict a writer's range and imagination, steal away those moments of intimacy and contemplation without which a literary text does not amount to very much. I have often caught myself wondering—if I were to be incarcerated or driven underground, would it liberate my writing? Would what I write become simpler, more lyrical perhaps, and less negotiated? It's possible. But right now, as we struggle to keep the windows open, I believe our liberation lies in the negotiation. Hope lies in texts that can accommodate and keep alive our intricacy, our complexity, and our *density* against the onslaught of the terrifying, sweeping simplifications of fascism. As they barrel toward us, speeding down their straight, smooth highway, we greet them with our beehive, our maze. We keep our complicated world, with all its seams exposed, alive in our writing.

After twenty years of writing fiction and nonfiction that tracks the rise of Hindu nationalism, after years of reading about the rise and fall of European fascism, I have begun to wonder why fascism—although it is by no means the *same* everywhere—is so recognizable across histories and cultures. It's not just the fascists that are recognizable—the strong man, the ideological army, the squalid dreams of Aryan superiority, the dehumanization and ghettoization of the "internal enemy," the massive and utterly ruthless propaganda machine, the false-flag attacks and assassinations, the fawning businessmen and film stars, the attacks on universities, the fear of intellectuals, the specter of detention camps, and the hate-fueled zombie population that chants the Eastern equivalent of "Heil! Heil! Heil!" It's also the rest of us—the exhausted, quarreling opposition, the vain, nit-picking Left, the equivocating liberals who spent years building the road that has led to the situation we find ourselves in, and are now behaving like shocked, righteous rabbits who never imagined that rabbits were an important ingredient of the rabbit stew that was always on the menu. And, of course, the wolves who ignored the decent folks' counsel of moderation and sloped off into the wilderness to howl unceasingly, futilely—and, if they were female, then "shrilly" and "hysterically"—at the terrifying, misshapen moon. All of us are recognizable.

So, at the end of it all, is fascism a kind of *feeling*—in the way anger, fear, and love are feelings—that manifests itself in recognizable ways across cultures? Does a country fall into fascism the way a person falls in love? Or, more accurately, in hate? Has India fallen in hate? Because truly, the most palpable feeling in the air is the barbaric hatred the current regime and its supporters show toward a section of the population. Equally palpable now is the love that has risen to oppose this. You can see it in people's eyes, hear it in protesters' song and speech. It's a battle of those who know how to think against those who know how to hate. A battle of lovers against haters. It's an unequal battle, because the love is on the street and vulnerable. The hate is on the street, too, but it is armed to the teeth, and protected by all the machinery of the state.

The violence in Uttar Pradesh under Adityanath has not yet approached anything like the violence of the anti-Muslim pogroms in Gujarat in 2002 under its chief minister at the time, Narendra Modi. Uttar Pradesh is still a work in progress. Adityanath, unlike Modi, is still a prime minister-in-waiting. The 2017 election campaign that delivered him to power in Uttar Pradesh came to be known as the Kabristan-versus-Shamshan (the Graveyard-versus-the Cremation Ground) campaign. The BJP's rabble-rousing, spearheaded by Modi himself, involved pitting

Muslim graveyards against Hindu cremation grounds, and accusing the opposition of "appeasing" Muslims by developing one but not the other. This obsession with "burial versus cremation" runs deep. Babu Bajrangi, one of the lynchpins of the 2002 pogroms in Gujarat, was caught on camera in a sting operation by a journalist for *Tehelka* magazine, boasting of his deeds and of his proximity to Modi: "We didn't spare a single Muslim shop, we set everything on fire, we set them on fire and killed them . . . hacked, burnt, set on fire . . . because these bastards say they don't want to be cremated, they're afraid of it."[18] The tapes are still online.

Years after the massacre, Babu Bajrangi was convicted for the murder of ninety-seven Muslims in the Naroda Patiya neighborhood. He spent some years in jail but is out on bail now, on grounds of ill health, along with some fellow mass murderers. In all, the pogroms saw more than two thousand people murdered, dismembered, raped, and burnt alive, and more than 150,000 driven from their homes. Just days ago, on January 28, 2020, the Supreme Court granted interim bail to fourteen people convicted of burning twenty-three Muslims to death during the Gujarat pogroms.[19] The chief justice has asked the government to find them useful "social and spiritual service." The difficulty here is that, for many Hindu fascists, killing Muslims *is* considered social and spiritual service.

After the 2002 pogroms, Modi's popularity soared. When, in 2014, he was sworn in as prime minister, many liberals—writers, journalists, and public intellectuals—greeted him ecstatically as an embodiment of hope for a new India. Many are deeply disillusioned now, but their disillusionment only begins after 2014.

Because questioning Modi's deeds before that would involve questioning themselves. So Gujarat in 2002 is rapidly being erased from public memory. That ought not happen. It deserves a place in history, as well as in literature. Anjum ensures that.

In *The Ministry*, Anjum gets caught by the mob in Gujarat. She is there with her father's old friend Zakir Mian, who earns his living in a street-side stall in Old Delhi, making wedding garlands out of small currency notes folded into little birds. The two of them have gone on a little pilgrimage to the shrine of the poet Wali Dakhani. When they don't return, even weeks after the murdering has tailed off, Zakir Mian's son goes looking for his father. He finds Anjum in a refugee camp—doubly traumatized by having to live in the men's section. She returns home with him but finds herself unable to cope with life as usual. She is unable to continue living in the Khwabgah, the House of Dreams in Old Delhi where she has lived for years with an adopted family of souls like her, all having seceded from the *duniya*—the real world. She is unable to get on with Ustad Kulsoom Bi, stern head of the Khwabgah. Unable to be a good mother to her foundling daughter, Zainab. So, Anjum packs her things and moves into the nearby graveyard, where her family is buried:

> The smack addicts at the northern end of the graveyard—shadows just a deeper shade of night—huddled on knolls of hospital waste in a sea of old bandages and used syringes, didn't seem to notice her at all. On the southern side, clots of homeless people sat around fires cooking their meagre, smoky meals. Stray dogs, in better health than the humans, sat at a polite distance, waiting politely for scraps.
>
> In that setting, Anjum would ordinarily have been in some

danger. But her desolation protected her. Unleashed at last from social protocol, it rose up around her in all its majesty—a fort, with ramparts, turrets, hidden dungeons and walls that hummed like an approaching mob. She rattled through its gilded chambers like a fugitive absconding from herself. She tried to dismiss the cortège of saffron men with saffron smiles who pursued her with infants impaled on their saffron tridents, but they would not be dismissed. She tried to shut the door on Zakir Mian, lying neatly folded in the middle of the street, like one of his crisp cash-birds. But he followed her, folded, through closed doors on his flying carpet. She tried to forget the way he had looked at her just before the light went out of his eyes. But he wouldn't let her.

She tried to tell him that she had fought back bravely as they hauled her off his lifeless body.

But she knew very well that she hadn't.

She tried to un-know what they had done to all the others— how they had folded the men and unfolded the women. And how eventually they had pulled them apart limb from limb and set them on fire.

But she knew very well that she knew.

They.

They, who?

Newton's Army, deployed to deliver an Equal and Opposite Reaction. Thirty thousand saffron parakeets with steel talons and bloodied beaks, all squawking together:

Mussalman ka ek hi sthan! Qabristan ya Pakistan!

Only one place for the Mussalman! The Graveyard or Pakistan!

Anjum, feigning death, had lain sprawled over Zakir Mian. Counterfeit corpse of a counterfeit woman. But the parakeets, even though they were—or pretended to be—pure vegetarian (this was the minimum qualification for conscription), tested the breeze with the fastidiousness and proficiency of bloodhounds. And of course they found her. Thirty thousand voices chimed together, mimicking Ustad Kulsoom Bi's Birbal:*

Ai Hai! Saali randi Hijra! Sister-fucking Whore Hijra. Sister-fucking Muslim Whore Hijra.

Another voice rose, high and anxious, another bird:

Nahi yaar, mat maro, Hijron ka maarna apshagun hota hai.

Don't kill her, brother, killing Hijras brings bad luck.

Bad luck!

Nothing scared those murderers more than the prospect of bad luck. After all, it was to ward off bad luck that the fingers that gripped the slashing swords and flashing daggers were studded with lucky stones embedded in thick gold rings. It was to ward off bad luck that the wrists wielding iron rods that bludgeoned people to death were festooned with red puja threads lovingly tied by adoring mothers. Having taken all these precautions, what would be the point of willfully courting bad luck?

So they stood over her and made her chant their slogans.

Bharat Mata Ki Jai! Vande Mataram!

She did. Weeping, shaking, humiliated beyond her worst nightmare.

Victory to Mother India! Salute the Mother!

They left her alive. Unkilled. Unhurt. Neither folded nor unfolded. She alone. So that *they* might be blessed with good fortune.

Butchers' Luck.

That's all she was. And the longer she lived, the more good luck she brought them.

---

* Birbal is Ustad Kulsoom Bi's foul-mouthed pet parakeet.

She tried to un-know that little detail as she rattled through her private fort. But she failed. She knew very well that she knew very well that she knew very well.

The Chief Minister with cold eyes and a vermillion forehead would go on to win the next elections. Even after the Poet-Prime Minister's government fell at the Center, he won election after election in Gujarat. Some people believed he ought to be held responsible for mass murder, but his voters called him Gujarat ka Lalla. Gujarat's Beloved.[20]

Anjum lives in the graveyard for years, at first as "a ravaged, feral specter, out-haunting every resident djinn and spirit, ambushing bereaved families who came to bury their dead with a grief so wild, so untethered, that it clean outstripped theirs."[21] Gradually, she recovers and begins to build a house for herself, each room enclosing a grave. This eventually turns into the Jannat Guest House. When municipal authorities say that it is illegal for squatters to live in the graveyard and threaten to demolish it, she tells them that she isn't living in the graveyard, she is dying in it. The Jannat Guest House blossoms when Saddam Hussain—former mortuary worker, watchman, and now small-time entrepreneur—arrives to live there with his horse, Payal. And when Anjum's old friend, the blind Imam Ziauddin, moves in, the enterprise expands into the Jannat Guest House and Funeral Services. Guest rooms and funeral services are offered entirely on the whims of the CEO. Those whims are unashamedly partial to people and animals, living as well as deceased, for whom the the duniya has no place.

Sometimes I feel that my world, too, is divided very simply into two kinds of people—those whom Anjum will agree to accommodate in her guest house or inter in her graveyard, and those she will not.

Anjum knows that the place she has created is not merely a physical shelter. It's not your run-of-the-mill poorhouse. Because it is not only the poor and hard-done-by who gather around her. Here she is, explaining to Saddam Hussain the meaning of the place they call their home. The Biroo she refers to is her dog, whom she rescued off the streets:

> "Once you have fallen off the edge like all of us have, including our Biroo," Anjum said, "you will never stop falling. And as you fall you will hold on to other falling people. The sooner you understand that the better. This place where we live, where we have made our home, is the place of falling people. Here there is no *haqeeqat. Arre*, even *we* aren't real. We don't really exist."[22]

People come and go, live and die in the Place of Falling People. Life germinates between the graves. Anjum's graveyard boasts a vegetable garden and even a small swimming pool for poor people. Even though it has no water, local people are proud of it and bring their children to see it. At funerals and weddings, all manner of prayers are murmured and sung, all manner of vows exchanged. They include a reading of the Islamic Fateha, a recitation of Shakespeare's *Henry V*, and the singing of the Hindi translation of "The "Internationale."

One day, Dr. Azad Bhartiya—who translates his own name to mean the Free Indian—tireless pamphleteer and hunger striker and steadfast friend to Falling People, reads Anjum a long letter, translating it into Urdu for her. The letter is from a Comrade

Maase Revathy, the biological mother of a baby whom Anjum found abandoned in a place called Jantar Mantar—Delhi's gathering place for protesters and hunger strikers, and home to Dr. Azad Bhartiya, who has lived there on the pavement for seventeen years. Anjum adopts the baby and brings her to the graveyard. The letter Dr. Bhartiya reads is a long account of the mother's life as a guerrilla fighter in the forests of central India, the circumstances that led to the birth of her baby, and the reasons that have compelled her to abandon it. At first Anjum—who longs to be a mother—is hostile, because she cannot countenance the idea of a woman who has abandoned her child. But gradually she begins to listen to the story of this faraway woman, whose concerns are so different from her own but whose grief is just as wild and just as complicated. The letter ends with a Lal Salaam, a red salute:

> "Lal Salaam Aleikum," was Anjum's inadvertent, instinctive response to the end of the letter. That could have been the beginning of a whole political movement, but she had only meant it in the way of an "Ameen" after listening to a moving sermon.[23]

There it is then—between Anjum, Saddam, and their companions, the political compact of today's uprising, assembled in Anjum's graveyard. Jai Bhim. Inquilab Zindabad. Lal Salaam Aleikum. But these are only the soul of the revolution. Not the revolution itself. Because there is none of the stuff of which revolutions are made in Anjum's graveyards. There are no flags. There is no flag-waving, no pledge-taking. No slogans. No hard borders between male and female, human and animal, nation and nation, or even life and death.

The presiding deity in the Jannat Guest House is Hazrat Sarmad, who blessed Anjum when she was a newborn. Hazrat Sarmad was a Jewish Armenian who traveled from Persia to Delhi three hundred years ago. He renounced Judaism for Islam and then renounced orthodox Islam for Love. He lived naked on the streets of Old Delhi, reciting poems of love until he was beheaded on the steps of Delhi's Jama Masjid by the Mughal emperor Aurangzeb. Sarmad's shrine is clamped like a limpet to the sheer face of the Jama Masjid. To Anjum and those who seek her shelter, Sarmad is the Saint of the Unconsoled, Solace of the Indeterminate, Blasphemer among Believers, Believer among Blasphemers. He is the battered angel who keeps watch over his battered charges, who holds the doors between worlds open (illegally) and who never allows the circle to close. And so it is that through that illegal crack, that unclosed circle, Kashmir comes drifting into Anjum's graveyard. And the forbidden conversation begins.

Kashmir, the land of the living dead and the talking graves—city graveyards, village graveyards, mass graves, unmarked graves, double-decker graves. Kashmir, whose truth can only be told in fiction—because only fiction can tell about air that is so thick with fear and loss, with pride and mad courage, and with unimaginable cruelty. Only fiction can try to describe the transactions that take place in such a climate. Because the story of Kashmir is not only a story about war and torture and rigged elections and human rights violations. It's a story about love and poetry, too. It cannot be flattened into news.

Here is Musa Yeswi, architect and obsessive sketcher of horses. Musa, who wanders in and out of Anjum's graveyard through the battered angel's illegal portal. Musa, who struggles to hold on to some semblance of sanity as he is drawn inexorably into the vortex of Kashmir's filthy war, and eventually disappears into its dark heart. Like many young men of his generation, circumstance drives him underground, where he morphs into many people, takes on many identities, attends his own funeral, and barely knows who he really is any more. In a letter to Miss Jebeen, his five-year-old daughter who is killed when the security forces open fire on an unarmed procession, Musa describes her own funeral to her. He tells her about the sloth bear that came down the mountain, the *hangul* (Kashmir stag) that watched from the woods, the kites that circled in the sky supervising everything, and the one hundred thousand mourners who covered the ground like snow. "What I know for sure is only this," he writes, "in our Kashmir the dead will live forever; and the living are only dead people, pretending."[24] This is a description of Miss Jebeen's funeral:

> Miss Jebeen and her mother were buried along with fifteen others, taking the toll of their massacre to seventeen.
>
> At the time of their funeral the Mazar-e-Shohadda was still fairly new, but was already getting crowded. However, the Intizamiya Committee, the Organizing Committee, had its ear to the ground from the very beginning of the insurrection and had a realistic idea of things to come. It planned the layout of the graves carefully, making ordered, efficient use of the available space. Everyone understood how important it was to bury martyrs' bodies in collective burial grounds and not leave them scattered (in their thousands), like birdfeed, up in the moun-

tains, or in the forests around the army camps and torture centers that had mushroomed across the Valley. When the fighting began and the Occupation tightened its grip, for ordinary people the consolidation of their dead became, in itself, an act of defiance. . . .

As the bodies were lowered into their graves the crowd began to murmur its prayer.

> *Rabbish rahlee sadree; Wa yassir lee amri*
> *Wahlul uqdatan min lisaanee; Yafqahoo qawlee*

My Lord! Relieve my mind. And ease my task for me
And loose a knot from my tongue. That they may understand my saying

The smaller, hip-high children in the separate, segregated section for women, suffocated by the rough wool of their mothers' garments, unable to see very much, barely able to breathe, conducted their own hip-level transactions: *I'll give you six bullet casings if you give me your dud grenade.*

A lone woman's voice climbed into the sky, eerily high, raw pain driven through it like a pike.

> *Ro rahi hai yeh zameen! Ro raha hai asmaan . . .*
> Another joined in and then another:

This earth, she weeps! The heavens too . . .
The birds stopped their twittering for a while and listened, beady-eyed, to humansong. Street dogs slouched past checkposts unchecked, their heartbeats rock steady. Kites and griffons circled the thermals, drifting lazily back and forth across the

> Line of Control, just to mock the tiny clot of humans gathered
> down below.[25]

This conversation between Anjum's graveyard and Miss Jebeen's, disallowed in the duniya, the real world, cannot be prevented from taking place in our collective Khwabgah, our House of Dreams.

Just as I wrote that last line, a quiet little seven-year-old fellow called Esthappen, an interloper from another novel called *The God of Small Things*, came up to me and whispered in my ear: "If you eat fish in a dream, does it count? Does it mean you've eaten fish?"[26]

But if that conversation between graveyards does not, cannot, or will not be allowed to take place in the duniya—then perhaps the one I describe next ought to be taken seriously.

Musa and Garson Hobart, the intelligence officer, now retired, meet for the first time after decades. From being rival suitors for the attentions of a woman in college, they have been shadowy antagonists in Kashmir's endless war. As Musa leaves, Hobart walks down to the street with him to see him off. He wants to ask him one last question that has tormented him, and he knows that once Musa disappears he will never know the answer. It's about Major Amrik Singh—a notorious army officer involved in a series of killings in Kashmir during the 1990s, one of which was thought to have been the custodial killing of Musa himself. When huge protests broke out against him, Amrik Singh vanished from Kashmir without a trace. Hobart knows that he was secretly spirited away by the Indian government, sent first to Canada from where he disappeared into the United States. He surfaced after some years when the fact that he had been arrested in California for domestic violence made the news. Months later, Singh and his family were found dead. He appeared to have shot himself, his wife, and his children in their little suburban home. Hobart, whose own past and the story of the woman he loves are intricately connected with Amrik Singh, is not convinced of the official story. Based on wisps of evidence and some papers he has come across, he believes that Kashmir, and Musa in particular, had something to do with Amrik Singh's tragic and gruesome end:

"Did you kill Amrik Singh?"

"No." He looked at me with his green-tea-colored eyes. "I didn't."

He said nothing for a moment, but I could tell from his gaze that he was assessing me, wondering if he should say more or not. I told him I'd seen the asylum applications and the boarding passes of flights to the US with a name that matched one of his fake passports. I had come across a receipt from a car-hire company in Clovis. The dates matched too, so I knew that he had something to do with that whole episode, but I didn't know what.

"I'm just curious," I said. "It doesn't matter if you did. He deserved to die."

"I didn't kill him. He killed himself. But we made him kill himself."

I had no idea what the hell that was supposed to mean.

"I didn't go to the US looking for him. I was already there on some other work when I saw the news in the papers that he had been arrested for assaulting his wife. His residential address became public. I had been looking for him for years. I had some unfinished business with him. Many of us did. So I went to Clovis, made some inquiries and finally found him at a truck-washing garage and workshop where he would go to have his truck serviced. He was a completely different person from the murderer we knew, the killer of Jalib Qadri and many others. He did not have that infrastructure of impunity within which he operated in Kashmir. He was scared and broke. I almost felt sorry for him. I assured him that I was not going to harm him, and that I was only there to tell him that we would not allow him to forget the things that he had done."

Musa and I were having this conversation out on the street. I had come down to see him off.

"Other Kashmiris had also read the news. So they began to arrive in Clovis to see how the Butcher of Kashmir lived now. Some were journalists, some were writers, photographers, lawyers . . . some were just ordinary people. They turned up at his workplace, at his home, at the supermarket, across the street, at his children's school. Every day. He was forced to look at us. Forced to remember. It must have driven him crazy. Eventually it made him self-destruct. So . . . to answer your question . . . no, I did not kill him."

What Musa said next, standing against the backdrop of the school gates with the painting of the ogre nurse giving a baby a polio vaccine, was like . . . like an ice-injection. More so because it was said in that casual, genial way he had, with a friendly, almost-happy smile, as though he was only joking.

"One day Kashmir will make India self-destruct in the same way. You may have blinded all of us, every one of us, with your pellet guns by then. But you will still have eyes to see what you have done to us. You're not destroying us. You are constructing us. It's yourselves that you are destroying. Khuda Hafiz, Garson bhai."[27]

The destruction—it has begun.

And, yes, if in a dream you've eaten fish, it means you've eaten fish.

CHAPTER 8

There Is Fire in the Ducts, the System Is Failing

Beloved friends, comrades, and my fellow writers—this place where we are gathered today is only a short bus ride away from where four days ago a fascist mob—fired up by speeches made by members of the ruling party, backed up and actively assisted by the police, assured of round-the-clock support by a vast section of the electronic mass media, and comforted by the belief that the courts would do nothing to come in their way—mounted an armed, murderous attack on Muslims in the working-class colonies of northeast Delhi.

The attack had been in the air for a while, so people were somewhat prepared, and so defended themselves. Markets, shops, homes, mosques, and vehicles have been burned out. The streets are full of stones and debris. The hospitals are full of the wounded and dying.

* Statement at Hum Dekhenge All India Convention of Writers and Artists Against CAA-NPR-NRC, delivered in New Delhi, March 1, 2020.

The morgues are full of the dead—both Muslim and Hindu, including a policeman and a young staffer of the Intelligence Bureau. Yes, people on both sides have shown themselves capable of horrifying brutality as well as unbelievable courage and kindness.

However, there can be no equivalence here. None of this alters the fact that the attack was begun by lumpen mobs chanting "Jai Shri Ram!" and backed by the apparatus of this now nakedly fascist state. Notwithstanding these slogans, this is not what people like to label a Hindu–Muslim "riot." It is a manifestation of the ongoing battle between fascists and anti-fascists—in which Muslims are the first among the fascists' "enemies." To call it a riot or a *danga*, or "left" versus "right" or even "right" versus "wrong," as many are doing, is dangerous and obfuscatory. We have all seen the videos of the police standing by and sometimes participating in the arson. We have seen them smashing CCTV cameras, just as they did when they vandalized the Jamia Millia Islamia University library on December 15. We have seen them beat wounded Muslim men as they lay piled up against each other and force them to sing the National Anthem. We know that one of those young men is dead.[1] All the dead, wounded, and devastated, Muslim as well as Hindu, are victims of this regime headed by Narendra Modi, our nakedly fascist prime minister who himself is no stranger to being at the helm of affairs in a state when eighteen years ago a massacre on a much larger scale went on for weeks.

The anatomy of this particular conflagration will be studied for years to come. But the local detail will only be a matter of historical record because the ripples, based on hateful rumors fueled on social media, have begun to eddy outwards, and we can already smell more blood on the breeze. Although there have been no more killings in North Delhi, yesterday (February 29) saw mobs of people in Central Delhi chanting the slogan that built up to the attacks: *Desh ke gaddaron ko, Goli maaron saalon ko!*—What's to be done with traitors of the nation? Shoot the bastards! Only a few days ago, the Delhi High Court judge S. Muralidhar was furious with the Delhi police for having taken no action against Kapil Mishra, the former BJP MLA candidate who had earlier in the presence of the police issued a blatant threat to protestors peacefully sitting on the road in Jafarabad. On the night of February 26, the judge was given midnight orders to take up his new assignment in the Punjab High Court. Kapil Mishra is back on the streets with his supporters who are once again chanting *Desh ke gaddaron ko, Goli maaron saalon ko!* That slogan can now be used until further notice. Fun and games with judges isn't new. We know the story about Justice Loya.[2] We may have forgotten the story of Babu Bajrangi, convicted of participating in the killing of ninety-seven Muslims in Naroda Patiya, in Gujarat in 2002. You can listen to him in a YouTube video.[3] He'll tell you how "Narendra bhai" got him out of jail by "setting" the judges.

We have learned to expect massacres such as this one before elections—they have become a sort of barbaric election campaign to polarize votes and build constituencies. But the Delhi massacre happened just days after an election, after the BJP-RSS suffered a humiliating defeat. It is a punishment for Delhi and an announcement for the coming elections in Bihar.

Everything is on record. Everything is available for everyone to see and hear—the provocative speeches of Kapil Mishra, Parvesh Verma, Union Minister Anurag Thakur, Chief Minister of UP Yogi Adityanath, Home Minister Amit Shah, and even the prime minister himself. And yet everything has been turned upside down—it's being made to appear as though all of India is a victim of the absolutely peaceful, mostly female, mostly—but not only—Muslim protesters who have been out on the streets for almost seventy-five days, in their tens of thousands, to protest against the Citizenship Amendment Act.

The CAA, which offers a fast-track route to citizenship for non-Muslim minorities, is blatantly unconstitutional and blatantly anti-Muslim. Coupled with the National Population Register and the National Register of Citizens, it is meant to delegitimize, destabilize, and criminalize not just Muslims but hundreds of millions of Indians who do not have the requisite documents—including those who are chanting *Goli maaro saalon ko* today. Once citizenship comes into question, everything comes into question—your children's rights, your voting rights, your land rights. As Hannah Arendt said, "Citizenship gives you the right to have rights." Anybody who thinks this is not the case, please turn your attention to Assam and see what has happened to two million people—Hindus, Muslims. Dalits, Adivasis. Now trouble has started between local tribes and the non-tribal population in the state of Meghalaya. There is curfew in Shillong. The state borders are closed to non-locals.

The sole purpose of the NPR-NRC-CAA is to destabilize and divide people not just in India but across the whole subcontinent.

If they do indeed exist, these phantom millions of human beings whom India's current home minister calls Bangladeshi "termites" cannot be kept in detention centers and cannot be deported. By using such terminology and by thinking up such a ridiculous, diabolic scheme, this government is actually endangering the tens of millions of Hindus who live in Bangladesh, Pakistan, and Afghanistan whom they pretend to be concerned about, but who could suffer the backlash of this bigotry emanating from New Delhi.

Look where we have ended up.

In 1947 we won independence from colonial rule that was fought for by almost everybody with the exception of our current rulers. Since then all manner of social movements, anti-caste struggles, anti-capitalist struggles, feminist struggles have marked our journey up to now.

In the 1960s the call to revolution was a demand for justice, for the redistribution of wealth, and the overthrow of the ruling class.

By the 1990s we were reduced to fighting against the displacement of millions of people from their own lands and villages, people who became the collateral damage for the building of a new India in which India's sixty-three richest people have more wealth than the annual budget outlay for 1.3 billion people.

Now we are reduced to pleading for our rights as citizens from people who have had nothing to do with building this country. And as we plead, we watch the state withdraw its protection, we watch the police get communalized, we watch the judiciary gradually abdicate its duty, we watch the media that is meant to afflict the comfortable and comfort the afflicted do the very opposite.

Today is the 210th day since Jammu and Kashmir was uncon-stitutionally stripped of its special status. Thousands of Kashmiris including three former chief ministers continue to be in jail. Seven million people are living under a virtual information siege, a novel exercise in the mass violation of human rights. On February 26, the streets of Delhi looked like the streets of Srinagar. That was the day that Kashmiri children went to school for the first time in seven months. But what does it mean to go to school, while everything around you is slowly throttled?

A democracy that is not governed by a constitution and one whose institutions have all been hollowed out can only ever become a majoritarian state. You can agree or disagree with a constitution as a whole or in part—but to act as though it does not exist as this government is doing is to completely dismantle democracy. Perhaps this is the aim. This is our version of the coronavirus. We are sick.

There's no help on the horizon. No well-meaning foreign country. No UN.

And no political party that intends to win elections will or can afford to take a moral position. Because there is fire in the ducts. The system is failing.

What we need are people who are prepared to be unpopular. Who are prepared to put themselves in danger. Who are prepared to tell the truth. Brave journalists can do that, and they have. Brave lawyers can do that, and they have. And artists—beautiful, brilliant, brave writers, poets, musicians, painters, and filmmakers can do that. That beauty is on our side. All of it.

We have work to do. And a world to win.

CHAPTER 9

The Pandemic Is a Portal

Who can use the term "gone viral" now without shuddering a little? Who can look at anything anymore—a door handle, a cardboard carton, a bag of vegetables—without imagining it swarming with those unseeable, undead, unliving blobs dotted with suction pads waiting to fasten themselves on to our lungs? Who can think of kissing a stranger, jumping on to a bus, or sending their child to school without feeling real fear? Who can think of ordinary pleasure and not assess its risk? Who among us is not a quack epidemiologist, virologist, statistician, and prophet? Which scientist or doctor is not secretly praying for a miracle? Which anti-science priest is not—secretly, at least—submitting to science? And even while the virus proliferates, who could not be thrilled by the swell of birdsong in cities, peacocks dancing at traffic crossings, and the silence in the skies?

* First published in the *Financial Times*, April 4, 2020.

The number of cases worldwide is creeping perilously close to a million. Almost 50,000 people have died already. Projections suggest that number will swell to hundreds of thousands, perhaps more. The virus has moved freely along the pathways of trade and international capital, and the terrible illness it has brought in its wake has locked humans down in their countries, their cities, and their homes.

But unlike the flow of capital, this virus seeks proliferation, not profit, and has, therefore, inadvertently, to some extent, reversed the direction of the flow. It has mocked immigration controls, biometrics, digital surveillance, and every other kind of data analytics, and struck hardest—thus far—in the richest, most powerful nations of the world, bringing the engine of capitalism to a juddering halt. Temporarily perhaps, but at least long enough for us to examine its parts, make an assessment, and decide whether we want to help fix it, or look for a better engine.

The mandarins who are managing this pandemic are fond of speaking of war. They don't even use war as a metaphor, they use it literally. But if it really were a war, then who would be better prepared than the United States? If it were not masks, swabs, and gloves that its frontline soldiers needed but guns, smart bombs, bunker busters, submarines, fighter jets, and nuclear bombs, would there be a shortage?

Night after night, from halfway across the world, some of us watch the New York governor's press briefings with a fascination that is hard to explain. We follow the statistics, and hear the stories of overwhelmed hospitals in the United States, of underpaid, overworked nurses having to make masks out of garbage bags and old raincoats, risking everything to bring succor to the sick. About states being forced to bid against each other for ventilators, about doctors' dilemmas over which patient should get one and which left to die. And we think to ourselves, "My God! This is *America*!"

The tragedy is immediate, real, epic, and unfolding before our eyes. But it isn't new. It is the wreckage of a train that has been careening down the track for years. Who doesn't remember the videos of "patient dumping"—sick people, still in their hospital gowns, butt naked, being surreptitiously dumped on street corners? Hospital doors have too often been closed to the less fortunate citizens of the United States. It hasn't mattered how sick they've been, or how much they've suffered. At least not until now—because now, in the era of The Virus, a poor person's sickness can affect a wealthy society's health. And yet, even now, Bernie Sanders, the senator who has relentlessly campaigned for health care for all, is considered an outlier in his bid for the White House, even by his own party.

And what of my country, my poor-rich country, India, suspended somewhere between feudalism and religious fundamentalism, caste and capitalism, ruled by far-right Hindu nationalists? In December, while China was fighting the outbreak of the virus in Wuhan, the government of India was dealing with a mass uprising by hundreds of thousands of its citizens protesting against the brazenly discriminatory anti-Muslim citizenship law it had just passed in Parliament.

The first case of Covid-19 was reported in India on January 30, only days after the honorable chief guest of our Republic Day

Parade, Amazon forest-eater and Covid-denier Jair Bolsonaro, had left Delhi. But there was too much to do in February for The Virus to be accommodated in the ruling party's timetable. There was the official visit of president Donald Trump scheduled for the last week of the month. He had been lured by the promise of an audience of one million people in a sports stadium in the state of Gujarat. All that took money, and a great deal of time.

Then there were the Delhi Assembly elections that the Bharatiya Janata Party was slated to lose unless it upped its game, which it did, unleashing a vicious, no-holds-barred Hindu nationalist campaign, replete with threats of physical violence and the shooting of "traitors."

It lost anyway. So then there was punishment to be meted out to Delhi's Muslims, who were blamed for the humiliation. Armed mobs of Hindu vigilantes, backed by the police, attacked Muslims in the working-class neighborhoods of northeast Delhi. Houses, shops, mosques, and schools were burnt. Muslims who had been expecting the attack fought back. More than fifty people, Muslims and some Hindus, were killed. Thousands moved into refugee camps in local graveyards. Mutilated bodies were still being pulled out of the network of filthy, stinking drains when government officials had their first meeting about Covid-19 and most Indians first began to hear about the existence of something called hand sanitizer.

March was busy too. The first two weeks were devoted to toppling the Congress government in the central Indian state of Madhya Pradesh and installing a BJP government in its place. On

March 11 the World Health Organization declared that Covid-19 was a pandemic. Two days later, on March 13, the health ministry said that coronavirus "is not a health emergency." Finally, on March 19, the prime minister addressed the nation. He hadn't done much homework. He borrowed the playbook from France and Italy. He told us of the need for "social distancing" (easy to understand for a society so steeped in the practice of caste) and called for a day of "people's curfew" on March 22. He said nothing about what his government was going to do in the crisis, but he asked people to come out on their balconies and ring bells and bang their pots and pans to salute health workers. He didn't mention that, until that very moment, India had been exporting protective gear and respiratory equipment, instead of keeping it for Indian health workers and hospitals.

Not surprisingly, Narendra Modi's request was met with great enthusiasm. There were pot-banging marches, community dances, and processions. Not much social distancing. In the days that followed, men jumped into barrels of sacred cow dung, and BJP supporters threw cow-urine drinking parties. Not to be outdone, many Muslim organizations declared that the Almighty was the answer to The Virus and called for the faithful to gather in mosques in numbers. On March 24, at 8pm, Modi appeared on TV again to announce that, from midnight onwards, all of India would be under lockdown. Markets would be closed. All transport, public as well as private, would be disallowed. He said he was taking this decision not just as a prime minister but as our family elder. Who else can decide, without consulting the state governments that would have to deal with the fallout of this decision, that a nation of 1.38 billion people should be locked down with zero preparation and with four hours' notice? His methods definitely give the impression that India's prime minister thinks of citizens as a hostile force that needs to be ambushed, taken by surprise, but never trusted.

Locked down we were. Many health professionals and epidemiologists have applauded this move. Perhaps they are right in theory. But surely none of them can support the calamitous lack of planning or preparedness that turned the world's biggest, most punitive lockdown into the exact opposite of what it was meant to achieve.

The man who loves spectacles created the mother of all spectacles.

As an appalled world watched, India revealed herself in all her shame—her brutal, structural, social and economic inequality, her callous indifference to suffering. The lockdown worked like a chemical experiment that suddenly illuminated hidden things. As shops, restaurants, factories, and the construction industry shut down, as the wealthy and the middle classes enclosed themselves in gated colonies, our towns and megacities began to extrude their working-class citizens—their migrant workers—like so much unwanted accrual. Many driven out by their employers and landlords, millions of impoverished, hungry, thirsty people, young and old, men, women, children, sick people, blind people, disabled people, with nowhere else to go, with no public transport in sight, began a long march home to their villages. They walked for days, toward Badaun, Agra, Azamgarh, Aligarh, Lucknow, Gorakhpur—hundreds of miles away. Some died on the way.

They knew they were going home potentially to slow starvation. Perhaps they even knew they could be carrying the virus with them, and would infect their families, their parents, and grandparents back home, but they desperately needed a shred of familiarity, shelter, and dignity, as well as food, if not love. As they walked some were beaten brutally and humiliated by the police, who were charged with strictly enforcing the curfew. Young men were made to crouch and frog jump down the highway. Outside the town of Bareilly, one group was herded together and hosed down with chemical spray. A few days later, worried that the fleeing population would spread the virus to villages, the government sealed state borders even for walkers. People who had been walking for days were stopped and forced to return to camps in the cities they had just been forced to leave.

Among older people it evoked memories of the population transfer of 1947, when India was divided and Pakistan was born. Except that this current exodus was driven by class divisions, not religion. Even still, these were not India's poorest people. These were people who had (at least until now) work in the city and homes to return to. The jobless, the homeless, and the despairing remained where they were, in the cities as well as the countryside, where deep distress was growing long before this tragedy occurred. All through these horrible days, the home affairs minister, Amit Shah, remained absent from public view.

When the walking began in Delhi, I used a press pass from a magazine I frequently write for to drive to Ghazipur, on the border between Delhi and Uttar Pradesh.

The scene was biblical. Or perhaps not. The Bible could not have known numbers such as these. The lockdown to enforce physical distancing had resulted in the opposite—physical compression on an unthinkable scale. This is true even within India's towns and cities. The main roads might be empty, but the poor are sealed into cramped quarters in slums and shanties.

Every one of the walking people I spoke to was worried about the virus. But it was less real, less present in their lives than looming unemployment, starvation, and the violence of the police. Of all the people I spoke to that day, including a group of Muslim tailors who had only weeks ago survived the anti-Muslim pogrom, one man's words especially troubled me. He was a carpenter called Ramjeet, who planned to walk all the way to Gorakhpur, near the Nepal border.

"Maybe when Modiji decided to do this, nobody told him about us. Maybe he doesn't know about us," he said. "Us" means approximately 460 million people.

State governments in India (as in the United States) have showed more heart and understanding in the crisis. Trade unions, private citizens, and other collectives are distributing food and emergency rations. The central government has been slow to respond to their desperate appeals for funds. It turns out that the prime minister's National Relief Fund has no ready cash available. Instead, money from well-wishers is pouring into the somewhat mysterious new PM-CARES fund.[1] Prepackaged meals with Modi's face on them have begun to appear. In addition to this, the prime minister has shared his yoga nidra videos, in which a morphed, animated Modi with a dream body demonstrates yoga asanas to help people deal with the stress of self-isolation.

The narcissism is deeply troubling. Perhaps one of the asanas could be a request-asana in which Modi requests the French prime minister to allow us to renege on the very troublesome Rafale fighter jet deal and use that $8.5 billion for desperately needed emergency measures to support a few million hungry people. Surely the French will understand.

As the lockdown enters its second week, supply chains have broken, medicines and essential supplies are running low. Thousands of truck drivers are still marooned on the highways, with little food and water. Standing crops, ready to be harvested, are slowly rotting. The economic crisis is here. The political crisis is ongoing. The mainstream media has incorporated the Covid story into its 24/7 toxic anti-Muslim campaign. An organization called the Tablighi Jamaat, which held a meeting in Delhi before the lockdown was announced, has turned out to be a "super spreader." That is being used to stigmatize and demonize Muslims. The overall tone suggests that Muslims invented the virus and have deliberately spread it as a form of jihad.

The Covid crisis is still to come. Or not. We don't know. If and when it does, we can be sure it will be dealt with, with all the prevailing prejudices of religion, caste, and class completely in place. Today (April 2) in India, there are almost 2,000 confirmed cases and 58 deaths. These are surely unreliable numbers, based on woefully few tests. Expert opinion varies wildly. Some predict millions of cases. Others think the toll will be far less. We may never know the real contours of the crisis, even when it hits us. All we know is that the run on hospitals has not yet begun.

India's public hospitals and clinics are unable to cope with the almost one million children who die of diarrhea and malnutrition every year, with the more than two million tuberculosis patients (a quarter of the world's cases), with a vast anemic and malnourished population vulnerable to any number of minor illnesses that prove fatal for them.[2] It will be impossible for them to cope with a crisis that is on a scale anything like what Europe and the United States are dealing with now. All health care is more or less on hold as hospitals have been turned over to the service of The Virus. The trauma center of the legendary All India Institute of Medical Sciences (AIIMS) in Delhi is closed, the hundreds of cancer patients known as cancer refugees, who live on the roads outside that huge hospital, driven away like cattle.

People will fall sick and die at home. We may never know their stories. They may not even become statistics. We can only hope that the studies that say The Virus likes cold weather are correct (though other researchers have cast doubt on this). Never have a people longed so irrationally and so much for a burning, punishing Indian summer.

What is this thing that has happened to us? It's a virus, yes. In and of itself it holds no moral brief. But it is definitely more than a virus. Some believe it's God's way of bringing us to our senses. Others that it's a Chinese conspiracy to take over the world.

Whatever it is, coronavirus has made the mighty kneel and brought the world to a halt like nothing else could. Our minds are still racing back and forth, longing for a return to "normality," trying to stitch our future to our past and refusing to acknowledge the rupture. But the rupture exists. And in the midst of this terrible despair, it offers us a chance to rethink the doomsday machine we have built for ourselves. Nothing could be worse than a return to normality. Historically, pandemics have forced humans to break with the past and imagine their world anew. This one is no different. It is a portal, a gateway between one world and the next.

We can choose to walk through it, dragging the carcasses of our prejudice and hatred, our avarice, our data banks and dead ideas, our dead rivers and smoky skies behind us. Or we can walk through lightly, with little luggage, ready to imagine another world. And ready to fight for it.

CHAPTER 10

A Battle for Love

I thank the organizers of the 2021 Elgar Parishad for inviting me to speak at this forum to mark what would have been Rohit Vemula's thirty-second birthday and the 1818 victory of the battle of Bhima Koregaon. Not far from here, Mahar troops fighting in the British Army defeated the Peshwa King Bajirao II, under whom Mahars and other Dalit castes were cruelly persecuted and ritually debased in indescribable ways.

From this platform let me join the other speakers to express my solidarity with the farmers' protest that is calling for the immediate withdrawal of the three farm bills that have been rammed down the throats of millions of farmers and farm workers and brought them onto the streets. We are here to express our sorrow and anger for the many who have died during the course of the protest.

We are also here to demand the release of the dozens of political prisoners—including those who have come to be known as the Bhima Koregaon Sixteen—jailed on ludicrous charges under

* First published in *Clarion India*, January 31, 2021.

draconian anti-terror laws. Many of them are not just comrades but personal friends of mine with whom I have laughed, walked, and broken bread. Nobody, not even their captors, probably believes that they have committed the hackneyed crimes they are being accused of—planning the assassination of the prime minister, or plotting murder. Everybody knows they are in jail for their intellectual clarity and moral courage—both of which are viewed by this regime as a significant threat. To make up for nonexistent evidence, the charge sheets against some of the accused run into tens of thousands of pages. It could take a judge several years to just *read* these, let alone adjudicate upon them.

It's as hard to defend yourself against trumped-up charges as it is to wake up a person who is pretending to sleep. In India we have learned that relying on legal redress is a risky proposition. In any case, where and when have courts ever turned back the tide of fascism? In our country, laws are selectively applied depending on your class, caste, ethnicity, religion, gender, and political beliefs. So while poets and priests, students, activists, teachers, and lawyers are in prison, mass murderers, serial killers, daylight lynch mobs, dishonest judges, and venomous TV anchors are handsomely rewarded and can aspire to high office. The highest, even.

Over the last two years the Elgar Parishad as an event and an organization has been relentlessly defamed and demonized by the corporate media. Elgar Parishad: to many ordinary people those two words conjure up a shady cabal of radicals—terrorists, jihadis, Urban Naxals, Dalit Panthers—plotting to destroy India. In this climate of name-calling, of threat, dread, and anxiety, just to have organized this meeting is in itself an act of courage and defiance that deserves to be saluted. It's incumbent on those of us up here on the stage to speak as candidly as we can.

§

Roughly three weeks ago, on January 6, as we watched an outlandish mob storm through the US Capitol carrying Confederate flags, weapons, gibbets, and crucifixes, some wearing furs and antlers—the thought that ran through my head was, "My goodness, in our country we are already *ruled* by the Indian equivalent of these people. They've taken our Capitol Hill. They've won." Our institutions have been overrun by them. Our leader appears before us in a different set of furs and antlers every day. Our favored elixir is cow urine. They are well on their way toward destroying every democratic institution in this country. The US might have managed to claw itself back from the brink to some semblance of imperial "normalcy." But we in India are being dragged back centuries into a past that we have tried so hard to escape.

It isn't us—it isn't this gathering of the Elgar Parishad that is radical or extreme. It isn't us who are acting illegally and unconstitutionally. It isn't us who have looked away from or overtly encouraged pogroms in which Muslims have been killed in their thousands. It isn't us who benignly watch while Dalits are publicly flogged on city streets. It isn't us who are pitting people against one another, ruling through hatred and divisiveness. That is being done by those that we have elected as our government and by their propaganda machine that calls itself the media.

§

Two hundred years have gone by since the battle of Bhima Koregaon. The British have gone, but a form of colonialism that predates them by centuries lives on. The Peshwas are gone, but Peshwai—Brahminism—has not. Brahminism—I don't need to clarify to this audience, but I do for others who many not know—is the term the anti-caste movement has historically used for the jaa-ti-vyavastha. The caste system. It does not refer to Brahmins alone. Brahminism has been to the workshop, though, and has emerged fitted out with a modern, democratic-sounding vocabulary and a streamlined caste-management manual and program (not new, but overhauled) that has mounted an existential challenge to the Dalit-Bahujan-led political parties that once offered some hope. Right now, the chosen *vaahan* (vehicle) of twenty-first-century Brahminism is the far-right, Brahmin-controlled RSS, which, after a century of unceasing labor, has, through its best-known member, Narendra Modi, taken power in Delhi.

Many, including Karl Marx himself, believed that modern capitalism would end or at least override caste in India. Has it? Across the world, capitalism has ensured that wealth is concentrated in fewer and fewer hands. In India, the sixty-three richest people have more money than the 2018–2019 Union Budget for 1.3 billion people. A recent Oxfam study has found that in India during the corona pandemic, while hundreds of millions lost their jobs during the lockdown—170,000 people lost their jobs every hour in April 2020—India's billionaires increased their wealth by 35 percent. One hundred of the richest among them—let's call them the corporate class—made enough to be able to distribute, if they wanted to, almost 100,000 rupees each to 138 million of India's poorest people. A mainstream newspaper headlined this news as follows: "Covid deepened inequalities: wealth, education, gender." The missing word in the report as well as in the newspaper headline, is of course, caste.

The question is, does this tiny corporate class—which owns ports, mines, gas fields, refineries, telecommunication, high-speed data and cell phone networks, universities, petrochemical plants, hotels, hospitals, food distribution outlets, and television cable networks—does this class, which virtually owns and runs India, also have a caste? To a great extent, yes. Many of the biggest Indian corporations are family owned. To name a few of the biggest—Reliance Industries Ltd (Mukesh Ambani), Adani Group (Gautam Adani), Arcelor Mittal (Lakshmi Mittal), O. P. Jindal Group (Savitri Devi Jindal), Birla Group (K. M. Birla). They all call themselves Vaishyas, the trader caste. They are only doing their divinely ordained duty—making money.

Empirical studies about the ownership of corporate media and the caste breakdown of their editors, columnists, and senior journalists reveal the stranglehold of the privileged castes, mainly Brahmin and Bania, on designing and disseminating the news—real as well as fake. Dalits, Adivasis, and increasingly Muslims are almost absent from this landscape. The situation is no different in the higher and lower judiciary, the upper echelons of the civil services, the foreign service, the world of chartered accountants, or plum jobs in education, health, publishing, or in any sphere of governance. Between them the population of Brahmins and Vaishyas is probably less than 10 percent of the population. Caste and capitalism have fused to create a peculiarly lethal, peculiarly Indian alloy.

§

Prime Minister Modi, so relentless in his attack on the dynastic politics of the Congress Party, is entirely dedicated to supporting and enriching these corporate dynasties. The palanquin in which he is showcased, for better or for worse, also rests on the shoulders of mostly Vaishya and Brahmin family-owned corporate media dynasties. To name a few—*Times of India*, *Hindustan Times*, *Indian Express*, the *Hindu*, *India Today*, *Dainik Bhaskar*, *Dainik Jagran*. Reliance Industries has a controlling share in twenty-seven channels. I use the verb "showcased" because Modi has never directly addressed the press in his nearly seven years as prime minister. Not once.

While the rest of us are having our personal data mined and our irises scanned, an opaque system has been put in place to allow the corporate world to repay the unflinching loyalty that has been shown to them. In 2018 an electoral bond scheme was introduced which allows anonymous donations to be made to political parties. So we now have an actual, institutionalized, hermetically sealed pipeline that circulates money and power between the corporate and political elite. Small wonder then that the BJP is the richest political party in the world.

Smaller wonder then that while this tiny class-caste elite consolidates its hold on this country in the name of the people, in the name of Hindu nationalism, it has begun to treat people, including its own voters, as an enemy force, to be managed, manipulated, waylaid, taken by surprise, attacked by stealth, and ruled with an iron fist. We have been turned into a nation of ambush announcements and illegal ordinances.

Demonetization broke the back of the economy, overnight.

The Abrogation of Article 370 in Jammu and Kashmir led to seven million people suddenly locked down for months under a military and digital siege—a crime against humanity being committed in our name—and played out for the world to see. A year later, a stubbornly defiant people continue their struggle for freedom even as every bone in Kashmir's collective body is being broken, official fiat by official fiat.

The blatantly anti-Muslim Citizenship Amendment Act and the National Register of Citizens led to months of protest led by Muslim women. It ended with an anti-Muslim pogrom in North East Delhi, fueled by vigilantes and backed by the police, for which Muslims are being blamed. Hundreds of young Muslim men, students, and activists, including Umar Khalid, Khalid Saifi, Sharjeel Imam, Meran Haider, Natasha Narwal, and Devangana Kalita, are in jail. The protests are portrayed as an Islamist jihadi plot. The women who led the iconic Shaheen Bagh sit-in, the backbone of the nationwide uprising, were, we're told, being used for "gender cover," and the public pledges to the Constitution that took place at almost every protest site have been dismissed as "secular cover." The inference is that everything to do with Muslims is by default "jihadi" (used incorrectly as a euphemism for terrorism) and anything that is contraindicative is just details. The policemen who forced grievously wounded Muslim men to sing the National Anthem, even as they lay piled up against each other on the street, have not even been identified, let alone charged. One of the injured subsequently died from having a patriotic police lathi pushed down his throat. This month the home minister praised the Delhi police for its handling of the "riots."

And now, a year after the massacre, while a battered community is trying to get back on its feet, the Bajrang Dal and VHP are announcing Rath Yatras and motorcycle parades to raise money for the Ram Mandir in Ayodhya, in those very same colonies where the pogrom took place,

We also had the Lockdown Ambush—1.3 billion of us locked down with four hours' notice. Millions of urban workers forced to walk thousands of kilometers towards home, while being beaten like criminals.

While the pandemic raged, responding to the change of status of the disputed State of Jammu and Kashmir, China occupied swathes of Indian territory in Ladakh. Our hapless government has been forced to pretend that it hasn't happened. Whether there is or isn't a war, a negative growth economy must now hemorrhage money to keep thousands of troops equipped and permanently battle ready. In sub-zero temperatures, many soldiers' lives will be lost just to the weather.

On top of that list of induced calamities we now have the three farm bills that will break the back of Indian agriculture, hand the controls to corporations, and blatantly deny farmers legal recourse without even a nod to their constitutional rights.

It's like watching a vehicle being dismantled, its engine broken, its wheels removed, its upholstery stripped, the vandalized shell left on the highway, while other cars, driven by people who aren't wearing antlers and furs, whizz by.

§

This is why we desperately need this Elgar—this consistent, collective, defiant expression of rage—against Brahminism, against capitalism, against Islamophobia, and against patriarchy. Patriarchy, the underpinning of it all—because if men don't or can't control women, they know they control nothing.

While the pandemic rages, while farmers are on the streets, states ruled by the BJP are rushing through anti-religious conversion ordinances. I will take a moment to talk about these because they are a compendium of insights into this regime's anxieties about caste, about masculinity, about Muslims and Christians, about love, women, demography, and history.

The UP Prohibition of Unlawful Conversion of Religion Ordinance 2020 (popularly known as the Ordinance against Love Jihad) is barely a month old. Already weddings have been disrupted, families have had cases filed against them, and dozens of young Muslim men are in jail. So now, in addition to being lynched for beef they haven't eaten, cows they haven't killed, crimes they haven't committed (although for Muslims, being murdered is increasingly being viewed as a criminal act), in addition to being jailed for jokes they haven't made (as in the case of the young comedian Munawer Faruqui), Muslims can now be jailed for committing the crime of falling in love and getting married. In our reading of this Ordinance I will leave aside some basic questions, such as how do you define "religion"? Would someone who persuaded a person of faith to become an atheist become liable for prosecution?

The 2020 UP ordinance provides "for prohibition of unlawful conversion from one religion to another by misrepresentation, force, undue influence, coercion, allurement or by any fraudulent means or by marriage. . ." The definition of allurement includes gifts, gratification, free education in reputed schools, or the promise of a better lifestyle. (Which roughly describes the transactions involved in almost every arranged marriage in India.)

The accused (the person who has caused the conversion to take place) faces a jail sentence of between one and five years. The accusers can be any family member including a distant relative. The burden of proof rests on the accused. The "victim" may be granted a 500,000-rupee compensation by the court, payable by the accused. You can imagine the infinite possibilities of extortion and blackmail that this sets up.

Now for the best part: if the converted person is a minor, a woman, or belongs to a Scheduled Caste or Scheduled Tribe, the punishment to the "Religion Convertor" is doubled—that is, two to ten years. In other words, this Ordinance accords women, Dalits, and Adivasis the same status as minors. It infantilizes us: we are not considered to be adults responsible for our own actions. In the eyes of the UP government, only the privileged-caste Hindu male has full agency. It's the same spirit in which the Chief Justice of India asked why women (who are in more ways than one the backbone of Indian agriculture) were being "kept" at the farmers' protests. And the government of Madhya Pradesh proposed that working women who don't live with their families be registered at police stations and tracked by the police for their own safety.

If Mother Teresa were alive, under this Ordinance she'd be serving a jail sentence for sure. My guess is ten years and a lifetime of debt, given how many people she converted to Christianity. This could become the fate of every Christian priest working among the poor in India.

Also, what about the person who said:

> Because we have the misfortune of calling ourselves Hindus we are treated thus. If we were members of another faith, none would dare treat us such. Choose any religion which gives you equality of status and treatment. We shall repair our mistake now.

Those were the words, many of you will know, of Babasaheb Ambedkar. A clear call for mass conversion with the promise of a better lifestyle. Under this Ordinance, in which "mass conversion" is defined as when "two or more people convert," those words would make Ambedkar criminally liable. Mahatma Phule, too, would likely be indicted for his overt approval of mass conversion when he said:

> The Muslims, destroying the carved stone images of the cunning Arya Bhats, forcibly enslaved them and brought the Shudras and Ati-Shudras in great numbers out of their clutches and made them Muslims, including them in the Muslim religion. Not only this, but they established interdining and intermarriage with them and gave them all equal rights. . .

A great part of the millions of Sikhs, Muslims, Christians, and Buddhists who make up the population of this subcontinent are testimony to historical change and to mass conversion. The rapid depletion in numbers of the "Hindu population" is what initially gave rise to privileged-caste anxiety about demography and galvanized the politics of what is today called Hindutva.

Today, however, with the RSS in power, the tide has turned. The only mass conversions happening at scale are those being conducted by the Vishwa Hindu Parishad—the process known as "Ghar Wapsi" (returning home) which began with Hindu Reformist groups in the late nineteenth century. Ghar Wapsi involves forest-dwelling tribespeople being "returned" to Hinduism. But not before undergoing a Shuddhi (purification) ceremony to purge the pollution they have incurred by straying from "home."

How does the UP ordinance then deal with this inconvenience that ought, by logic, to criminalize this practice? It includes a clause that says: "Provided that, if any person reconverts to his/ her immediate previous religion the same shall not be deemed to be a conversion under this Ordinance." By doing this the ordinance perpetuates and legalizes the myth that Hinduism is an ancient autochthonous religion that predates and subsumes the religions of the hundreds of indigenous tribes and Dalit and Dravidian peoples of the Indian subcontinent. An outright falsehood.

§

In India, these are the ways in which mythology is turned into history and history into mythology. Privileged-caste chroniclers see no contradiction whatsoever in simultaneously claiming to be indigenous as well as the descendants of Aryan conquerors, depending on what suits them. At the beginning of his career in South Africa, while campaigning for a separate entrance for Indians in the Durban post office—so that they would not have to share the same entrance as Black Africans, whom he often called "Kaffirs" and "savages"—Gandhi argued that Indians and the English sprang from "common stock, called the Indo-Aryan." He made sure to distinguish the privileged-caste "passenger Indians" from oppressed-caste indentured laborers. That was in 1893. But the circus hasn't stopped.

The range of speakers present today shows the Elgar Parishad's intellectual ability to see the concerted attack that is coming at us from all directions—not just one or the other. Nothing makes this regime happier than when we seal ourselves into silos, into little tanks in which we splash around angrily, each for ourselves or our communities—never seeing the big picture, our anger often directed at one another. It is only when we breach the banks of our designated tanks that we can turn into a river. And flow as an unstoppable current. To do that we have to exceed our brief, we have to dare to dream like Rohit Vemula did. He is here today with us, among us, an inspiration to a whole new generation even in death, because he died dreaming. He died insisting on his right to expand into the fullness of his humanity, his ambitions, his intellectual curiosity. He refused to shrink, to contract, to fit the mold that was offered to him. He refused the labels the real world wanted to pin on him. He knew that he was made up of nothing less than stardust. He has become stardust.

We have to be watchful of the traps that limit and essentialize us. None of us are just the sum of our identities. We are that, too, but much, much more. While we square off against our foes, we must be able to recognize our friends. We must look for allies because none of us can fight this battle alone. The audacious anti-CAA protests last year and the grand farmers' protest that surrounds us now has shown that. The many farmers' unions that have come together represent people with different ideological beliefs, different histories. There are deep contradictions between big and small farmers, between landlords and landless agricultural workers, between Jat Sikhs and Mazhabi Sikhs, between the Left Unions and the Centrists. There are caste contradictions, too, and horrifying caste violence, as Bant Singh, who had both his legs and an arm hacked off in 2006, has told you today. Those differences are not buried. They are spoken about—as Randeep Maddoke has spoken, both here today and in his brave documentary film *Landless*. Yet they have come together to confront this state to fight what we know is an existential battle.

§

Perhaps here in this city, where Ambedkar was literally blackmailed into signing the Poona Pact, and where Jotiba and Savitribai Phule did their revolutionary work, we can give our struggle a name. Perhaps it should be the Satya Shodhak Resistance—SSR to the RSS.

The battle of Love against Hate. A battle *for* Love. It must be militantly waged and beautifully won.

Thank you.

CHAPTER 11

Freedom Side

Tribunal against State Terror
and White Supremacy

I am honored and privileged to serve as a juror on this Peoples' Tribunal against state terrorism and white supremacy in the United States alongside others I have admired for a very long time. I have lived all my life in India, where British colonialism ended in 1947. With that, white racism was more or less removed from our daily lives. But another, some would say equally or more cruel form of colonialism and social hierarchy—the ancient Hindu caste system—continues to be the engine that runs modern India. Today, it has fused with what we call modern "democracy" and neoliberal capitalism to create a dangerous new alloy. I mention this because it is necessary to speak about the

---

* This essay originally presented as testimony to the Rising Majority People's Tribunal and Congress, "Rising Against White Supremacist Terror: Toward a Just World," October 17, 2020.

awfulness of what goes on in one's own country before criticizing another. Too often have I seen elite Indians, Bollywood actors and actresses, who promote fairness creams and Hindu nationalism and its corollary—Islamophobia—who will never breathe a word about what goes on in India but will gladly tweet "I can't breathe." Not because they care, but because they think it's cool. They haven't thought to pay attention to the fact that there are millions of people in their home country who are being systematically brutalized, lynched, raped, and dehumanized, and cannot breathe. Or to introspect at the very least about the part they play in the caste apartheid that Hindu society is and always has been. Or to say one single word about the military occupation and cruel subjugation of people in Kashmir.

The United States has a much longer history of exclusionary nationalism, xenophobia, and exceptionalism, believing itself an "indispensable nation." Many who criticize its government's policies and social practices in the domestic sphere remain silent about its brutal history beyond its own borders. In your country and mine, this deeply entrenched, unquestioning nationalism gives our governments cover to unleash all manner of destruction that must be called out.

I expect that what I hear during the course of this tribunal will not only give me an insight into the United States but also deepen my understanding of both what is unique as well as what is universal in my own country. I look forward to hearing the testimonials today because I believe that the only way to enhance our understanding of the overarching structures in modern society that cause such unspeakable suffering to so many, is to understand the latticework of that suffering—across and between genders, communities, races, classes, landscapes, countries, and continents. Only once we understand it, its width, breadth, depth, span, scope, and texture, can we hope to know what it even means to move toward justice.

§

First of all, let me perform the peculiar job of thanking the participants in this tribunal for their harrowing testimonies. Nobody should have to go through what you have been through. Each testimony in and of itself is mind-numbing, but when heard collectively, sequentially, they teach us a grave and vital lesson—and this illuminates why this tribunal has been put together. It tells us plenty about the acumen and discernment of the organizers. Together these testimonies show us how the ghosts of genocide, slavery, bigotry, and white supremacy, far from being exorcised, have adapted, modernized, made themselves acceptable, and taken up residence in the spaces between democratic-sounding words in a liberal-sounding discourse.

From the testimony of John Vasquez we learned how the mass incarceration of African Americans and other ethnic and racial minorities in the US prison-industrial complex incentivizes incarceration-for-profit, how the dehumanization and disenfranchisement of prisoners and people who have served prison sentences is a way of making sure they will never play a role in the shaping of public life and the power structure in the country in which they live, and how the use of prison labor is nothing more than modern slavery. From Valencia Gunder, we heard how women are subject to routine but unspeakable humiliation in these prisons. Jamal Jones, speaking of the presence of police on school campuses, used the chilling phrase "school-to-prison pipeline"—none of us are in any doubt about which schools and whose children play the starring roles in that movie. In her testimony about racism and sexism in schools, Su Han told us of students from disadvantaged families having "mountains of debt" to pay back in return for the favor of getting themselves an education. What choice do those students have once they leave other than to join that exploitative system and never question it in order to earn enough to pay back their loans? From other testimonies, we learned that thinking of the planet we live on and the forests and rivers that sustain life on earth as "resources" to be exploited is only an extension of the idea of stealing land and exterminating or subjugating the people who live on it. We know now that the logical end to that way of thinking is climate change. The endgame.

The engine of that endgame is the country built on stolen land, which is now guarded against "outsiders" and "immigrants" with the most sophisticated surveillance and border patrols in the world. Yet it thinks nothing of waging war, raining destruction, or supporting settler-colonialism and dictatorships in other countries, all in the name of Democracy and Freedom. We learned something of the ways in which this is done with haunting testimonies from Haiti, Palestine, and Bolivia. We heard from Sevonna, a birth worker, about the national crisis of the preventable deaths of poor Black mothers with no access to health care. "This is violence. It's state violence. It's obstetric violence. . . . It's coerced reproductive violation," she says about a woman who was being forced to have her baby sooner than she naturally would have because she was being treated like a package on a conveyor belt. We heard Dr. Sami Schalk, who is differently abled herself, talk about the links between ableism and white supremacy. Nobody could illuminate this point better than the president of the United States. Back home in the White House after being diagnosed with Covid and being treated with the best medical care on earth while more than two hundred thousand Americans died of the disease, a disproportionate number of them African American, Donald Trump said: "I'm back because I'm a perfect physical specimen and I'm extremely young."

We heard from Brittany Ramos DeBarros, who describes herself as Latina, Black, queer, and a combat veteran whose father was Puerto Rican. She calls the twelve-year military contract she signed at the age of eighteen an agreement to "kill on command for access to education." She was deployed in Afghanistan as part of the machinery of the US War on Terror. Remember, that was the war in which the US was going to bomb feminism into Afghanistan and bomb Afghanistan back to the Stone Age. Brittany says, "What I saw there made it impossible to deny that we were doing anything but catastrophic harm. . . . I'll never fully heal from knowing that I am part of the reason that over eight hundred thousand people are dead in the so-called War on Terror, and more than 37 million are wounded, poisoned, and displaced. And yet,

I'm also painfully clear that I was used and betrayed by politicians and corporations loyal only to power and profit."

What an incisive and devastating statement. How many countries in which Black and Brown people live have been destroyed, how many regimes toppled by the United States' and NATO's War on Terror? How many millions starved and killed by their economic sanctions?

What are we to make of the fact that today the US government is in talks with the Taliban, whom they first empowered, then toppled, and now, after nineteen years of war, will once again make way for?

Surely a part of fighting white supremacy should involve refusing to fight in those wars.

§

The challenge for us today is to understand how all the testimonies and stories from Valencia Gunder, Su Han, Julia Burnham, Angelo, Brittany Ramos DeBarros, Christopher Colleen, Nik, Lara Sharif, Doria Robinson, Osama Tanous, Alejandra Laprea, Dr. Sami Schalk, Jamal Jones, Joseph Jacques, John Vasquez, and Sevonna fit together.

What they did was to shine a light on the latticework of their experiences and their suffering. That light casts a sharp shadow on the wall that actually reveals the overarching superstructure of the system that causes it.

In facing down this system, one of the great difficulties is that pain and suffering can be isolating experiences. They tend to make us withdraw into silos, lock ourselves in, and make those walls thick and unbreachable. They can make us suspicious of empathy and solidarity. But we must know that if Brittany, Joseph, John, Nik, Lara, Alejandra, and the others who have given testimony here fight alone, they will never win. That is what the system wants and encourages. If they fight alone, they may perhaps be given space and spurious sympathy. Maybe even some funding. They will be encouraged to attack and disparage and police each other, and valorize their suffering over the suffering of others. But if they fight together with understanding and solidarity, they will be considered dangerous.

Reverend Martin Luther King Jr. was tolerated until he made the connections between racism, war, and capitalism. When he did, he was assassinated.

People in the United States are making these connections— and many more—once again. The witnesses and jurors in this tribunal are making these connecstions.

That is dangerous business. This tribunal is dangerous business. As it should be.

To listen to accounts of suffering only in order to sympathize is not political. Now that we have listened, we must act. Quickly, cleverly, and furiously.

Thank you, once again, for giving me this opportunity to deepen my understanding and express my solidarity. It's all a writer could ever hope for.

POSTSCRIPT

I saw the testimony of M Adams only after I had filmed my reflections and uploaded them. That testimony is both the vortex of hell and the prism through which we must view the world we would like to live in and work toward. I think it ought to be one of the fundamental building blocks of our vision of a world in which we see gender not as boxes we tick in forms we have to fill out, but as a fluid, infinite spectrum where each of us can find our place with joy and dignity. And without judgment.

CHAPTER 12

Two Conspiracies and a Cremation

A s Diwali approaches and Hindus prepare to celebrate the triumphant return of Lord Ram to his kingdom (and the spanking new temple that is being built for him in Ayodhya), the rest of us must be content to celebrate this season of serial triumphs for Indian Democracy. Between the breaking news of a disturbing cremation, the laying to rest of one great conspiracy and the inauguration of another, how can we not be proud of ourselves, our cultural and civilizational values, both ancient and modern?

In mid-September 2020, reports came in of a nineteen-year-old Dalit girl who was gang-raped, mutilated, and left for dead by dominant-caste men in her village in Hathras, Uttar Pradesh. Her family was one of fifteen Dalit families in a village where a majority of the six hundred households were Brahmin and

*First published at Scroll.in, October 3, 2020.

Thakur—the same caste as Ajay Singh Bisht, the saffron-robed Uttar Pradesh chief minister who calls himself Yogi Adityanath. (He is, by all accounts, being groomed to replace Narendra Modi as prime minister in the near future.) The girl had been stalked and terrorized by her assailants for a while. She had nobody to turn to for help. Nobody to protect her. So, she stayed at home and rarely went out. She and her family were aware of what was in store for them. But awareness didn't help. Her mother found her daughter's bleeding body in the field where she took her cows to graze. Her tongue had been almost severed, her spine broken, leaving her paralyzed.

The girl survived for two weeks, first in a hospital in Aligarh and then, as her condition worsened, in a hospital in Delhi. On the night of September 29, she died. The UP police, best known for pulling off 400 custodial killings last year—almost a fourth of the all-India total of nearly 1,700[1]— whisked the girl's body away in the dead of night and drove all the way back to the outskirts of her village. They locked up the traumatized family, denying the girl's mother a final farewell, a chance to gaze upon her daughter's face, and denying the community the dignity of performing the last rites for a beloved who has departed this world. Denying them even the definite knowledge that it was indeed their daughter's body that was cremated.

The murdered girl's broken body was laid on a hurriedly put together pyre, and the smoke rose into the night sky from behind a wall of khaki police uniforms. The girl's family huddled together, clearly terrified by the blaze of media attention. Terrified because they knew very well that when the lights faded, they would be punished for that attention, too.

If they manage to survive, they will go back to the lives they have grown used to—victims of medieval cruelty and indignity meted out to them in their medieval caste–ridden village where they are considered untouchable and subhuman.

A day after the cremation, confident that the body had been safely dispatched, the police announced that the girl had not been raped. She had only been murdered. Only. This marks the beginning of the standard operating procedure in which the caste angle is quickly excised from caste atrocities. Courts, hospital records, and the mainstream media can all be expected to cooperate in this process of gradually turning a hate-fueled caste atrocity into just another unfortunate but ordinary crime. In other words, absolving our society, letting our culture and social practices off the hook. We have seen it time and time again, most graphically in the 2006 massacre and brutalization of Surekha Bhotmange and her two children in Khairlanji.

As part of our effort to return to our country to her glorious past as the Bharatiya Janata Party promises it will do, in the next election, if you can, please don't forget to vote for Ajay Singh Bisht. If not him, then for the nearest Muslim-baiting, Dalit-hating politician, whoever he or she may be. Remember to "like" the next lynching video that's uploaded, and to keep watching your favorite venom-spewing TV anchor, because he or she is the Keeper of our collective conscience. Also, please don't forget to be grateful that we can still vote, that we live in the world's largest democracy, and that unlike what we like to call the "failed states" in our neighborhood, in India we have neutral courts that administer the Rule of Law.

Only a few hours after that shameful, horrifying cremation outside the village in Hathras, on the morning of September 30, 2020, a CBI special court gave us a robust demonstration of just such neutrality and probity.

After twenty-eight years of careful deliberation, it acquitted all the thirty-two people who had been accused of conspiring to demolish the Babri Masjid in 1992, an event that changed the course of the history of Modern India. The acquitted included a former home minister, a former cabinet minister, and a former chief minister. In effect, it appears that nobody demolished the Babri Masjid. At least not legally. Perhaps the mosque demolished itself. Perhaps all those years ago, it picked that day, December 6, Babasaheb Ambedkar's death anniversary, to hammer itself into dust, to crumble under the collective willpower of the saffron-scarfed thugs who called themselves devotees that had gathered there that day.

It turns out that the videos and photographs we all saw of the men hammering down the old mosque's domes, the witness testimonies that we read and heard, the news reports that filled the media in the months that followed, were figments of our imagination. L. K. Advani's Rath Yatra, when he traveled the length and breadth of India in an open truck, addressing huge crowds, shutting down city roads, exhorting true Hindus to converge on Ayodhya and participate in building a Ram temple at the exact spot where the mosque stood—all of that never really happened. Neither did the death and destruction that his Yatra left in its wake. Nobody chanted *Ek dhakka aur do, Babri Masjid tod do*. We were experiencing a collective, nationwide hallucination. What were we all smoking? Why aren't we being summoned by the NCB? Why are only Bollywood folks being summoned? Are we not all equal in the eyes of the law?

The Special Court judge has written a detailed, 2,300-page judgment about how there was no plan to destroy the mosque. That's a feat, you have to admit—2,300 pages about the *absence* of a plan. He describes how there is absolutely no evidence to say that the accused had met "in a room" to plan the demolition. Perhaps that's because it happened outside a room, on our streets, at public meetings, on our TV screens for all of us to watch and participate in? Or heck—is it just that "maal" again, giving us these ideas?

Anyway, the Babri Masjid conspiracy is out for now. But there's another one that's "in" and "trending": the conspiracy of the 2020 Delhi massacre, in which 53 people (40 of them Muslim) were killed and 581 injured in the working-class neighborhoods of North East Delhi. Mosques, graveyards, and madrassas were specifically targeted. Homes, shops, and businesses, for the most part Muslim, were firebombed and razed to the ground.

In the case of this conspiracy, the Delhi police charge sheet, which runs into thousands of pages, even has a photograph of a few people sitting around a table—Yes! in a *room,* a sort of office basement—plotting. You can clearly tell by their expressions that they're plotting. What's more, there are accusing arrows pointing at them, identifying them, telling us their *names*. It's devastating. Far more alarming than those men with sledgehammers on the dome of the Babri Masjid. Some of the people sitting around the table are already in jail. The rest probably soon will be. The arrests took just a few months. The acquittals could take years—if the Babri judgment is anything to go by, then maybe twenty-eight years, who knows. Under the UAPA (Unlawful Activities Prevention Act), under which they have been charged, almost everything is a crime, including thinking anti-national thoughts. The onus is on you to prove your innocence. The more I read about it and the modus operandi the police adopt around it, the more it sounds like asking a sane person to establish her sanity before a committee of lunatics.

The Delhi conspiracy, we are asked to believe, was hatched by Muslim students and activists, Gandhians, "Urban Naxals," and "leftists," who were all protesting against the implementation of the National Population Register (NPR), the National Register of Citizens, and the Citizenship Amendment Act, which they believed combine together to cut the very ground from under the feet of the Muslim community and India's poor who do not have "legacy papers." I believe that, too. And I believe that if the government decides to push ahead with that project, the protests will start again. As they should.

According to the police, the idea behind the Delhi conspiracy was to embarrass the Indian government by inciting violence and creating a bloody, communal conflagration during US president Donald Trump's state visit to India in February. The non-Muslims who are named in the charge sheet are accused of conspiring to give the protests a "secular color." The thousands of Muslim women who were leading the sit-ins and protests are accused of being "brought in" to give the protests "gender cover." All the flag-waving and public readings of the preamble to the Indian Constitution, and the outpouring of poetry and music and love that marked these protests, are dismissed as some sort of insincere fakery designed to disguise malign intent. In other words, the core of the protest is jihadi (and male)—the rest is just garnishing and decoration.

The young scholar Dr. Umar Khalid, whom I know well and who has been persecuted, hounded, and fake-newsed by the media for years, is, according to the police, one of the chief conspirators. The evidence they have collected against him, the police say, runs into more than one million pages.[2] (This is the same government that declared it had no data on the ten million workers who had to walk hundreds—and, for some, thousands—of miles home to their villages in March 2020, after Modi announced the world's most cruel Covid lockdown—no idea of how many died, how many starved, how many fell sick.) Not included in the one million pages of evidence against Umar Khalid is the CCTV footage of the Jafrabad Metro station—the site of his supposedly egregious plotting and provocation—which activists appealed to the Delhi High Court to preserve, as early as February 25, even as the violence was raging. It has been inexplicably erased.[3] Umar is now in jail along with hundreds of other Muslims who have been recently arrested, charged under the UAPA as well as with murder, attempt to murder, and rioting. How many lifetimes will it take for courts and lawyers to wade through one million pages of "evidence"?

Similar to the way in which the Babri Masjid appears to have decided to demolish itself, in the police version of the 2020 Delhi massacre, Muslims conspired to murder themselves, burn their own mosques, destroy their own homes, orphan their own children, all in order to show Donald Trump what a terrible time they're having in India.

To bolster their case, the police have annexed to their charge sheet hundreds of pages of WhatsApp conversations between students and activists and activist support groups that are trying to support and coordinate between the scores of sites of protests and peaceful sit-ins that had sprung up in Delhi. It could not be more different from another set of WhatsApp conversations by a group of people who call themselves Kattar Hindu Ekta, or Hardline Hindu Unity, in which they actually boast about killing Muslims and openly praise BJP leaders. That is part of a separate charge sheet.

The student–activist conversations are, for the most part, full of spirit and purpose as young people, buoyed by a sense of righteous anger, go about their business. Reading them is energizing and returns you to those heady pre-Covid days and the excitement of watching a new generation come into its own. Time and again, more experienced activists intervene to caution them about the need to stay peaceful and calm. They also argue and bicker in petty ways as activists tend to—that's part of the business of being democratic. The main bone of contention in the conversations, unsurprisingly, is whether or not to try and replicate the stunning success of the protest by the thousands of women of Shaheen Bagh, who had, for weeks together, braving the bitter winter cold, squatted on a main road, blocking traffic, creating chaos but drawing a huge amount of attention to themselves and their cause. Bilkis Bano, the Dadi ("Granny") of Shaheen Bagh, made it to *TIME* magazine's most influential people of 2020. (Don't confuse her with the other Bilkis Bano, the nineteen-year-old who survived a 2002 anti-Muslim pogrom in Gujarat when Narendra Modi was chief minister of that state. She witnessed a massacre in which fourteen members of her family, including her three-year-old daughter, were killed by a rampaging mob of Hindu vigilantes. She was pregnant and gang-raped. Only.[4])

The Delhi activists' WhatsApp chatter has people divided over whether to go for a "chakka jam"—a road block—in North East Delhi or not. There's nothing new about planning a chakka jam—farmers have done it time and again. They are doing it right now, in Punjab and Haryana, to protest the recently passed farm bills that corporatize Indian agriculture and threaten to deliver small farmers into an existential crisis.

In the case of the Delhi protests, some activists on the chat groups argued that blocking roads would be counterproductive. Given the climate of open threats by BJP leaders in the area that was fueled by their rage at having been humiliated in the Delhi elections just weeks before, some local activists feared that blocking roads would incite anger and direct the ensuing violence toward their communities. They knew that farmers or Gujjars or even

Dalits doing it is one thing. Muslims doing it is quite another. That's the reality in India today. Others argued that unless roads were blocked and the city was forced to pay attention, the protesters would just be sidelined and ignored. As it turned out, in some protest sites, roads were blocked. As predicted, it gave Hindu vigilante mobs armed with weapons and murderous chants the opportunity they were looking for.

Over the next few days they unleashed a kind of brutality that took our breath away. Videos showed them being openly backed and supported by the police. Muslims fought back. Lives and property were lost on both sides. But entirely unequally. No equivalence can be made here. The violence was allowed to swell and spread. We watched in disbelief the spectacle of grievously injured young Muslim men lying on a road surrounded by police who forced them to sing the National Anthem. One of them, Faizan, died soon after. Hundreds of distress calls were ignored by the police. When the arson and slaughter cooled down, and the hundreds of complaints were finally entertained, victims claimed that the police forced them to remove the names and identities of their attackers and the communal slogans raised by the gun- and sword-wielding mobs. Specific complaints were turned into generic ones designed to be inconclusive and protect the guilty. (Hate was excised from hate crimes.) On one of the WhatsApp chats, one particular Muslim activist, who lived in North East Delhi and had repeatedly warned the others about the perils of a chakka jam, exited the group after posting a final bitter, recriminatory message. It is this message the police and the media have seized and built upon to spin their sordid web and tar the whole group—among them India's most respected activists, teachers, and filmmakers—as a set of violent conspirators with murderous intent. Can there be anything more ridiculous? But it could take years for innocence to be established. Until then they could be in jail, their lives completely ruined, while the real murderers and provocateurs roam free and win elections. The process is intended to be the punishment.

Meanwhile, several independent media reports, citizens' fact-finding reports, and human rights organizations have held the Delhi police complicit in the violence that took place in North East Delhi. In an August 2020 report, after having had some of the disturbingly violent videos that we all saw forensically examined, Amnesty International said that the Delhi police were guilty of beating and torturing protestors and acting with the mob. Since then, Amnesty has been accused of financial irregularities and its bank accounts have been frozen. It has had to close its India offices and let go of all 150 of its staff in India.

When things begin to get dire, the first to leave or be forced to leave are international observers. In which countries have we seen this pattern before? Think. Or Google.

India wants a permanent place on the UN Security Council, a say in world affairs. But it also wants to be one of the five countries in the world that will not ratify the international Convention against Torture. It wants to be a one-party democracy (an oxymoron) with zero accountability.

The real purpose of the absurd, police-manufactured 2020

Delhi conspiracy, and equally absurd 2018 Bhima-Koregaon conspiracy (the absurdity is part of the threat and the humiliation),
is to imprison and pin down activists, students, lawyers, writers,
poets, professors, trade-unionists, and noncompliant NGOs. It
has to do not just with erasing the horrors of the past and present
but also with clearing the decks for what is still to come.

I suppose we ought to be grateful for these one-million-page
evidence gatherings and two-thousand-page court judgments.
Because they are proof that the carcass of democracy is still being
dragged around. It hasn't been cremated yet, unlike the murdered
girl in Hathras, Uttar Pradesh. Even as a carcass, it's pulling its
weight, slowing things down. The day is not far off when it will be
jettisoned and things will speed up. The unspoken slogan amongst
those who rule us may well be *Ek dhakka aur do, Democracy gaad
do.* Bury it.

When that day comes, 1,700 custodial killings in a year will
seem like a rosy recollection of our recent, glorious past.

Let that small fact not deter us. Let's keep voting for the people who are leading us into penury and war, tearing us apart limb
from limb.

At least they are building us a grand temple. And that's not
nothing.

CHAPTER 13

India's Day of Shame

On August 5, 2019, a year ago today, seven million people in the valley of Kashmir were locked into their homes under a strict military curfew. Thirteen thousand people, ranging from young children and teenage stone pelters to former chief ministers and major pro-India politicians, were arrested and put into preventive detention, where many of them still remain.[1] At midnight on August 4, phones went dead and internet connections were cut. On August 6, a bill was passed in parliament stripping the State of Jammu and Kashmir of its autonomy and special status enshrined in the Indian Constitution. It was divested of statehood and downgraded into two Union Territories, Ladakh and Jammu and Kashmir. Ladakh would have no legislature and would be governed directly by New Delhi.

The problem of Kashmir, we were told, had been finally solved once and for all. In other words, Kashmir's decades-long struggle for self-determination, which has cost tens of thousands

*First published in *Progressive International*, December 8, 2020.

of lives of soldiers, militants and civilians, thousands of enforced "disappearances" and cruelly tortured bodies—was over. On the floor of the House, home minister Amit Shah went further. He said he was prepared to lay down his life to take over the territories of what India calls Pakistan Occupied Kashmir (POK) and what Kashmiris call Azad Kashmir, as well as the frontier provinces of Gilgit-Baltistan. He also threw in Aksai Chin, once part of the erstwhile Kingdom of Jammu and Kashmir, now a part of China. He was wading into dangerous territory, literally as well as figuratively. The borders he was talking about lie between three nuclear powers. Amid the unseemly celebrations on India's streets, the extra wattage generated by Kashmir's humiliation intensified the glow of prime minister Narendra Modi's already godlike halo. Provocatively, the Indian Meteorological Department began to include Gilgit-Baltistan into its weather reports. Few of us in India paid attention to the Chinese government when it urged India to "be cautious in its words and deeds on the border issue."

In the year that has gone by, the struggle in Kashmir has by no means ended. In just the last few months, media reports say that 34 soldiers, 154 militants, and 17 civilians have been killed.[2] A world traumatized by the coronavirus has understandably paid no attention to what the Indian government has done to the people of Kashmir. The curfew and communication siege, and everything else that such a siege entails (no access to doctors, hospitals, work, no business, no school, no contact with loved ones), lasted for months. Even the United States didn't do this during its war against Iraq.

Just a few months of coronavirus lockdown, without a military curfew or communications siege, has brought the world to its knees and hundreds of millions to the limits of their endurance and sanity. Think of Kashmir under the densest military deployment in the world. On top of the suffering coronavirus has laid on you, add a maze of concertina wire on your streets, soldiers breaking into your homes, beating the men and abusing the women, destroying your food stocks, amplifying the cries of humans being tortured on Public Address Systems.

Add to this a judicial system—including the Supreme Court of India—that has for a whole year allowed the internet siege to continue and ignored the six hundred habeas corpus petitions by distraught people seeking the whereabouts of their family members.[3] Add further a new Domicile Law that opens the floodgates by allowing Indians a right of residence in Kashmir. The precious State Subject Certificates of Kashmiris are now legally void except as backup evidence to bolster their applications to the Indian government for domicile status in their own homeland. Those whose applications are rejected can be denied residency and shipped out. What Kashmir faces is nothing less than cultural erasure.

Kashmir's new Domicile Law is a cognate of India's new blatantly anti-Muslim Citizenship Amendment Act (CAA) passed in December 2019 and the National Register of Citizens (NRC) that is supposed to detect "Bangladeshi infiltrators" (Muslim of course) who the home minister has called "termites." In the state of Assam, the NRC has already wreaked havoc. Millions have been struck off the citizens register. While many countries are dealing with a refugee crisis, the Indian government is turning citizens into refugees, fueling a crisis of statelessness on an unimaginable scale.

The CAA, NRC, and Kashmir's new Domicile Law require even bona fide citizens to produce a set of documents approved by the state in order to be granted citizenship. (The Nuremberg Laws passed by the Nazi Party in 1935 decreed that only those citizens who could provide legacy papers approved by the Third Reich were eligible for German citizenship.)

What should all this be called? A war crime? Or a crime against humanity?

And what should the collusion of institutions and the celebrations on the streets of India be called? Democracy?

A year down the line, these celebrations over Kashmir are distinctly muted. For good reason. We have a dragon on our doorstep and it isn't happy. On June 17, 2020, we awoke to the horrifying news that twenty Indian soldiers including a colonel had been brutally killed by the Chinese People's Liberation Army (PLA) in the icy reaches of the remote Galwan Valley on the Ladakh border. Over the next few days reports in sections of the Indian press suggested that there had been several points of ingress. Army veterans and respected defence correspondents have said that the PLA has occupied hundreds of square kilometers of what India considers to be its territory.[4] Was it just naked aggression as portrayed by the Indian media? Or have the Chinese moved to protect what they see as their vital interests—a road through the high mountains of Aksai Chin and a trade route through Pakistan Occupied/Azad Kashmir? Both under threat, if the belligerent statements made by India's home minister were to be taken seriously, and how can they not be?

For a ferociously nationalist government such as ours to concede what it thinks of as sovereign territory has to be its worst nightmare. It cannot be countenanced. But what can be done? A simple solution was found. Just days after the Galwan Valley tragedy, Prime Minister Modi addressed the nation. "Not an inch of land has been occupied by anyone," he said, "no one has entered our borders," and "none of our posts have been occupied by anyone." Modi's critics fell about laughing. The Chinese government was quick to welcome his statement, because that's what they were saying, too. But Modi's statement isn't as stupid as it sounds. While army commanders of both countries are discussing withdrawal and the "disengagement" of troops and social media is full of jokes about the art of exiting without entering, and while the Chinese continue to hold territory they claim to be their own, to the vast, uniformed majority of India's population, Modi has won. It was on TV. And who's to say which is more important? TV or territory?

Whichever way you slice it, in the long term, India now requires a battle-ready army on two fronts—the western frontier with Pakistan and the eastern frontier with China. In addition, the government's hubris has alienated its neighbors Nepal and Bangladesh. We have been reduced to boasting that in the event of war, the United States—reeling from its own crises—will come to India's rescue. Really? Like it rescued the Kurds in Syria and Iraq? Like it rescued the Afghans from the Soviets? Or the South Vietnamese from the North Vietnamese?

Last night a Kashmiri friend messaged me: "Will India, Pakistan and China fight over our skies without seeing us?" It's not an unlikely scenario. None of these countries is morally superior or more humane than the other. None of them is in this for the greater good of humanity.

But even without an official war, for India to keep a standing army on the Ladakh border, supplied and equipped for high-altitude warfare, for it to even remotely match China's arsenal, India's defense budget would probably have to double or triple in size. Even that won't be enough. It will come as a huge blow to an economy that was already in steep decline (with unemployment at a forty-five-year high) *before* the Covid-19 lockdown, and is now predicted to shrink between 3.2 and 9.5 percent.[5] Modi is not doing too well in the early rounds of this game of Chinese checkers.

The first week of August comes with some other milestones, too. Despite the ill-planned, draconian, back-breaking lockdown, despite woefully few tests compared to other countries, confirmed cases of coronavirus in India are now growing at perhaps the fastest rate in the world. Among its victims is our saber-rattling home minister, who is spending August 5 in a hospital bed. Not for him the cures being peddled by the quacks, god men, and members of Parliament in his party—drinking cow urine, a magic potion called Coronil, blowing conch shells and banging pots and pans, reciting the Hanuman Chalisa, chanting, "Go, corona, go!" in the flat intonations of a Sanskrit Sloka. Oh, no. For him the most expensive private hospital *and* the best (allopathic) government doctors on call.

And where will India's prime minister be on August 5?

If Kashmir had really been "solved" once and for all, he would be there to be feted by adoring socially distanced crowds. But Kashmir isn't solved. It's shut down again. And Ladakh is almost a battle front. So Modi has wisely decided to retreat from those troubled borders to a very safe place to make good another long-standing election promise. By the time you read this, he will, accompanied by prayers from priests and people across the country, as well as the blessings of India's Supreme Court, have laid a silver slab that weighs 40 kilograms as the foundation for the Ram Mandir, a temple that will rise from the ruins of the Babri Masjid, a mosque that was hammered into the dust by Hindu vigilantes led by members of Modi's Bharatiya Janata Party in 1992. It's been a long journey. Let's call it a Triumph of the Will.

Lockdown or no lockdown, as I write this, I can sense the very air trembling in anticipation of the historic moment. Only the naïve or the hopelessly indoctrinated can still believe that hunger and joblessness will lead to revolution—that temples and monuments cannot feed people. They can. The Ram Mandir is food for millions of starved Hindu souls. The further humiliation of the already humiliated Muslims and other minorities only sharpens the taste of victory on the tongue. How can bread compete?

It would be easy to look at the 365 days between August 5, 2019, and August 5, 2020—the final "integration" of Kashmir into India, the passing of the CAA and NRC, and the inauguration of the Ram Mandir—as the defining period in which India under Modi has formally declared itself a Hindu nation, the dawning of a new era. But declarations can contain unacknowledged defeats. And showy beginnings can contain unforeseen ends. It's worth remembering that despite Modi's larger-than-life presence and the BJP's massive majority in Parliament, only 17.2 percent of India's population voted for them.[6] Perhaps, as the Chinese suggest, in this matter we should proceed with caution. Think a little. Why did Modi decide to inaugurate the Ram Mandir now? After all, it's not Dussehra or Diwali, and the date has no particular relevance in the Ramayana or the Hindu calendar. And there's a partial lockdown in most parts of India—many of the priests and policemen preparing and securing the site have already tested Covid positive. The massive crowds that could turn out at a later date will be missing. So why August 5? Is it to rub salt into Kashmir's wounds, or is it to put balm on India's? Because, whatever they tell us on TV, there's been a tectonic shift on the borders. Big plates are moving. The world order is changing. You can't bully people and act like the top dog in the neighborhood when you're not top dog. That's not a Chinese saying. It's just common sense.

Could it be that August 5, 2020, is not actually what it's being cracked up to be? Could it be instead the little limpet of shame clamped to the soaring cliff of glory?

When and if India, China, and Pakistan fight over Kashmir's skies, the least the rest of us can do is to keep our eyes on its people.

CHAPTER 14

My Post-Lockdown Reverie

What do I most look forward to as we emerge from the lockdown? Most urgently, a carefully drawn-up ledger of accountability.

On March 24, India's prime minister, Narendra Modi, announced the most punitive and least-planned lockdown in the world, giving 1.38 billion people just four hours' notice. After fifty-five days of lockdown, the graph of Covid-positive cases in India is still rising sharply. Fortunately, a great number of patients are asymptomatic, and when compared to the US and Europe, relatively few have needed intensive care. After all the military metaphors, the fear-mongering, hatemongering, and stigmatization around the disease, we have now been informed that, as the lockdown is eased, we will have to learn to live with the virus. In India, we are good at living with illness. So far, according to government figures, about 3,000 people have died of Covid-19 in India. During the same period (starting

* First published as "After the Lockdown, We Need a Reckoning" in *Financial Times*, May 23, 2020.

January 30, 2020) extrapolating from existing data, 150,000 people, most of them poor, would have died from that other infectious respiratory illness, tuberculosis, much of it the drug-resistant variety.

The zero-planning lockdown has meant that in these last fifty-five days India has witnessed a nightmare from which we may never fully recover. Unemployment was at a forty-five-year high before the lockdown. The lockdown is estimated to have cost 135 million jobs.[1] Millions of workers found themselves stranded in cities with no food, shelter, money, or means of transport. The exodus of traumatized people walking hundreds of miles from cities to their villages that began on March 25 is now, all these weeks later, a deluge. Stripped of dignity and hope, these once self-respecting people travel hundreds of miles on foot, on bicycles, or crammed illegally into private trucks like so much cargo. Many have died of hunger and exhaustion or been killed in accidents on their desperate journeys. To escape being brutalized by the police as they walked on the highways, they began to trek on railways tracks. After sixteen people were crushed to death by a goods train,[2] the police started to patrol those routes, too. Now, we see people wading across rivers and streams, their luggage and little children held aloft. They are going home to hunger and unemployment. We see stampedes for food, and tens of thousands swarming bus stops and train stations (where social distancing is a cruel joke), hoping to get on the few trains and buses that the government organized weeks after the reverse migration crisis began. For now, we only have a rough idea of the scale of the horror. We know little of its depth and texture.

In his various addresses to the nation, Modi has only once

mentioned this desolate exodus, even then obliquely, dressing it up in Hindu notions of tapasya and tyaag—penance, self-mortification, and sacrifice.

In the meantime, in the hugely publicized Operation Vande Bharat (Operation Salute India), Indians stranded abroad were flown back home. In order to reassure the socially distanced flying classes about how much is being done to make travel safe in the future, TV reports showcase the elaborate sanitization protocol in airports and planes. In the era of Covid, such attentiveness toward one class and such overt cruelty toward another only makes sense if, in the future, India's flying classes and walking classes are to be sealed off from each other and almost never encounter each other physically. We have lived with caste apartheid for centuries. Religious apartheid is in an advanced stage of preparation. We have a new anti-Muslim citizenship law and a new citizenship register in the works. Those who protested against it, mostly young Muslims, are being arrested under draconian nonbailable laws. Muslim ghettos and massive detention centers are already a reality in India. Now we can welcome class apartheid. The era of touchlessness, in which the very bodies of one class are seen as a biohazard to another. Are we, under cover of Covid-19, going to accelerate toward a digitized, robotized, virtually workerless world? What will become of the surplus working class—the bulk of the world's population—not just in India, but worldwide? Who is going to be held accountable for this apocalypse? Not a virus, I hope.

We need Covid Trials. In an international court. At the very least. That's my post-lockdown reverie.

We Are Witnessing a Crime against Humanity

The Politics of India's Covid Catastrophe

D uring a particularly polarizing election campaign in the state of Uttar Pradesh in 2017, India's prime minister, Narendra Modi, waded into the fray to stir things up even further. From a public podium, he accused the state government—which was led by an opposition party—of pandering to the Muslim community by spending more on Muslim graveyards (*kabristans*) than on Hindu cremation grounds (*shamshans*). With his customary braying sneer, in which every taunt and barb rises to a high note mid sentence before it falls away in a menacing echo, he stirred up the crowd. "If a kabristan is built in a village, a shamshan should also be constructed there," he said.[1]

"Shamshan! Shamshan!" the mesmerized, adoring crowd echoed back.

* First published in the *Guardian*, April 28, 2021.

Perhaps he is happy now that the haunting image of the flames rising from the mass funerals in India's cremation grounds is making the front page of international newspapers. And that all the kabristans and shamshans in his country are working properly, in direct proportion to the populations they cater to, and far beyond their capacities.

"Can India, population 1.3 billion, be isolated?" the *Washington Post* asked rhetorically in a recent editorial about India's unfolding catastrophe and the difficulty of containing new, fast-spreading Covid variants within national borders.[2] "Not easily," it replied. It's unlikely this question was posed in quite the same way when the coronavirus was raging through the UK and Europe just a few months ago. But we in India have little right to take offense, given our prime minister's words at the World Economic Forum in January this year.[3]

Modi spoke at a time when people in Europe and the US were suffering through the peak of the second wave of the pandemic. He had not one word of sympathy to offer, only a long, gloating boast about India's infrastructure and Covid preparedness. I downloaded the speech because I fear that when history is rewritten by the Modi regime, as it soon will be, it might disappear or become hard to find. Here are some priceless snippets:

> Friends, I have brought the message of confidence, positivity and hope from 1.3 billion Indians amid these times of apprehension. . . . It was predicted that India would be the most affected country from corona all over the world. It was said that there would be a tsunami of corona infections in India, somebody said

700 to 800 million Indians would get infected while others said 2 million Indians would die.

Friends, it would not be advisable to judge India's success with that of another country. In a country which is home to 18 percent of the world population, that country has saved humanity from a big disaster by containing corona effectively.

Modi the magician takes a bow for saving humanity by containing the coronavirus effectively. Now that it turns out he has not contained it, can we complain about being viewed as though we are radioactive? That other countries' borders are being closed to us and flights are being canceled? That we're being sealed in with our virus and our prime minister, along with all the sickness, the antiscience, the hatred, and the idiocy that he, his party, and its brand of politics represent?

§

When the first wave of Covid came to India and then subsided last year, the government and its supportive commentariat were triumphant. "India isn't having a picnic," tweeted Shekhar Gupta, the editor in chief of the online news site ThePrint.[4] "But our drains aren't choked with bodies, hospitals aren't out of beds, nor crematoriums & graveyards out of wood or space. Too good to be true? Bring data if you disagree. Unless you think you're god." Leave aside the callous, disrespectful imagery—did we need a god to tell us that most pandemics have a second wave?

This one was predicted, although its virulence has taken even scientists and virologists by surprise. So where is the Covid-specific infrastructure and the "people's movement" against the virus that Modi boasted about in his speech? Hospital beds are unavailable. Doctors and medical staff are at a breaking point. Friends call with stories about wards with no staff and more dead patients than live ones. People are dying in hospital corridors, on roads, and in their homes. Crematoriums in Delhi have run out of firewood. The forest department has had to give special permission for the felling of city trees. Desperate people are using whatever kindling they can find. Parks and car parks are being turned into cremation grounds. It's as if there's an invisible UFO parked in our skies, sucking the air out of our lungs. An air raid of a kind we've never known.

Oxygen is the new currency on India's morbid new stock exchange. Senior politicians, journalists, lawyers—India's elite—are on Twitter pleading for hospital beds and oxygen cylinders. The hidden market for cylinders is booming. Oxygen saturation machines and drugs are hard to come by.

There are markets for other things, too. At the bottom end of the free market, a bribe to sneak a last look at your loved one, bagged and stacked in a hospital mortuary. A surcharge for a priest who agrees to say the final prayers. Online medical consultancies in which desperate families are fleeced by ruthless doctors. At the top end, you might need to sell your land and home and use up every last rupee for treatment at a private hospital. Just the deposit alone, before they even agree to admit you, could set your family back a couple of generations.

None of this conveys the full depth and range of the trauma, the chaos, and, above all, the indignity that people are being subjected to. What happened to my young friend T. is just one of hundreds, perhaps thousands of similar stories in Delhi alone. T., who is in his twenties, lives in his parents' tiny flat in Ghaziabad, on the outskirts of Delhi. All three of them tested positive for Covid. His mother was critically ill. Since it was in the early days, he was lucky enough to find a hospital bed for her. His father, diagnosed with severe bipolar depression, turned violent and began to harm himself. He stopped sleeping. He soiled himself. His psychiatrist was online trying to help, although she also broke down from time to time because her husband had just died from Covid. She said T.'s father needed hospitalization, but since he was Covid positive there was no chance of that. So T. stayed awake, night after night, holding his father down, sponging him, cleaning him up. Each time I spoke to him I felt my own breath falter. Finally, the message came: "Father's dead." He did not die of Covid but of a massive spike in blood pressure induced by a psychiatric meltdown induced by utter helplessness.

What to do with the body? I desperately called everybody I knew. Among those who responded was Anirban Bhattacharya, who works with the well-known social activist Harsh Mander. Bhattacharya is about to stand trial on a charge of sedition for a protest he helped organize on his university campus in 2016. Mander, who has not fully recovered from a savage case of Covid last year, is being threatened with arrest and the closure of the orphanages he runs after he mobilized people against the National Register of Citizens and the Citizenship Amendment Act passed in December 2020, both of which blatantly discriminate against Muslims. Mander and Bhattacharya are among the many citizens who, in the absence of all forms of governance, have set up helplines and emergency responses, and are running themselves ragged organizing ambulances and coordinating funerals and the transport of dead bodies. It's not safe for these volunteers to do what they're doing. In this wave of the pandemic, it's the young who are falling, who are filling the intensive care units.[5] When young people die, the older among us lose a little of our will to live.

T.'s father was cremated. T. and his mother are recovering.

§

Things will settle down eventually. Of course they will. But we don't know who among us will survive to see that day. The rich will breathe easier. The poor will not. For now, among the sick and dying, there is a vestige of democracy. The rich have been felled, too. Hospitals are begging for oxygen. Some have started bring-your-own-oxygen schemes. The oxygen crisis has led to intense, unseemly battles between states, with political parties trying to deflect blame from themselves.

On the night of April 22, 2021, twenty-five critically ill coronavirus patients on high-flow oxygen died in one of Delhi's biggest private hospitals, Sir Ganga Ram. The hospital issued several desperate SOS messages for the replenishment of its oxygen supply. A day later, the chair of the hospital board rushed to clarify matters: "We cannot say that they have died due to lack of oxygen support."[6] On April 24, twenty-five more patients died when oxygen supplies were depleted in another big Delhi hospital, Jaipur Golden.[7] That same day, in the Delhi high court, Tushar Mehta, India's solicitor general, speaking for the government of India, said: "Let's try and not be a crybaby. . . . so far we have ensured that no one in the country was left without oxygen."[8]

Yogi Adityanath, the chief minister of Uttar Pradesh, has declared that there is no shortage of oxygen in any hospital in his state and that rumormongers will be arrested without bail under the National Security Act and have their property seized.[9]

Yogi Adityanath doesn't play around. Siddique Kappan, a Muslim journalist from Kerala, jailed for months in Uttar Pradesh when he and two others traveled there to report on the gang rape and murder of a Dalit girl in Hathras district, is critically ill and has tested positive for Covid. His wife, in a desperate petition to the chief justice of the supreme court of India, says her husband is lying chained "like an animal" to a hospital bed in the Medical College hospital in Mathura. (The supreme court has now ordered the Uttar Pradesh government to move him to a hospital in Delhi.) So if you live in Uttar Pradesh, the message seems to be, please do yourself a favor and die without complaining.

The threat to those who complain is not restricted to Uttar Pradesh. A spokesperson for the fascist Hindu nationalist organization the Rashtriya Swayamsevak Sangh—of which Modi and several of his ministers are members, and which runs its own armed militia[10]—has warned that "anti-India forces" would use the crisis to fuel "negativity" and "mistrust" and asked the media to help foster a "positive atmosphere."[11] Twitter has helped them out by deactivating accounts critical of the government.[12]

Where shall we look for solace? For science? Shall we cling

to numbers? How many dead? How many recovered? How many infected? When will the peak come? On April 27, the report was 323,144 new cases, 2,771 deaths.[13] The precision is somewhat reassuring. Except—how do we know? Tests are hard to come by, even in Delhi. The number of Covid-protocol funerals from grave-yards and crematoriums in small towns and cities suggest a death toll up to thirty times higher than the official count. Doctors who are working outside the metropolitan areas can tell you how it is.

If Delhi is breaking down, what should we imagine is hap-pening in villages in Bihar, in Uttar Pradesh, in Madhya Pradesh? Where tens of millions of workers from the cities, carrying the virus with them, are fleeing home to their families, traumatized by their memory of Modi's national lockdown in 2020. It was the strictest lockdown in the world, announced with only four hours' notice.[14] It left migrant workers stranded in cities with no work, no money to pay their rent, no food, and no transport. Many had to walk hundreds of miles to their homes in far-flung villages. Hundreds died on the way.

This time around, although there is no national lockdown, the workers have left while transport is still available, while trains and buses are still running. They've left because they know that even though they make up the engine of the economy in this huge country, when a crisis comes, in the eyes of this administration, they simply don't exist. This year's exodus has resulted in a different kind of chaos: there are no quarantine centers for them to stay in before they enter their village homes. There's not even the meager pretense of trying to protect the countryside from the city virus.

These are villages where people die of easily treatable diseases like diarrhea and tuberculosis. How are they to cope with Covid? Are Covid tests available to them? Are there hospitals? Is there oxygen? More than that, is there love? Forget love, is there even concern? There isn't. Because there is only a heart-shaped hole filled with cold indifference where India's public heart should be.

§

Early this morning, on April 28, news came that our friend Prabhubhai had died. Before he died, he showed classic Covid symptoms. But his death will not register in the official Covid count because he died at home without a test or treatment. Prabhubhai was a stalwart of the anti-dam movement in the Narmada Valley. I stayed several times at his home in Kevadia, where, decades ago, the first group of indigenous tribespeople was thrown off their lands to make room for the dam-builders and officers' colony. Displaced families like Prabhubhai's still remain on the edges of that colony, impoverished and unsettled, transgressors on land that was once theirs.

There is no hospital in Kevadia. There's only the Statue of Unity, built in the likeness of the freedom fighter and first deputy prime minister of India, Sardar Vallabhbhai Patel, for whom the dam is named. At 182 meters high, it's the tallest statue in the world and cost US $42 million. High-speed elevators inside take tourists up to view the Narmada Dam from the level of Sardar Patel's chest. Of course, you cannot see the river valley civilization that lies destroyed, submerged in the depths of the vast reservoir, or hear the stories of the people who waged one of the most beautiful, profound struggles the world has ever known—not just against that one dam, but against the accepted ideas of what constitutes civilization, happiness, and progress. The statue was Modi's pet project. He inaugurated it in October 2018.

The friend who messaged about Prabhubhai had spent years as an anti-dam activist in the Narmada Valley. She wrote: "My hands shiver as I write this. Covid situation in and around Kevadia Colony grim."

The precise numbers that make up India's Covid graph are like the wall that was built in Ahmedabad to hide the slums Donald Trump would drive past on his way to the "Namaste Trump" event that Modi hosted for him in February 2020.[15] Grim as those numbers are, they give you a picture of the India that matters, but certainly not the India that is. In the India that is, people are expected to vote as Hindus but die as disposables.

"Let's try and not be a crybaby."

Try not to pay attention to the fact that the possibility of a dire shortage of oxygen had been flagged as far back as April 2020, and then again in November by a committee set up by the government itself.[16] Try not to wonder why even Delhi's biggest hospitals don't have their own oxygen-generating plants. Try not to wonder why the PM Cares Fund—the opaque organization that has recently replaced the more public Prime Minister's National Relief Fund,[17] and which uses public money and government infrastructure but functions like a private trust with zero public accountability[18]—has suddenly moved in to address the oxygen crisis. Will Modi own shares in our air supply now?

"Let's try and not be a crybaby.

Understand that there were and are so many far more pressing issues for the Modi government to attend to. Destroying the last vestiges of democracy, persecuting non-Hindu minorities, and consolidating the foundations of the Hindu nation makes for a relentless schedule. There are massive prison complexes, for example, that must be urgently constructed in Assam for the 2 million people who have lived there for generations and have suddenly been stripped of their citizenship.[19] (On this matter, our independent supreme court came down hard on the side of the government and leniently on the side of the vandals.)[20]

There are hundreds of students and activists and young Muslim citizens to be tried and imprisoned as the primary accused in the anti-Muslim pogrom that took place against their own community in North East Delhi last March.[21] If you are Muslim in India, it's a crime to be murdered. Your folks will pay for it. There was the inauguration of the new Ram temple in Ayodhya, which is being built in place of the mosque that was hammered to dust by Hindu vandals watched over by senior BJP politicians. (On this matter, our independent supreme court came down hard on the side of the government and the vandals.)[22] There were the controversial new farm bills to be passed, corporatizing agriculture.[23] There were hundreds of thousands of farmers to be beaten and teargassed when they came out on to the streets to protest.

Then there's the multi-multi-multimillion-dollar plan for a grand new replacement for the fading grandeur of New Delhi's imperial center to be urgently attended to. After all, how can the government of the new Hindu India be housed in old buildings? While Delhi is locked down, ravaged by the pandemic, construction work on the "Central Vista" project, declared as an essential service, has begun.[24] Workers are being transported in. Maybe they can alter the plans to add a crematorium.

There was also the Kumbh Mela to be organized, so that millions of Hindu pilgrims could crowd together in a small town to bathe in the Ganges and spread the virus even-handedly as they returned to their homes across the country, blessed and purified.[25] This Kumbh rocks on, although Modi has gently suggested that it might be an idea for the holy dip to become "symbolic"—whatever that means. (Unlike what happened with those who attended a conference for the Islamic organization Tablighi Jamaat last year, the media has not run a campaign against them calling them "corona jihadis" or accusing them of committing crimes against humanity.)[26] There were also those few thousand Rohingya refugees who had to be urgently deported back to the genocidal regime in Myanmar from where they had fled—in the middle of a coup. (Once again, when our independent supreme court was petitioned on this matter, it concurred with the government's view.)[27]

So, as you can tell, it's been busy, busy, busy.

Over and above all this urgent activity, there is an election to be won in the state of West Bengal. This required our home minister, Modi's man Amit Shah, to more or less abandon his cabinet duties and focus all his attention on Bengal for months, to disseminate his party's murderous propaganda, to pit human against human in every little town and village. Geographically, West Bengal is a small state. The election could have taken place in a single day, and has done so in the past. But since it is new territory for the BJP, the party needed time to move its cadres, many of who are not from Bengal, from constituency to constituency to oversee the voting. The election schedule was divided into eight phases, spread out over a month, the last on April 29. As the count of corona infections ticked up, the other political parties pleaded with the election commission to rethink the election schedule. The commission refused and came down hard on the side of the BJP, and the campaign continued.[28] Who hasn't seen the videos of the BJP's star campaigner, the prime minister himself, triumphant and maskless, speaking to the maskless crowds, thanking people for coming out in unprecedented numbers?[29] That was on April 17, when the official number of daily infections was already rocketing upward of two hundred thousand.

Now, as voting closes, Bengal is poised to become the new corona cauldron, with a new triple mutant strain known as—guess what—the "Bengal strain."[30] Newspapers report that every second person tested in the state capital, Kolkata, is Covid positive.[31] The BJP has declared that if it wins Bengal, it will ensure people get free vaccines. And if it doesn't?

"Let's try and not be a crybaby."

§

Anyway, what about the vaccines? Surely they'll save us? Isn't India a vaccine powerhouse? In fact, the Indian government is entirely dependent on two manufacturers, the Serum Institute of India

(SII) and Bharat Biotech. Both are being allowed to roll out two of the most expensive vaccines in the world to the poorest people in the world.[32] This week they announced that they will sell to private hospitals at a slightly elevated price, and to state governments at a somewhat lower price.[33] Back-of-the-envelope calculations show the vaccine companies are likely to make obscene profits.

Under Modi, India's economy has been hollowed out, and hundreds of millions of people who were already living precarious lives have been pushed into abject poverty. A huge number now depend for survival on paltry earnings from the National Rural Employment Guarantee Act (NREGA), which was instituted in 2005 when the Congress Party was in power. It is impossible to expect that families on the verge of starvation will pay most of a month's income to have themselves vaccinated. In the UK, vaccines are free and a fundamental right. Those trying to get vaccinated out of turn can be prosecuted. In India, the main underlying impetus of the vaccination campaign seems to be corporate profit.

As this epic catastrophe plays out on our Modi-aligned Indian television channels, you'll notice how they all speak in one tutored voice. The "system" has collapsed, they say, again and again. The virus has overwhelmed India's health care "system."

The system has not collapsed. The "system" barely existed. The government—this one, as well as the Congress government that preceded it—deliberately dismantled what little medical infrastructure there was. This is what happens when a pandemic hits a country with an almost nonexistent public health care system. India spends about 1.25 percent of its gross domestic product on health care, far lower than most countries in the world, even the poorest ones. Even that figure is thought to be inflated, because things that are important but do not strictly qualify as health care have been slipped into it. So the real figure is estimated to be more like 0.34 percent.[34] The tragedy is that in this devastatingly poor country, as a 2016 *Lancet* study shows, 78 percent of the health care in urban areas and 71 percent in rural areas is now handled by the private sector.[35] The resources that remain in the public sector are systematically siphoned into the private sector by a nexus of corrupt administrators and medical practitioners, corrupt referrals and insurance rackets.

Health care is a fundamental right. The private sector will not cater to starving, sick, dying people who don't have money. This massive privatization of India's healthcare is a crime.

The system hasn't collapsed. The government has failed. Perhaps "failed" is an inaccurate word, because what we are witnessing is not criminal negligence but an outright crime against humanity. Virologists predict that the number of cases in India will grow exponentially to more than 500,000 a day.[36] They predict the death of many hundreds of thousands in the coming months, perhaps more. My friends and I have agreed to call each other every day just to mark ourselves present, like roll call in our school classrooms. We speak to those we love in tears, and with trepidation, not knowing if we will ever see each other again. We write, we work, not knowing if we will live to finish what we started. Not knowing what horror and humiliation awaits us. The indignity of it all. That is what breaks us.

§

The hashtag #ModiMustResign is trending on social media. Some of the memes and illustrations show Modi with a heap of skulls peeping out from behind the curtain of his beard. Modi the Messiah speaking at a public rally of corpses. Modi and Amit Shah as vultures, scanning the horizon for corpses to harvest votes from. But that is only one part of the story. The other part is that the man with no feelings, the man with empty eyes and a mirthless smile, can, like so many tyrants in the past, arouse passionate feelings in others. His pathology is infectious. And that is what sets him apart. In north India, which is home to his largest voting base, and which, by dint of sheer numbers, tends to decide the political fate of the country, the pain he inflicts seems to turn into a peculiar pleasure.

Frederick Douglass said it right: "The limits of tyrants are prescribed by the endurance of those whom they oppress." How we in India pride ourselves on our capacity to endure. How beautifully we have trained ourselves to meditate, to turn inward, to exorcise our fury as well as justify our inability to be egalitarian. How meekly we embrace our humiliation.

When he made his political debut as Gujarat's new chief minister in 2001, Modi ensured his place in posterity after what has come to be known as the 2002 Gujarat pogrom. Over a period of a few days, Hindu vigilante mobs, watched over and sometimes actively assisted by the Gujarat police, murdered, raped, and burned alive thousands of Muslims as "revenge" for a gruesome arson attack on a train in which more than fifty Hindu pilgrims had been burned alive.[37] Once the violence subsided, Modi, who had until then only been appointed as chief minister by his party, called for early elections. The campaign in which he was portrayed as Hindu Hriday Samrat ("The Emperor of Hindu Hearts") won him a landslide victory. Modi hasn't lost an election since.

Several of the killers in the Gujrat pogrom were subsequently captured on camera by the journalist Ashish Khetan, boasting of how they hacked people to death, slashed pregnant women's stomachs open, and smashed infants' heads against rocks. They said they could only have done what they did because Modi was their chief minister. Those tapes were broadcast on national TV. While Modi remained in the seat of power, Khetan, whose tapes were submitted to the courts and forensically examined, appeared as a witness on several occasions. Over time, some of the killers were arrested and imprisoned, but many were let off. In his recent book, *Undercover: My Journey Into the Darkness of Hindutva*, Khetan describes in detail how, during Modi's tenure as chief minister, the Gujarat police, judges, lawyers, prosecutors, and inquiry committees all colluded to tamper with evidence, intimidate witnesses and transfer judges.

Despite knowing all this, many of India's so-called public intellectuals, the CEOs of its major corporations, and the media houses they own worked hard to pave the way for Modi to become the prime minister. They humiliated and shouted down those of us who persisted in our criticism. "Move on," was their mantra. Even today, they mitigate their harsh words for Modi with praise for his oratory skills and his "hard work." Their denunciation and bullying contempt for politicians in opposition parties are far more strident. They reserve their special scorn for Rahul Gandhi of the Congress Party, the only politician who consistently warned of the coming Covid crisis and repeatedly asked the government to prepare itself as best it could. To assist the ruling party in its campaign to destroy all opposition parties amounts to colluding with the destruction of democracy.

So here we are now, in the hell of their collective making, with every independent institution essential to the functioning of a democracy compromised and hollowed out, and a virus that is out of control.

The crisis-generating machine that we call our government is incapable of leading us out of this disaster. Not least because one man makes all the decisions in this government, and that man is dangerous—and not very bright. This virus is an international problem. To deal with it, decision-making, at least on the control and administration of the pandemic, will need to pass into the hands of some sort of nonpartisan body consisting of members of the ruling party, members of the opposition, and health and public policy experts.

As for Modi, is resigning from your crimes a feasible proposition? Perhaps he could just take a break from them—a break from all his hard work. There's that $564 million Boeing 777, Air India One, customized for VVIP travel—for him, actually—that's been sitting idle on the runway for a while now. He and his men could just leave. The rest of us will do all we can to clean up their mess.

No, India cannot be isolated. We need help.

CHAPTER 16

We Need a Government

We need a government. Desperately. And we don't have one. We are running out of air. We are dying. We don't have systems in place to know what to do with help even when it's on hand.

What can be done? Right here, right now?

We cannot wait till 2024. Never would people like myself have imagined the day would come when we would find ourselves appealing to Prime Minister Narendra Modi for anything. Personally, I would rather have gone to prison than do that. But today, as we die in our homes, on the streets, in hospital car parks, in big cities, in small towns, in villages and forests and fields—I, an ordinary private citizen, am swallowing my pride to join millions of my fellow citizens in saying please, sir, please, step aside. At least for now. I beseech you, step down.

This is a crisis of your making. You cannot solve it. You can only make it worse. This virus prospers in an atmosphere of fear

* First published at Scroll.in, May 4, 2021.

and hatred and ignorance. It prospers when you clamp down on those who speak out. It prospers when you manage the media to such an extent that the real truth is only reported in the international media. It prospers when you are a prime minister who has never held a single press conference in all your years in office, who is incapable of fielding questions, even now in this moment of numbing horror.

Hundreds of thousands of us will die, unnecessarily, if you don't go. So, go now. *Jhola utha ke.* With your dignity intact. You can have a great life ahead, of meditation and solitude. You yourself have said that's what you want. That won't be possible if you allow this mass dying to continue.

There are many in your party who can take your place for now. People who know they must get on even with political opponents in this moment of crisis. Whoever that person is—from your party, with the approval of the Rashtriya Swayamsevak Sangh—can head the government and a crisis management committee.

The state chief ministers can elect a few representatives so that all parties feel represented. The Congress by virtue of being a national party can be on the committee, too. And then scientists, public health experts, doctors, experienced bureaucrats. You may not understand this, but this is what is known as democracy. You cannot have an Opposition-mukt democracy. That is known as a tyranny. This virus loves tyrannies.

If you don't do this now, as this outbreak is increasingly viewed as an international problem, as a threat to the world, which it is—your incompetence is giving other countries a legitimate excuse to try and interfere in our affairs, try and take charge. This will compromise our hard-fought-for sovereignty. We will become a colony again. This is a serious possibility. Do not disregard it.

So please go. It is the most responsible thing for you to do. You have forfeited the moral right to be our prime minister.

ACKNOWLEDGMENTS

For their foresight, their insight, their work, and for long conversations that helped me write these essays, I thank: Aijaz Hussain, Tarun Bhartiya, Parvaiz Bukhari, Mayank Austen Soofi, Abdul Kalam Azad, Ahraful Hussain, Bonojit Hussain, Sanghamitra M. Misra, Harsh Mander, Teesta Setalvad, Prashant Bhushan, Kancha Illiah Shepherd, Alok Rai, Shaj Mohan, Divya Dwivedi, Shohini Ghosh, and Roman Gautam.

David Godwin, who has been there from the beginning.

Simon Prosser, my publisher who makes all things possible.

Lisette Verhagen, without whom my mind would be a ball of wax.

For being my comrade and my intellectual family, Anthony Arnove.

Sanjay Kak, who walks with me.

Notes

INTRODUCTION

1. Anumeha Yadav, "Ground Report: Delhi Police Actions Caused Death of Man in Infamous National Anthem Video," *HuffPost India*, March 1, 2020, updated March 2, 2020, https://www.huffingtonpost.in/entry/delhi-riots-police-national-anthem-video-faizan_in_5e5bb8e1c5b6010221126276.

1. IN WHAT LANGUAGE DOES RAIN FALL OVER TORMENTED CITIES?

1. Devanagari, known earlier as Nagari, which means "belonging to a city"—or, in the case of language, "spoken in a city"—was the script used primarily by Brahmins in the northern and western regions of the Indian subcontinent. It is the script in which Sanskrit, the language of the scriptures traditionally recited by Brahmin priests, is written. That is why it came to be known as Devanagari. Deva means "god" or "divine."

2. Geeta Pandey, "An 'English Goddess' for India's Down-Trodden," BBC News, February 15, 2011, https://www.bbc.com/news/world-south-asia-12355740.

3. The English policy in my mother's school has since been completely reversed. Now, only Malayalam is taught in junior classes.

4. See Arundhati Roy, "Why I Am Returning My Award," *Indian Express*, November 5, 2015, https://indianexpress.com/article/opinion/columns/why-i-am-returning-my-award/.

5. Arundhati Roy, *The God of Small Things* (New York: Random House, 1997), 78.

6. Arundhati Roy, "The End of Imagination," in *My Seditious Heart: Collected Nonfiction* (Chicago: Haymarket Books, 2019), 10, 11.

7. While NGOs and news reports suggest a toll of two thousand persons (see "A Decade of Shame" by Anupama Katakam, *Frontline*, March 9, 2012), then Union Minister of State for Home, Shriprakash Jaiswal (of the Congress Party), told Parliament on May 11, 2005, that 790 Muslims and 254 Hindus were killed in the riots; 2,548 were injured and 223 persons were missing. See "Gujarat Riot Death Toll Revealed," BBC News, May 11, 2005, http://news.bbc .co.uk/1/hi/world/south_asia/4536199.stm.

8. Arundhati Roy, *The Ministry of Utmost Happiness* (New York: Knopf, 2019), 7.

9. Roy, *Ministry of Utmost Happiness*, 8.

10. Roy, *Ministry of Utmost Happiness*, 11, 12.

11. Roy, *Ministry of Utmost Happiness*, 18–19.

12. This assertion was made by Badri Narain Upadhyaya "Premghan" while speaking at the Hindi Sahitya Sammelan in 1912. Alok Rai, *Hindi Nationalism* (Hyderabad: Orient Longman, 2001), 53.

13. Rai, *Hindi Nationalism*, 52.

14. Rai, *Hindi Nationalism*, 57.

15. Atul Chandra, "Language Row in UP Assembly: Sanskrit Allowed, Urdu Not," Catch News, March 30, 2017, http://www.catchnews .com/politics-news/language-row-in-up-assembly-sanskrit-allowed -urdu-not-56230.html.

16. "BSP Corporator Takes Oath in Urdu, Is Charged with 'Intent to Hurt Religious Sentiments,'" *The Hindu*, December 14, 2017, http://www.thehindu.com/news/national/other-states/bsp -corporator-takes-oath-in-urdu-is-charged-with-intent-to-hurt -religious-sentiments/article21665609.ece.

17. Roy, *Ministry of Utmost Happiness*, 47–48.

18. Roy, *Ministry of Utmost Happiness*, 49–50.

19. Jawed Naqvi, "The Lost Precious Pearls of Gujarat," *National Herald*, September 2, 2017, https://www.nationalheraldindia.com/opinion /the-lost-precious-pearls-of-gujarat.

20. See Roy, *Ministry of Utmost Happiness*, 175.

21. Roy, *Ministry of Utmost Happiness*, 67.

22. Roy, *Ministry of Utmost Happiness*, 101.

23. Pablo Neruda, "LXVI," *The Book of Questions*, trans. William O'Daly (Port Townsend, WA: Copper Canyon Press, 1991), 66.

2. ELECTION SEASON IN A DANGEROUS DEMOCRACY

1. Chandan Haygunde, "Elgaar Parishad Probe: Those Held Part of Anti-Fascist Plot to Overthrow Govt, Pune Police Tells Court," *Indian Express*, August 30, 2018, https://indianexpress.com/article /india/elgaar-parishad-probe-those-held-part-of-anti-fascist-plot-to -overthrow-govt-pune-police-tells-court-5331832/.

2. Lokniti-CSDS-ABP News Mood of the Nation Survey, Round 3, www.lokniti.org/otherstudies/lokniti-csds-abp-news-mood-of-the- nation-survey-round-3-18.

3. Michael Safi, "Demonetisation Drive That Cost India 1.5m Jobs Fails to Uncover 'Black Money,'" *The Guardian*, August 30, 2018, https://www.theguardian.com/world/2018/aug/30/india -demonetisation-drive-fails-uncover-black-money.

4. Amit Agnihotri, "Reliance Defence Granted Offset Contract in Rafale Deal without Licence: Congress," *New Indian Express*, July 27, 2018, https://www.newindianexpress.com/nation/2018/jul/27 /reliance-defence-granted-offset-contract-in-rafale-deal-without -licence-congress-1849429.html.

5. "1992: Mob Rips Apart Mosque in Ayodha," BBC "On This Day," http://news.bbc.co.uk/onthisday/hi/dates/stories/december/6

/newsid_3712000/3712777.stm.

6. Zeba Siddiqui, "India Leaves Four Million Off Assam Citizens' List, Triggers Fear," Reuters, July 31, 2018, https://in.reuters.com/article /nrc-assam-national-register-citizens/india-leaves-four-million-off -assam-citizens-list-triggers-fear-idINKBN1KL0CE.

3. OUR CAPTURED, WOUNDED HEARTS

1. Hilal Mir, "In Pulwama Bomber Adil Ahmad Dar's Village, It's Another Day, Another Death," *HuffPost India*, February 18, 2019, https://www.huffingtonpost.in/entry/pulwama-attack-just-another -detail-for-suicide-bomber-adil-dars-village_in _5c699d01e4b033a79943a0da.

2. "Pulwama Blast: At Least 40 CRPF Personnel Killed, Deadliest Attack in 20 Years," *HuffPost India*, February 14, 2019, https:// www.huffingtonpost.in/entry/pulwama-attack-at-least-30-crpf -personnel-dead-pm-modi-calls-attack-despicable_in _5c656f42e4b0bcddd40f3026.

3. "400 People Killed in Kashmir So Far in 2018, Highest in Almost 10 Years," Reuters, December 23, 2018, https://www.huffingtonpost .in/2018/11/23/400-people-killed-in-kashmir-so-far-in-2018-highest -in-almost-10-years_a_23597844/.

4. Aijaz Hussain, "In Life and Death, Fight against India Joins Kashmir Teens," Associated Press, January 16, 2019, https://apnews.com /06975c4b8a25470898cd9c1b6b7050d1.

5. Ankur Pathak, "'Abhinandan,' 'Balakot,' 'Pulwama': Bollywood Producers Fight to Register 'Patriotic' Movie Titles," *HuffPost India*, February 28, 2019, https://www.huffingtonpost.in/entry /abhinandan-balakot-pulwama-bollywood-producers-fight-to -register-patriotic-movie-titles_in_5c778498e4b0952f89de441b.

6. "PM Narendra Modi Can Trace 3 Kg Beef but Not '350 kg' RDX, Says Congress's Haroon Yusuf," *Indian Express*, February 22, 2019,

https://indianexpress.com/article/india/three-kg-beef-can-be-traced
-but-not-350-kg-rdx-haroon-yusuf-asks-5595856/.

7.   Ritu Sarin, "Pulwama Attack: Intelligence Failure . . . We Are at
      Fault Also, Admits Governor," *Indian Express*, February 15, 2019,
      https://indianexpress.com/article/india/kashmir-pulwama-crpf
      -attacks-intelligence-failure-governor-satya-pal-malik-5584865/.

8.   "Days Ahead of Pulwama Blast, Intelligence Warned of Possible IED
      Attacks: Report," *Outlook*, February 15, 2019, https://www
      .outlookindia.com/website/story/india-news-days-ahead-of
      -pulwama-blast-intelligence-warned-of-possible-suicide-attacks
      -report/325491.

9.   See Arundhati Roy, "#Me Too Urban Naxal," *HuffPost India*, August
      30, 2018, https://www.huffingtonpost.in/2018/08/30/arundhati
      -roy-says-me-too-urban-naxal_a_23512718/.

10.   Shubhajit Roy, "India Strikes Terror, Deep in Pakistan: Next Step,
      Diplomatic Outreach," *Indian Express*, February 27, 2019, https://
      indianexpress.com/article/india/iaf-air-strike-pakistan-india-balakot
      -jaish-e-mohammad-mirage-5602259/.

11.   "Villagers Near Balakot Say Indian Warplanes Missed Jaish-Run
      Madrasa by a Kilometre," Reuters, February 26, 2019,
      https://www.huffingtonpost.in/entry/villagers-balakot-india
      -warplanes-missed-jaish-run-madrasa-by-a-kilometre
      _in_5c752946e4b0bf1662033467.

12.   Muneeza Naqvi, "India Says It Has Struck Militants across Kashmir
      Frontier," Associated Press, September 29, 2016, https://apnews
      .com/6355e09f1f364ca7b94d535df29c99a7.

13.   Maria Abi-Habib and Austin Ramzy, "Indian Jets Strike in Pakistan
      in Revenge for Kashmir Attack," *New York Times*, February 25,
      2019, https://www.nytimes.com/2019/02/25/world/asia/india
      -pakistan-kashmir-jets.html.

14.   "Pakistani Jets Violate Indian Air Space, Drop Bombs on Way Out,"

HuffPost India, February 27, 2019, https://www.huffingtonpost
.in/entry/pakistani-jets-violate-indian-air-space-drop-bombs-on
-way-out_in_5c7625ebe4b0031d956348eb; "India Shot Down One
Pakistani Aircraft, One Indian Pilot Missing: MEA," *HuffPost India*,
February 27, 2019, https://www.huffingtonpost.in/entry
/india-shot-down-one-pakistani-aircraft-one-indian-pilot-missing
-mea_in_5c765df4e4b08c4f55559ce4; Maria Abi-Habib and Hari
Kumar, "Pakistani Military Says It Downed Two Indian Warplanes,
Capturing Pilot," *New York Times*, February 27, 2019, https://www
.nytimes.com/2019/02/27/world/asia/kashmir-india-pakistan
-aircraft.html.

4. THE LANGUAGE OF LITERATURE

1. Arundhati Roy, "The Doctor and the Saint," in *My Seditious Heart:
    Collected Nonfiction* (Chicago: Haymarket Books, 2019), 676, note 20.

5. THE SILENCE IS THE LOUDEST SOUND

1. Haseeb A. Drabu, "Modi's Majoritarian March to Kashmir," *New
    York Times*, August 8, 2019, https://www.nytimes.com/2019/08/08
    /opinion/modis-majoritarian-march-to-kashmir.html.

2. Sameer Yasir, Suhasini Raj, and Jeffrey Gettleman, "Inside Kashmir,
    Cut Off from the World: 'A Living Hell' of Anger and Fear," *New
    York Times*, August 10, 2019, https://www.nytimes.com
    /2019/08/10/world/asia/kashmir-india-pakistan.html.

3. See Vindu Goel, "What Is Article 370, and Why Does It Matter in
    Kashmir?," *New York Times*, August 5, 2019, https://www.nytimes.
    com/interactive/2019/world/asia/india-pakistan-crisis.html. See also
    A. G. Noorani, "Murder of Insaniyat, and of India's Solemn Com-
    mitment to Kashmir," *The Wire*, August 13, 2019, https://thewire
    .in/law/murder-of-insaniyat-and-of-indias-solemn-commitment
    -to-kashmir.

4. Drabu, "Modi's Majoritarian March to Kashmir."

5. See Sunil S. Amrith, "The Race to Dam the Himalayas," *New York Times*, December 1, 2018, https://www.nytimes.com/2018/12/01 /opinion/himalayas-mountains-dams.html.

6. See "Kashmir Special Status Explained: What Are Articles 370 and 35A?," Al Jazeera, August 5, 2019, https://www.aljazeera.com /news/2019/08/kashmir-special-status-explained-articles-370-35a -190805054643431.html. See also Venkatesh Nayak, "The Backstory of Article 370: A True Copy of J&K's Instrument of Accession," *The Wire*, October 26, 2016, https://thewire.in/history /public-first-time-jammu-kashmirs-instrument-accession-india.

7. "Haryana Chief Minister's Bizarre 'Joke' on Kashmiri Daughters-In-Law," NDTV, August 10, 2019, https://www.ndtv.com/india-news /haryana-chief-minister-manohar-lal-khattars-bizarre-joke-on -kashmiri-daughters-in-law-2083255.

8. See Mike Thomson, "Hyderabad 1948: India's Hidden Massacre," BBC News, September 24, 2013, https://www.bbc.com/news /magazine-24159594.

9. See Khalid Bashir Ahmad, "Circa 1947: A Long Story," *Kashmir Life*, November 5, 2014, https://kashmirlife.net/circa-1947-a-long -story-67652/.

10. See United Nations Security Council, Resolution 47 [S/726], April 21, 1948, pp. 3–8, https://undocs.org/S/RES/47(1948).

11. See Pankaj Mishra, "Death in Kashmir," *New York Review of Books*, September 21, 2000, https://www.nybooks.com/articles /2000/09/21/death-in-kashmir/.

12. Muzamil Jaleel, "Why Kashmiris Want a Fair Probe into the Killings of Pandits, Prosecution of Guilty," August 8, 2017, https:// indianexpress.com/article/explained/why-kashmiris-want-a-fair-probe-into-the-killings-of-pandits-prosecution-of-guilty-4786855/.

13. See Azad Essa's interview with Mridu Rai, "Kashmir: The Pandit

Question," Al Jazeera, August 1, 2011, https://www.aljazeera.com /indepth/spotlight/kashmirtheforgottenconflict/2011/07 /2011724204546645823.html.

14. See Azad Essa, "Kashmiri Pandits: Why We Never Fled Kashmir," Al Jazeera, August 2, 2011, https://www.aljazeera.com/indepth/spotlight /kashmirtheforgottenconflict/2011/07/201176134818984961.html,

15. Association of Parents of Disappeared Persons and Jammu Kash-mir Coalition of Civil Society, *Torture: Indian State's Instrument of Control in Indian Administered Jammu and Kashmir,* February 2019, http://jkccs.net/wp-content/uploads/2019/05/TORTURE-Indi-an-State%E2%80%99s-Instrument-of-Control-in-Indian-adminis-tered-Jammu-and-Kashmir.pdf. See also Judith Matloff, "Kashmiri Mothers Hunt for Lost Sons," *Christian Science Monitor,* February 1, 2008, https://www.csmonitor.com/World/Asia-South-Central /2008/0201/p07s03-wosc.html.

16. Ellen Barry, "An Epidemic of 'Dead Eyes' in Kashmir as India Uses Pellet Guns on Protesters," *New York Times,* August 28, 2016, https://www.nytimes.com/2016/08/29/world/asia/pellet-guns-used -in-kashmir-protests-cause-dead-eyes-epidemic.html.

17. See chapter 3, "Our Captured, Wounded Hearts," above. See also Basharat Peer, "The Young Suicide Bomber Who Brought India and Pakistan to the Brink of War," *New York Times,* March 2, 2019, https://www.nytimes.com/2019/03/02/opinion/sunday/kashmir -india-pakistan.html.

18. ANI, "Before Abolishing Article 370, Indian Army Identified Pos-sible Trouble Spots in Kashmir," *Economic Times,* August 8, 2019, https://economictimes.indiatimes.com/news/defence/before -abolishing-article-370-indian-army-identified-possible-trouble -spots-in-kashmir/articleshow/70583869.cms.

19. See Alasdair Pal, "India Boosts Hindu Pilgrimage to Holy Cave in Conflict-Torn Kashmir," Reuters, July 28, 2019, https://uk

.reuters.com/article/uk-india-kashmir-pilgrimage/india-boosts
-hindu-pilgrimage-to-holy-cave-in-conflict-torn-kashmir
-idUKKCN1UN04Q.

20. Vishnu Som, "Pak[istan] Army Landmine, Sniper Rifle Found in
Amarnath Yatra Route: Army," NDTV, August 2, 2019, https://
www.ndtv.com/india-news/army-says-confirmed-intel-of-terrorists
-backed-by-pakistan-army-trying-to-disrupt-amarnath-yatra
-2079339.

21. "Leave Kashmir ASAP: J&K Govt Issues Advisory for Amarnath Yatra
Pilgrims and Tourists," *India Today*, August 2, 2019, https://www
.indiatoday.in/india/story/leave-kashmir-j-k-administration-issues
-security-advisory-for-amarnath-pilgrims-1576494-2019-08-02.

22. Shaswati Das, "Mehbooba Mufti, Omar Abdullah Arrested after
Scrapping of Article 370," Mint, August 5, 2019, https://www
.livemint.com/politics/news/mehbooba-mufti-omar-abdullah
-arrested-after-scrapping-of-article-370-1565015217174.html.

23. Muzaffar Raina, "Disarmed Fall Guys of Article 370," *The Telegraph*,
August 10, 2019, https://www.telegraphindia.com/india/disarmed
-fall-guys-of-article-370/cid/1696748.

24. Promit Mukherjee, "India's Modi Trumpets Kashmir, Muslim
Marriage Moves in Independence Day Speech," Reuters, August 15,
2019, https://uk.reuters.com/article/uk-india-independenceday
-modi/indias-modi-trumpets-kashmir-muslim-marriage-moves
-in-independence-day-speech-idUKKCN1V50K4.

25. Indrajit Kundu, "Kashmir Effect: Rebel Groups Ban Independence
Day Celebrations in Northeast," *India Today*, August 14, 2019,
https://www.indiatoday.in/india/story/kashmir-effect
-rebel-groups-ban-independence-day-celebrations-in-northeast
-1580947-2019-08-14.

26. See Charlie Phillips, "The Hour of Lynching: The Killing of Muslim
Cow Farmers in India," *The Guardian*, May 24, 2019, https://www

.theguardian.com/news/2019/may/24/the-hour-of-lynching-the
-killing-of-muslim-cow-farmers-in-india.

27. See Pankaj Mishra, "The Other Face of Fanaticism," *New York Times
Magazine*, February 2, 2003, https://www.nytimes.com/2003
/02/02/magazine/the-other-face-of-fanaticism.html. See also
Dhirendra K. Jha, "How the RSS Became Involved in Running the
Bhonsala Military School," *Caravan*, April 26, 2017, https://
caravanmagazine.in/vantage/the-rss-bhonsala-military-school
-dhirendra-k-jha.

28. See Rollo Romig, "Railing Against India's Right-Wing Nationalism
Was a Calling. It Was Also a Death Sentence," *New York Times Magazine*, March 14, 2019, https://www.nytimes.com/2019/03/14
/magazine/gauri-lankesh-murder-journalist.html.

29. Ram Madhav, "This Election Result Is a Positive Mandate in Favour of
Narendra Modi," *Indian Express*, May 24, 2019, https://indianexpress
.com/article/opinion/columns/lok-sabha-elections-result-narendra
-modi-bjp-government-congress-5745313/.

30. "Rajya Sabha: UAPA Bill Passed despite Opposition Fears," *The
Hindu*, August 2, 2019, https://www.thehindubusinessline.com
/news/uapa-amendment-bill-gets-rajya-sabha-approval
/article28796520.ece.

31. Siddharth Varadarajan, "Allowing the State to Designate Someone as
a 'Terrorist' without Trial Is Dangerous," *The Wire*, August 2, 2019,
https://thewire.in/rights/uapa-bjp-terrorist-amit-shah-nia.

32. See Geeta Pandey, "Jai Shri Ram: The Hindu Chant That Became a
Murder Cry," BBC News, July 10, 2019, https://www.bbc.com
/news/world-asia-india-48882053.

33. See Abhishek Angad, "Tabrez Ansari 18th Mob Violence Victim in
Jharkhand in Three Years," *Indian Express*, July 1, 2019, https://
indianexpress.com/article/india/tabrez-ansari-18th-mob-violence
-victim-in-jharkhand-in-three-years-5808122/.

6. INTIMATIONS OF AN ENDING

1. Ephrat Livni, "Nearly 2 Million People in India Have Just Been Rendered Stateless by a Bureaucratic Act," Quartz India, August 31, 2019, https://qz.com/1699761/indias-national-register-of -citizens-makes-nearly-2-million-stateless/.

2. Annalisa Merelli, "The BJP's Threat to Restrict Indian Citizenship Unmasks the Ugliest Side of Nationalism," Quartz India, April 11, 2019, https://qz.com/india/1591557/bjp-threat-to-restrict-indian -citizenship-targets-muslims/.

3. Rebecca Ratcliffe, "India Set to Withdraw Kashmir's Special Status and Split It in Two," *The Guardian,* August 5, 2019, https://www .theguardian.com/world/2019/aug/05/india-revoke-disputed -kashmir-special-status.

4. See Masha Gessen, "'The Right to Have Rights' and the Plight of the Stateless," *New Yorker,* May 3, 2018, https://www.newyorker.com /news/our-columnists/the-right-to-have-rights-and-the-plight-of -the-stateless.

5. Narendra Modi, "Full Text of Modi's First Speech after Historic Election Victory," *Business Insider,* May 26, 2019, https://www .businessinsider.in/full-text-of-modi-speech-lok-sabha-election -2019/articleshow/69467611.cms.

6. Krishna N. Das, "Hindu Group behind Modi's Rise in India Opens Up as Elections Near," Reuters, September 18, 2018, https://www .reuters.com/article/us-india-election-rss/hindu-group-behind-modis -rise-in-india-opens-up-as-elections-near-idUSKCN1LY1GI.

7. Avinash Dutt Garg, "Muzaffarnagar: Tales of Death and Despair in India's Riot-Hit Town," BBC News, September 25, 2013, https:// www.bbc.com/news/world-asia-india-24172537.

8. Sruthi Gottipati and Annie Banerji, "Modi's 'Puppy' Remark Triggers New Controversy over 2002 Riots," Reuters, July 12, 2013, https://in.reuters.com/article/narendra-modi-puppy-reuters

-interview/modis-puppy-remark-triggers-new-controversy-over
-2002-riots-idINDEE96B08S20130712.

9. Sai Manish, "86% of Currency by Value in India Are of Rs 500 &
Rs 1,000 Denominations," *Business Standard*, November 9, 2016,
https://www.business-standard.com/article/economy-policy/86-of
-currency-by-value-in-india-are-of-rs-500-rs-1-000-denominations
-116110801416_1.html.

10. Asit Ranjan Mishra, "Arvind Subramanian Speaks Up, Says Demonetisation Was a Draconian Move," Mint, November 30, 2018, https://
www.livemint.com/Politics/Zwagzf4FCtXQsAdy0JLWpK/Arvind
-Subramanian-speaks-up-says-demonetisation-was-a-drac.html.

11. Anand Patel, "Cat Finally Out of the Bag: Unemployment at
45-Year High, Government Defends Data," *India Today*, May 31,
2019, https://www.indiatoday.in/business/story/india
-unemployment-rate-6-1-per-cent-45-year-high-nsso-report
-1539580-2019-05-31.

12. Concern Worldwide and Welthungerhilfe, *2019 Global Hunger
Index by Severity*, https://www.globalhungerindex.org/results.html.

13. Archis Mohan, "BJP Richest Political Party with Rs. 10.03 Billion
Income in FY17: ADR," *Business Standard*, April 11, 2018, https://
www.business-standard.com/article/politics/bjp-richest-political-party
-with-rs-10-03-billion-income-in-fy17-adr-118041001008_1.html.

14. Sanjay Singh, "Mohan Bhagwat Meets Diplomats: Signs of 'Secretive' Sangh Shedding Reticence," Firstpost, September 13, 2017,
https://www.firstpost.com/politics/mohan-bhagwat-meets-diplomats
-signs-of-secretive-sangh-shedding-reticence-4039533.html.

15. Sidharth Bhatia, "The Cruel Irony of the German Ambassador's Visit
to the RSS Headquarters," *The Wire*, July 20, 2019, https://thewire
.in/world/german-ambassador-walter-lindner-rss-headquarters.

16. Maria Abi-Habib and Sameer Yasir, "Court Backs Hindus on Ayodhya, Handing Modi Victory in His Bid to Remake India," *New York*

Times, November 8, 2019, https://www.nytimes.com/2019/11/08/world/asia/ayodhya-supreme-court-india.html.

17. Alison Saldanha and Chaitanya Mallapur, "Crime Rate against Dalits Increased by 25% from 2006 to 2016; Cases Pending Investigation Up by 99%," Firstpost, April 9, 2018, https://www.firstpost.com/india/crime-rate-against-dalits-increased-by-25-from-2006-to-2016-cases-pending-investigation-up-by-99-4419369.html.

18. Bilal Kuchay, "Dalit Children Beaten to Death in India for Defecating in Public," Al Jazeera, September 26, 2019, https://www.aljazeera.com/news/2019/09/dalit-children-beaten-death-india-defecating-public-190926110658711.html. See also Annalisa Merelli, "The Problem with the Gates Foundation's Award to Narendra Modi," Quartz India, September 27, 2019, https://qz.com/1714568/why-is-the-gates-foundations-award-to-narendra-modi-controversial/.

19. Samah Hadid, "A Gulf Red Carpet for Modi and Silence for Kashmir," *Asia Times*, August 22, 2019, https://www.asiatimes.com/2019/08/opinion/a-gulf-red-carpet-for-modi-and-silence-for-kashmir/.

20. "Kashmir under Lockdown: All the Latest Updates," Al Jazeera, October 27, 2019, https://www.aljazeera.com/news/2019/08/india-revokes-kashmir-special-status-latest-updates-190806134011673.html.

21. Satyajeet Kumar, "Tabrez Ansari Lynching: New Medical Report Suggests Cardiac Arrest Was Due to Skull Fracture, Other Injuries," *India Today*, September 13, 2019, https://www.indiatoday.in/india/story/tabrez-ansari-lynching-medical-report-cardiac-arrest-skull-fracture-jharkhand-police-1598668-2019-09-13.

22. Rupinder Kaur et al., "Hunted: India's Lynch Files," The Quint Lab. Special interactive report available online at https://www.thequint.com/quintlab/lynching-in-india/.

23. Michael D. Shear, "At Rally for India's Modi, Trump Plays Second

Fiddle but a Familiar Tune," *New York Times*, September 22, 2019, https://www.nytimes.com/2019/09/22/us/politics/trump-modi -houston-rally.html.

24. *A Night at the Garden*, directed by Marshall Curry (Field of Vision, 2019), https://anightatthegarden.com/

25. Kai Schultz, "India's Soundtrack of Hate, with a Pop Sheen," *New York Times*, November 10, 2019, https://www.nytimes.com /2019/11/10/world/asia/india-hindutva-pop-narendra-modi.html. See also Sheikh Saaliq, "India's 'Patriotism Pop' Songs Urge Hindus to Claim Kashmir," Associated Press, August 22, 2019, https:// apnews.com/3df3740cf2204553b66c8b5a0a3d08f5.

26. Scroll staff, "Jammu and Kashmir: 125 Projects Cleared on Forest Land since August, Only 97 Approved Last Year," *Scroll*, October 21, 2019, https://scroll.in/latest/941222/jammu-and-kashmir-125-projects -cleared-on-forest-land-since-august-only-97-approved-last-year.

27. Furquan Ameen, "Normalcy in Kashmir? Government Ad Says It All," *The Telegraph*, October 12, 2019, https://www.telegraphindia .com/india/normalcy-in-kashmir-government-ad-says-it-all/cid /1711019.

28. Suhasini Raj and Jeffrey Gettleman, "Abused by Soldiers and Militants, Kashmiris Face Dangers in Daily Life," *New York Times*, September 15, 2019, https://www.nytimes.com/2019/09/15/world /asia/kashmir-india-militants.html. Aijaz Hussain, "Kashmiris Allege Night Terror by Indian Troops in Crackdown," Associated Press, September 14, 2019, https://apnews.com /52b06a124a5a4469984793d3c208733d.

29. Mudasir Ahmad, "Fearing Arrest, Youth in Srinagar Avoid Hospitals, Treat Pellet Injuries Themselves," *The Wire*, September 2, 2019, https://thewire.in/rights/fearing-arrest-youth-in-srinagar-avoid -hospitals-treat-pellet-injuries-themselves.

30. Niha Masih and Joanna Slater, "Among the 3,000 Detained by

Indian Authorities in Kashmir: Children," *Washington Post*, August 29, 2019, https://www.washingtonpost.com/world/asia_pacific /among-the-3000-detained-by-indian-authorities-in-kashmir-childre n/2019/08/29/1616b5c0-c91c-11e9-9615-8f1a32962e04_story.html.

31. Ananthakrishnan G, "Restrictions Only in the Mind, Not in J&K: Amit Shah," *Indian Express*, September 30, 2019, https:// indianexpress.com/article/india/restrictions-only-in-the-mind-not -in-jk-amit-shah-6039579/; *India Today* Web Desk, "Phone Lines Are Not Important for Kashmiris, Their Lives Are Important: Satya Pal Malik," *India Today*, October 14, 2019, https://www.indiatoday .in/india/story/phones-not-important-for-kashmiris-j-k-governor -satya-pal-malik-1609175-2019-10-14; Press Trust of India, "People Moving Around Freely in J&K: General Rawat," *Economic Times*, September 25, 2019, https://economictimes.indiatimes.com/news /defence/people-moving-around-freely-in-jk-general-rawat /articleshow/71294201.cms?from=mdr.

32. Public Service Broadcasting Trust India, *What the Fields Remember*, directed by Subasri Krishna, YouTube, uploaded March 13, 2016, https://www.youtube.com/watch?v=599LmFwHJwU.

33. Abdul Kalam Azad, "The Struggle of 'Doubtful Voters' Has Intensified in BJP's Assam," *The Wire*, July 12, 2017, https://thewire.in /law/assam-doubtful-voters-sonowal.

34. *Outlook* Web Bureau, "1,000 'Foreigners' Lodged in 6 Detention Centres in Assam, 28 Died in 3 Years: Home Ministry," *Outlook*, November 27, 2019, https://www.outlookindia.com/website/story /india-news-1000-foreigners-lodged-in-6-detention-centres-in -assam-28-died-in-3-years-home-ministry/343142.

35. TNN, "SC Strikes Down IMDT Act as Unconstitutional," *The Economic Times*, July 13, 2005, https://economictimes.indiatimes.com /sc-strikes-down-imdt-act-as-unconstitutional/articleshow/1168803 .cms?from=mdr.

36. Dhananjay Mahapatra, "Don't Drag Your Feet Over Illegal Migrants, SC [Supreme Court] Tells Assam," *Times of India*, April 1, 2015, https://economictimes.indiatimes.com/news/politics-and -nation/Dont-drag-your-feet-over-illegal-migrants-SC-tells-Assam /articleshow/46766776.cms.

37. Ipsita Chakravarty, "In Assam, the Congress [Party] Spars with BJP over Its Chief Ministerial Candidate's Past," *Scroll*, March 29, 2016, https://scroll.in/article/805772/in-assam-the-congress-spars-with -bjp-spar-over-its-chief-ministerial-candidates-past.

38. "Original Petitioner Assam Public Works Unhappy with 'Flawed' NRC, Questions Software Used," News18, August 31, 2019, https://www.news18.com/news/india/original-petitioner-assam -public-works-unhappy-with-flawed-nrc-questions-software -used-2291933.html.

39. *Assam Sanmilita Mahasangha & Ors. v. Union of India & Ors.*, Supreme Court of India, December 17, 2014, http://www.nrcassam .nic.in/pdf/17%20Dec%202014%20Record%20Of%20Proceedings _SUPREME%20COURT.pdf.

40. "India Excludes Nearly 2 Million People from Assam Citizen List," Al Jazeera, August 31, 2019, https://www.aljazeera.com/news/2019 /08/nrc-list-19-million-excluded-india-citizens-list -190831044040215.html.

41. Press Trust of India, "1,000 Foreigners Tribunals to Be Established in Phases, Assam Govt to Set Up 200 Additional FTs by Sep 1," News18, July 12, 2019, https://www.news18.com/news/india /1000-foreigners-tribunals-to-be-established-in-phases-assam-govt -to-set-up-200-additional-fts-by-sep-1-2228343.html.

42. Syeda Ambia Zahan, "Assam NRC: 6 Kill Self in 13 Days as State Prepares Final List; Lack of Recourse Pushes Residents to Edge, Say Activists," Firstpost, July 12, 2019, https://www.firstpost.com/india /assam-nrc-6-kill-self-in-13-days-as-state-prepares-final-list-lack-of

-recourse-pushes-residents-to-edge-say-activists-6984691.html.

43. See Newsclick Team, "I Am 'Miya'—Reclaiming Identity Through Protest Poetry," *Newsclick*, July 1, 2019, https://www.newsclick.in /I-am-miya-reclaiming-identity-protest-poetry-karwan-e-mohabbat.

44. Helen Regan, Swati Gupta, and Omar Khan, "India Passes Controversial Citizenship Bill That Excludes Muslims," CNN, December 17, 2019, https://www.cnn.com/2019/12/11/asia/india-citizenship -amendment-bill-intl-hnk/index.html.

45. Rahul Tripathi, "National Population Register to Include Aadhaar Details," *Economic Times*, August 5, 2019, https://economictimes .indiatimes.com/news/politics-and-nation/national-population -register-to-include-aadhaar-details/articleshow/70528850.cms.

46. M. S. Golwalkar, *We or Our Nationhood Defined* (Nagpur: Baharat Publications, 1939), Hinduism E Books edition, 51–52, 99, 100, 104–05.

47. Golwalkar, *We or Our Nationhood Defined*, 87–88.

7. THE GRAVEYARD TALKS BACK

1. See chapter 6.

2. Roy, *Ministry of Utmost Happiness*, 184, 185.

3. Kritika Sharma Sebastian, "We Want Freedom in India, Not from India: Kanhaiya," *The Hindu*, March 5, 2016, https://www.thehindu .com/news/national/other-states/we-want-freedom-in-india-not -from-india-kanhaiya/article8315890.ece.

4. "Yogi's Revenge: UP Govt Sets up Panel to Seize Property of CAA Protesters," *Clarion India*, December 24, 2019, https://clarionindia .net/yogis-revenge-up-govt-sets-up-panel-to-seize-property-of-caa -protesters/.

5. Liz Mathew and Abhinav Rajput, "Minister Anurag Thakur Chants Desh Ke Gaddaron Ko, Poll Rally Crowd Completes Goli Maaro . . . ," *Indian Express*, January 28, 2020, https://indianexpress

.com/article/india/anurag-thakur-slogan-rithala-rally-6238566/.

6. "Hours after Man Shot at Jamia Students, Amit Shah Asks Delhi Voters, 'With Modi or Shaheen Bagh?'" *Scroll India*, January 31, 2020, https://amp.scroll.in/latest/951665/hours-after-man-shot-at -jamia-students-amit-shah-asks-delhi-voters-with-modi-or-shaheen -bagh.

7. Agence France-Presse, "India Can Now Defeat Pakistan 'In 7–10 Days,' Says Narendra Modi," *Live Mint*, January 29, 2020, https:// www.livemint.com/news/india/india-can-now-defeat-pakistan-in-7 -10-days-says-narendra-modi-11580304232357.html.

8. Kai Schultz, "Indian Children's Book Lists Hitler as Leader 'Who Will Inspire You,'" *New York Times*, March 17, 2018, https://www .nytimes.com/2018/03/17/world/asia/india-hitler-childrens-book .html.

9. Arundhati Roy, *The Doctor and The Saint: Caste, Race, and* Annihilation of Caste*, the Debate Between B. R. Ambedkar and M. K. Gandhi* (Chicago: Haymarket Books, 2018).

10. Dhirendra K. Jha, "The Apostle of Hate," *Caravan*, January 1, 2020, https://caravanmagazine.in/reportage/historical-record-expose-lie -godse-left-rss.

11. M. K. Gandhi, *The Collected Works of Mahatma Gandhi* (Electronic Book) (New Delhi: Government of India, Publications Division, 1999), vol. 1, 192–93.

12. "'Go to Pakistan,' Says India Officer as Leader Praises Crackdown," Al Jazeera, December 28, 2019, https://www.aljazeera.com /news/2019/12/pakistan-india-officer-leader-praises-crackdown -191228080506372.html.

13. Arup Roychoudhury, "India's Top 63 Billionaires Have More Wealth Than 2018–19 Budget Outlay," *Business Standard*, January 21, 2020, https://www.business-standard.com/article/economy-policy/india -s-top-63-billionaires-have-more-wealth-than-2018-19-budget

-outlay-120012100038_1.html.

14. "Mettupalayam Untouchability Wall: The Fall of It and the Rise of Islam," *Dalit Camera*, January 19, 2020, https://www.dalitcamera .com/mettupalayam-untouchability-wall-the-fall-of-it-and-the-rise -of-islam/.

15. Roy, *Ministry of Utmost Happiness*, 90–91.

16. Neethu Joseph, "Police Complaint against Kerala Critic for 'Offensive' Remarks against Arundhati Roy," *The News Minute*, February 2, 2020, https://www.thenewsminute.com/article/police-complaint -against-kerala-critic-offensive-remarks-against-arundhati -roy-117351.

17. "Human Shield: Paresh Rawal Wants Arundhati Roy [to] Be Tied to Army Jeep Instead of Stone Pelter," *Times of India*, May 22, 2017, https://timesofindia.indiatimes.com/india/human-shield-paresh -rawal-wants-arundhati-roy-be-tied-to-army-jeep-instead-of-stone -pelter/articleshow/58785670.cms.

18. Babu Bajrangi, "After Killing Them I Felt Like Maharana Pratap," *Tehelka*, September 1, 2001.

19. A. Vaidyanathan, "14 Gujarat Riots Convicts Get Interim Bail, Supreme Court Orders Social Service," NDTV, January 28, 2020, https://www.ndtv.com/india-news/gujarat-riots-supreme-court -grants-bail-to-14-convicted-in-a-case-orders-them-to-do-social-and -spiri-2170755.

20. Roy, *Ministry of Utmost Happiness*, 65–67.

21. Roy, *Ministry of Utmost Happiness*, 67.

22. Roy, *Ministry of Utmost Happiness*, 88.

23. Roy, *Ministry of Utmost Happiness*, 431–32.

24. Roy, *Ministry of Utmost Happiness*, 349.

25. Roy, *Ministry of Utmost Happiness*, 316–17, 334–35.

26. Arundhati Roy, *The God of Small Things* (New York: Random House, 1997), 208.

27. Roy, *Ministry of Utmost Happiness*, 438–40.

8. THERE IS FIRE IN THE DUCTS, THE SYSTEM IS FAILING

1. Anumeha Yadav, "Ground Report: Delhi Police Actions Caused Death of Man in Infamous National Anthem Video," *HuffPost India*, March 1, 2020, updated March 2, 2020, https://www .huffingtonpost.in/entry/delhi-riots-police-national-anthem -video-faizan_in_5e5bb8e1c5b6010221126276.
2. See chapter 5, "The Silence Is the Loudest Sound."
3. "The Truth: Gujarat 2002: Babu Bajrangi," YouTube, October 25, 2007, https://www.youtube.com/watch?v=mfnTl_Fwvbo.

9. THE PANDEMIC IS A PORTAL

1. National Herald Web Desk, "PM National Relief Fund Has Only 15% Funds as Cash," *National Herald*, March 30, 2020, https://www .nationalheraldindia.com/india/pm-national-relief-fund-has-only -15-funds-as-cash?fbclid=IwAR2ZtB4rzzpU1e6Oqjh4B7KVj_EIt _v8Rc33jIuysJ93E9zsmb7-XMKpK-s.
2. Child malnutrition: Fatima Khan, "Over 8.8 Lakh Deaths—India on Top in UNICEF Report on Under-5 Child Mortality in 2018," *The Print*, October 17, 2019, https://theprint.in/india/8-lakh- deaths-india-unicef-report-child-mortality-2018/306950; Tuber- culosis: Teena Thacker, "India Continues to Record Maximum Number of Tuberculosis (TB) Cases," *Economic Times*, October 17, 2019, https://economictimes.indiatimes.com/news/politics-and -nation/india-continues-to-record-maximum-number-of -tuberculosis-tb-cases-/articleshow/71638359.cms?from=mdr.

12. TWO CONSPIRACIES AND A CREMATION

1. Akshita Jain, "Uttar Pradesh Reported 400 Custodial Deaths Last Year, Highest in India," Huffington Post, September 16, 2020,

https://www.huffpost.com/archive/in/entry/uttar-pradesh-custodi-al-deaths_in_5f61fc06c5b68d1b09ca45ea

2. Times of India, "Northeast Delhi Violence: Have to Confront Umar Khalid with "11 Lakh Pages of Data, Say Cops," September 15, 2020, https://timesofindia.indiatimes.com/city/delhi/northeast-del-hi-violence-have-to-confront-umar-khalid-with-11-lakh-pages-of-data-say-cops/articleshow/78116759.cms

3. Betwa Sharma, "Umar Khalid Case: Delhi Police Months-Long Delay Means Vital Video Evidence Destroyed," Huffington Post, September 29, 2020, https://www.huffingtonpost.in/entry/umar-khalid-case-delhi-police-months-long-delay-means-vital-video-evi-dence-destroyed_in_5f72aeecc5b6117cd1037845

4. Sabrang India, "Bilkees Bano Case: Rejecting Appeals of 11 Accused Bombay High Court Upholds Convictions," NewsClick, May 4, 2017, https://www.newsclick.in/bilkees-bano-case-rejecting-appeals-11-accused-bombay-high-court-upholds-convictions

13. INDIA'S DAY OF SHAME

1. Sarangal Ugalmugle and Clifton Rozario, "*The Constitutional Courts and Kashmir*," in *Disintegration at Gunpoint: Yearly Report 2019-2020* (Kashmir Reading Room: 2020), 53, available at https://jklpp.org/kashmir-reading-room-report-aug-2019-aug-2020/

2. Manoj Joshi, "A Year On, Modi's Kashmir 'Master Stroke' Has Proven to be a Major Flop," The Wire, August 4, 2020, https://thewire.in/politics/narendra-modi-kashmir-master-stroke

3. Ugalmugle and Rozario, 53.

4. Ajai Shukla, "The Government Misleads Media on China, Engage-ment Reports Untrue, Army Spouting Doval's Line," The Interview with Karan Thapar, July 11, 2020, https://www.youtube.com/watch?v=vJuUj54ILos

5. *Economic Times*, "India's GDP Growth to Lose Momentum from

Third Quarter: Oxford Economics," July 8, 2020, https://economictimes.indiatimes.com/news/economy/finance/indias-gdp-growth-to-lose-momentum-from-third-quarter-oxford-economics/articleshow/77221478.cms

6. Ravish Tiwari, Liz Mathew, Krishn Kaushik, Sandeep Singh, "India Election Results 2019: Vote Surge from 17 to 22 Crore Scripts BJP's Historic Victory," Indian Express, May 24, 2019, https://indianexpress.com/elections/lok-sabha-election-results-vote-surge-bjps-historic-victory-pm-modi-amit-shah-5745571/

14. MY POST-LOCKDOWN REVERIE

1. *Economic Times*, "Covid-19 Could Cost 135 Million Jobs, Push 120 Million People into Poverty, " May 17, 2020, https://economictimes.indiatimes.com/news/economy/policy/covid-19-could-cost-135-million-jobs-push-120-million-people-into-poverty-in-india-report/articleshow/75785601.cms.

2. Express News Service, "Aurangabad Train Accident: 16 Migrant Workers Run Over, Probe Ordered," *Indian Express,* May 8, 2020, https://indianexpress.com/article/india/india-lockdown-maharashtra-aurangabad-migrant-workers-killed-train-6399556/.

15. WE ARE WITNESSING A CRIME AGAINST HUMANITY

1. Piyush Srivasatra, "Covid: Dead Having to Queue at 'Smashan' and "Kabristan,'" *Telegraph*, October 22, 2021, https://www.telegraphindia.com/india/covid-narendra-modi-pits-smashan-against-kabristan-in-polarising-elections-speech-in-uttar-pradesh/cid/1813065

2. Editorial Board, "India's Coronavirus Wave Is Not a Far-Away Problem," *Washington Post*, April 23, 2021, https://www.washingtonpost.com/opinions/global-opinions/indias-sudden-coronavirus-wave-is-not-a-far-away-problem/2021/04/23/f363bda2-a3a3-11eb-85fc-06664ff4489d_story.html

3. Government of India, Press Information Bureau, "English Rendering of PM's Address at the World Economic Forum Dialogue," January 28, 2021, https://pib.gov.in/PressReleseDetail.aspx-?PRID=1693019

4. Shekhar Gupta, tweet, April 18, 2020, https://twitter.com/shekhar-gupta/status/1251381206827950081

5. Euan Marshall, Joe Wallen, Anne Gulland, and Jennifer Rigby, "Mystery Shrouds Growth in Covid Cases in Young People," Telegraph, April 25, 2021, https://www.telegraph.co.uk/global-health/science-and-disease/mystery-shrouds-growth-covid-cases-young-people/

6. Astha Saxena, "Delhi Hospitals Seek Oxygen for 4th Day, 25 Covid Patients Die at Ganga Ram," Indian Express, April 24, 2021, https://indianexpress.com/article/cities/delhi/delhi-ganga-ram-hospital-deaths-oxygen-shortage-7285598/

7. Astha Saxena, Jignasa Sinha, "20 Die in Delhi Hospital's Covid Critical Care Unit, Officials Say Dip in Oxygen, Move Court," April 25, 2021, Indian Express, https://indianexpress.com/article/cities/delhi/delhi-jaipur-golden-hospital-covid-patients-oxygen-supply-shortage-7286997/

8. Arvind Gunasekar, "'Let's Try and Not Be a Cry Baby: Centre to Delhi on Oxygen Crisis," NDTV, April 24, 2021, https://www.ndtv.com/india-news/coronavirus-lets-try-and-not-be-a-cry-baby-centre-to-delhi-on-oxygen-crisis-amid-covid-19-2421034

9. Omar Rashid, "Oxygen Shortage / Seize Property of Those Spreading Rumours: Yogi Adityanath," April 25, 2021, The Hindu, https://www.thehindu.com/news/national/other-states/seize-property-of-those-spreading-rumours-up-cm/article34404518.ece

10. Subranth Subramanian, "How Hindu Supremacists Are Tearing India Apart," Guardian, February 20, 2020, https://www.theguardian.com/world/2020/feb/20/hindu-supremacists-nationalism-tearing-india-apart-modi-bjp-rss-jnu-attacks

11. Special Correspondent, "RSS Warns against 'Anti-Bharat' Forces amid Pandemic," The Hindu, April 24, 2021, https://www.thehindu.com/news/national/rss-warns-against-anti-bharat-forces-amid-pandemic/article34401183.ece

12. Kim Lyons, "Twitter Censored Tweets Critical of India's Handling of Pandemic at Its Government's Request," The Verge, April 24, 2021, https://www.theverge.com/2021/4/24/22400976/twitter-re-moved-tweets-critical-india-censor-coronavirus

13. Reuters and Rupam Jain, Shilpa Jamkhandikar, and Sanjeev Miglani, "Vital Medical Supplies Reach India as COVID Deaths near 200,000," Reuters, April 27, 2021, https://www.reuters.com/world/india/india-posts-323144-new-covid-19-cases-2021-04-27/

14. Jeffrey Gettleman and Kai Schultz, "Coronavirus in India: Modi Orders 3-Week Total Lockdown for All 1.3 Billion Indians," New York Times, March 24, 2020, https://www.nytimes.com/2020/03/24/world/asia/india-coronavirus-lockdown.html

15. Hannah Ellis-Petersen, "'Namaste Trump': India Welcomes US President at Modi Rally," Guardian, February 24, 2020, https://www.theguardian.com/world/2020/feb/24/namaste-donald-trump-india-welcomes-us-president-narendra-modi-rally

16. Harikishan Sharma, "April, November Last Year: Official House Panel Flagged Oxygen Need, Shortage,"

17. BBC News, "Coronavirus: Secrecy Surrounds India PM Narendra Modi's $1 bn Covid-19 Fund," June 30, 2020, https://www.bbc.com/news/world-asia-india-53151308

18. Scroll Staff, "PM-CARES 'Controlled by Government," but Doesn't Come Under RTI Act, Says Centre in New Response," Scroll.in, December 25, 2020, https://scroll.in/latest/982310/pm-cares-con-trolled-by-government-but-doesnt-come-under-rti-act-says-centre-in-new-response

19. Krithika Varagur, "'The Clock Is Ticking': Race to Save 2 Million

from Statelessness in Assam," Guardian, November 20, 2019, https://www.theguardian.com/global-development/2019/nov/20/race-to-stop-2-million-becoming-stateless-as-the-clock-starts-ticking-in-assam

20. Mannat Malhi, "How Covid-19 Measures Reinforce the Indefinite Detention of 'Foreigners,'" University of Oxford Faculty of Law, blog, July 3, 2020, https://www.law.ox.ac.uk/research-subject-groups/centre-criminology/centreborder-criminologies/blog/2020/07/how-covid-19-0

21. Kenan Malik, "The Violence in Delhi Is Not a 'Riot.' It is Targeted Anti-Muslim Brutality," *Guardian*, March 1, 2020, https://www.theguardian.com/commentisfree/2020/mar/01/violence-in-delhi-is-not-a-riot-it-is-targeted-anti-muslim-brutality

22. Hannah Ellis-Petersen, "India's BJP Leaders Acquitted over Babri Mosque Demolition," *Guardian*, September 30, 2020, https://www.theguardian.com/world/2020/sep/30/india-bjp-leaders-acquitted-babri-mosque-demolition-case

23. BBC News, "Bharat Bandh: India Farmers Strike to Press for Repeal of Laws," BBC.com, September 27, 2020, https://www.bbc.com/news/world-asia-india-54233080

24. Vijayata Lalwani, "As Covid-19 Devastates Delhi, Central Vista Project Declared an Essential Service, Work Continues," Scroll.in, April 27, 2021, https://scroll.in/article/993385/as-covid-19-devastates-delhi-central-vista-project-declared-an-essential-service-work-continues

25. Vineet Khare, "India's Kumbh Festival Attracts Big Crowds amid Devastating Second Covid Wave," BBC.com, April 17, 2021, https://www.bbc.com/news/world-asia-india-56770460

26. BBC News, Tablighi Jamaat: The Group Blamed for New Covid-19 Outbreak in India," BBC.com, April 2, 2020, https://www.bbc.com/news/world-asia-india-52131338

27. Chander Uday Singh, "Supreme Court Must Rethink Its Order for Deportation of Rohingya Refugees," Indian Express, April 26, 2021, https://indianexpress.com/article/opinion/columns/rohingya-refu-gees-crisis-india-supreme-court-7288913/

28. ET Bureau, "Madras High Court Blames EC for Covid Spread, Says Officials Ought to be Booked for Murder," *Economic Times*, April 26, 2021, https://economictimes.indiatimes.com/news/politics-and-nation/election-commission-responsible-for-covid-19-surge-madras-high-court/articleshow/82256082.cms

29. India Today, "PM Modi In Asansol Rally Says 'Your Votes To BJP Will End 'Mafia Raaj' In West Bengal,'" April 17, 2021, https://www.youtube.com/watch?v=Nf9qcgCAJtI

30. India Today Web Desk, "What Is the New 'Triple Mutant Vari-ant' of Covid-19 Virus Found in Bengal? How Bad Is It?" India Today, April 22, 2021, https://www.indiatoday.in/science/story/what-is-triple-mutant-variant-of-covid19-virus-bengal-strain-de-tails-1793991-2021-04-22

31. Sumati Yengkhom, "Every Second Person Getting Tested in Kolkata Is Positive," *Times of India*, April 25, 2021, https://timesofindia.indi-atimes.com/city/kolkata/every-second-person-getting-tested-in-kolk-ata-is-positive/articleshow/82236519.cms

32. Achal Prabhala and Leena Menghaney, "The World's Poorest Coun-tries Are at India's Mercy for Vaccines. It's Unsustainable," *Guardian*, April 2, 2021, https://www.theguardian.com/commentisfree/2021/apr/02/india-in-charge-of-developing-world-covid-vaccine-supply-unsustainable

33. Harshit Sabarwal, "Centre Tells Serum Institute, Bharat Biotech to Lower Their Covid Vaccine Prices," *Hindustan Times*, April 26, 2021, https://www.hindustantimes.com/india-news/centre-tells-serum-institute-bharat-biotech-to-lower-their-covid-vaccine-prices-101619444078473.html

34. Dipa Sinha, "Explained: Despite Govt Claims, India's Health Budget Only Around 0.34% of GDP," The Wire, January 2, 2021, https://science.thewire.in/health/union-health-budget-nirmala-sitha-raman-covid-19-pmasby-allocation-gdp-expert-analysis/

35. Maureen McIntosh, Amos Channnon, Anup Karan, Sakthivel Selvarag, Eleonora Cavagnero, and Hongwen Zhao, "What Is the Private Sector? Understanding Private Provision in the Health Systems of Low-Income and Middle-Income Countries," Lancet, June 26, 2016, https://doi.org/10.1016/S0140-6736(16)00342-1

36. John Snow, interview with Shahid Jameel, "500,000 to 900,000 Covid Cases a Day in India—Virologist Shahid Jameel," Channel4.com, April 26, 2021, https://www.channel4.com/news/500000-to-900000-covid-cases-a-day-in-india-virologist-shahid-jameel

37. Pankaj Mishra, "The Gujarat Massacre: New India's Blood Rite," Guardian, March 15, 2021, https://www.theguardian.com/commentisfree/2012/mar/14/new-india-gujarat-massacre

Index

9/11 attacks, 23, 102

1857 War of Independence, 18, 33

1989 Scheduled Caste and Scheduled Tribe (Prevention of Atrocities) Act, 52

Abdullah, Farooq, 91

Abdullah, Omar, 91

Adani, Gautam, 197

Adani Group, 197

Adityanath, Yogi, 143–44, 159, 178, 216–17, 245, 285

Adivasis, 24

  BJP and, 54

  education and, 52

  media and, 197

  NRC and, 178

  Singh on, 68

  UP ordinance and, 202

Advani, L. K., 218

Afghanistan, 26, 72, 88, 231

  CAA and, 130, 149

  US war on, 66, 211–12

Africa, 69

Agence France-Presse, 114

Ahmedabad, 248

Ahomiya Hindus, 118

Ahomiya Muslims, 118

Aksai Chin, 228

Aligarh, 216

Aligarh Muslim University, 140

Al Jazeera, 114

All Assam Students' Union, 123

All India Institute of Medical Sciences, 190

Amarnath Yatra, 26, 90–91

Amazon, 184

Ambani, Mukesh, 84, 197

Ambedkar, B. R., 11, 147, 153, 155, 203, 206, 218

Amnesty International, 225

Anandamath (Chattopadhyay), 42

Annihilation of Caste (Ambedkar), 11

Ansari, Tabrez, 96, 110

Arabic language, 12, 14, 33, 36

Arcelor Mittal, 197

Arendt, Hannah, 99, 178

Armed Forces Special Powers Act, 26

Article 370, 83, 199, 268–69, 270–71

Arunachal Pradesh, 129

Aryans, 148, 154, 158, 205

Assam, 15–16, 51, 86, 98, 117–23, 125–30, 178, 249

Assam Accord, 122
Assamese language, 118
Assam Public Works, 123
assimilation, 9, 86
Associated Press, 58, 62, 114
Aurangzeb, 167
Australia, 69
Awadhi, 37
Axomiya, 16
Ayemenem, 16, 20, 75
Ayodhya, 51, 106, 109, 154, 200,
    218, 249
Azad, Chandrashekhar, 52
Azadi, 1–2, 43
    BJP and, 143
    Kashmir and, 110, 140–42
    The Ministry and, 26, 141–42

Babri Masjid mosque, 51, 106,
    133, 218–22, 233
Baganiya, 16
Bahujan Samaj Party, 107
Bai, Rasoolan, 40
Bajirao II, King, 193
Bajrang Dal, 200
Bajrangi, Babu, 160, 177
Balakot, Pakistan, 57
Baldwin, James, 79–80
Bangalore, 156
Bangladesh, 12, 105, 109, 120,
    123, 131, 231
    CAA and, 130, 149, 179

Bano, Bilkis, 223
Bareilly, 187
Baroda, 40
Bastar, 28, 54, 55
Bayer, 133
BBC, 114
Bengali language, 12, 42, 118–21
Berger, John, 71
Bhagwat, Mohan, 101, 111
Bharadwaj, Sudha, 52, 55
Bharat Biotech, 251–52
Bharatiya Janata Party, 77, 102,
    105–7, 159, 233234
    2014 elections and, 103
    2019 elections and, 3, 48–49,
        61, 62, 74, 94, 223
    Adivasis and, 54
    Assam and, 123
    Ayodhya and, 51, 106, 249
    Azadi and, 143
    coronavirus and, 185
    Dalits and, 54, 107, 217
    Delhi pogrom and, 177
    demonetization policy and, 49
    Gujarat massacre and, 23
    Kashmir and, 60, 113, 117
    in Madhya Pradesh, 184
    Muslims and, 54, 60, 201, 217,
        222
    richest party in the world, 198
    RSS and, 100–101, 108–9, 139
    The Ministry and, 157

in Uttar Pradesh, 143
in West Bengal, 131, 144, 251
Bhattacharya, Anirban, 243244
Bhide, Sambhaji, 53
Bhima Koregaon battle, 52, 193, 196
Bhima Koregaon Sixteen, 193, 226
Bhim Army, 52, 155
Bhojpuri, 37
Bhotmange, Surekha, 217
Bible, 16, 111, 188
Bihar, 85, 107, 177, 246
Bi, Kauser, 53
Birla Group, 197
Birla, K. M., 197
Bisht, Ajay Singh.
    See Yogi Adityanath
Black Africans, 147–48, 205
Bodos, 118
Bolivia, 210
Bollywood, 4, 59, 93, 156, 157,
    208, 219
Bolsonaro, Jair, 184
Booker Prize, 76
Border Security Force, 60
Brahmaputra, 119, 124
Brahminism, 73, 146, 196, 201
Brahmins, 11, 35, 52, 73, 102,
    146, 196–98, 215
Braj Bhasha, 37
Brazil, 66
Britain, 97
British Airways, 44

British Army, 193
British Empire, 8–10, 33–34, 53,
    59, 83–86, 117–19, 148, 207
British Residency, 17
Buddhists, 129, 130
Burnham, Julia, 212

Cachar, 118
caste, 183, 185, 189, 196–98, 207–8
    Ambedkar on, 11
    anti-caste struggle, 155, 179
    Bhima Koregaon and, 193
    courts and, 194
    Gandhi on, 73–74
    The God of Small Things and, 151
    Hindu nationalism and, 107–8,
        146–48, 150, 198–205
    language and, 34–36
    sexual violence and, 215–17
    UP ordinance and, 202
Catalonia, 97, 104
Central Reserve Police Force, 60
Chattopadhyay, Bankim Chandra, 42
Chhattisgarh, 55
Chile, 97, 104
China, 120, 183, 191, 200, 228,
    230–32, 234
Chin, Aksai, 230
Chinese People's Liberation Army,
    230
Christianity, 34, 146
Christians, 15–17, 63, 136

CAA and, 130, 132
Hindu nationalism and, 73, 148
Travancore Christian Succession
      Act, 76
UP ordinance and, 201–4
Citizenship Amendment Act,
      130–32, 139–40, 149, 233
   Christians and, 130, 132
   Dalits and, 131, 155
   Domicile Law and, 229–30
   Muslims and, 155, 178, 199,
      220, 237, 243
   protests and, 4, 155, 178, 183,
      199–200, 206, 220, 243
climate change, 69, 99, 113, 152,
      210
Colleen, Christopher, 212
Communist Party, 43
Communist Party of India
      (Maoist), 28, 67
Communist Party of India
      (Marxist), 75
Congress Party, 50, 54, 105, 122,
      147, 184, 256, 258
   Modi and, 198
   NREGA and, 252
coronavirus, 1, 3, 180, 181–91
   borders and, 2, 240
   economy and, 196–97, 232
   fascism and, 3
   India's second wave of, 241–56
   in Europe, 235, 240

in the United States, 182–83,
      188, 190, 211, 235, 240
   Kashmir and, 229
   lockdown and, 5, 185–88, 200,
      221, 232, 235–37, 246
   Modi and, 235–37, 240–41,
      246, 257–59
Curry, Marshall, 112

Dabholkar, Narendra, 72
Daesh (ISIS), 67
Dainik Bhaskar, 198
Dainik Jagran, 198
Dakhani, Wali, 39–40, 161
Dalit Camera: Through
      Un-Touchable Eyes, 153
Dalit Panthers, 194
Dalits, 127, 132, 146, 195
   2019 elections an, 63
   activism of, 53
   Ambedkar and, 147
   Bhima–Koregaon victory and,
      52–53, 193
   BJP and, 54, 107–8, 217
   CAA and, 131, 155
   education and, 52
   English language and, 11
   Indian state and, 9
   Islam and, 153
   lynchings and, 20, 72, 107, 152
   media and, 197
   Modi and, 153

NRC and, 178
sexual violence against, 215–16, 245
The Ministry and, 152, 154
UP ordinance and, 202–4
Danish language, 15
Dar, Adil Ahmad, 57–58, 90
Deccan Plateau, 32, 33
Delhi, 4–5 10, 53, 85, 96, 137, 180, 216
2020 massacre in, 219, 222, 224–25, 249
All India Institute of Medical Sciences, 190
author's arrival in, 18
BJP in, 144
Bolsonaro in, 184
coronavirus in, 188, 242–46, 248, 250
elections in, 66, 223
independence celebration in, 83
Jama Masjid, 155, 167
Jamia Millia Islamia University, 140, 176
Khari Boli and, 33
pogroms in, 137, 175–77, 184, 199–200, 219, 249
Red Fort in, 93
Shaheen Bagh, 140
student activism in, 222–23
The Ministry and, 29, 44
Delhi Assembly, 184

Delhi High Court, 221
Delhi University, 19
Devanagari script, 10, 35–36
Dhaka, 120
Dhawale, Sudhir, 53
Disturbed Areas Act, 27
The Doctor and the Saint, 73, 145
Domicile Law, 229–30
Doordarshan, 20
Douglass, Frederick, 254
Dravidians, 204
Dussehra, 154

East Bengal, 119, 120
East India Company, 33
East Pakistan, 12, 120, 122
Ekbote, Milind, 53
Elgar Parishad, 52–54, 193–194, 201, 205
Eliot, T. S., 135–136
"The End of Imagination," 22–23, 77–78
English language, 7–11, 13–22, 43, 45, 125
The Ministry and, 26–30
Europe, 10, 34
coronavirus in, 190, 235, 240
fascism in, 73, 100–1, 111, 158
racism in, 73

Faruqui, Munawer, 201
fascism, 47, 67, 72, 95, 112, 146,

150–51, 158–59, 194
European, 73, 94, 100–101, 158
mob violence of, 137, 175–76
RSS and, 73, 94, 100–101, 144,
    245
feminism, 141, 179, 211. *See
    also* women's activism
Ferreira, Arun, 52
fiction, 1, 29, 70–72, 75, 79, 137–
    38, 145, 150-51, 158, 167
First Anglo-Burmese War, 118
Foreigners Tribunals, 122, 127,
    130, 132
Forest Advisory Committee, 113
France, 50, 97, 133, 135, 189

Gadling, Surendra, 53, 55
Galwan Valley, 230, 231
Gandhi (Attenborough), 147
Gandhi, Indira, 120–22
Gandhi, Mohandas, 5, 73–74, 145,
    147–48, 205
Gandhi, Rahul, 256
Ganges River, 250
Gates Foundation, 107
Geneva Convention, 64
Germany, 100–1, 106, 132–33, 139
Ghar Wapsi, 204
Ghazipur, 188
Gilgit-Baltistan, 228
Goalpara, 125
The God of Small Things, 13, 68

Ammu, 76–77, 151
    Booker Prize and, 76
    caste and, 151
    Comrade K. N. M. Pillai, 76
    criminal charges and, 76–77
    critique of the Left in, 76, 151
    Esthappen, 170
    Hindu nationalism and, 21–22
    Kalyani, 76
    Kolkata reading from, 7
    The Ministry and, 28, 79, 81
    setting of, 16, 20–21, 75
    Velutha, 76–77, 151
Godhra, 23
Gogoi, Justice Ranjan, 123, 128
Golwalkar, M. S., 131–32
Gonsalves, Vernon, 52
Goods and Services Tax, 104
Gorakhpur, 187, 188
Guardian, 49, 114
Gujarat, 95, 102, 164
    2002 massacre in, 23, 38–41,
        43, 103, 159–61, 177, 223,
        254–55
    Trump in, 184
Gunder, Valencia, 210, 212
Gupta, Shekhar, 241

Haider, Meran, 199
Haiti, 210
Hajela, Prateek, 128
Harlem, 66

Haryana, 24, 85, 130, 152, 223
Hathras, 215, 218, 226, 245
Hindi language, 10, 16, 18–19, 23, 37, 45, 112
    Hindus and, 2, 36–38
    The Ministry and, 14, 25, 28, 33, 37
Hindi Nationalism (Rai), 35
the *Hindu*, 198
Hinduism, 34, 73, 101, 147, 152, 153, 154, 155, 204, 237
Hindu nationalism, 145, 155, 234. *See also* Gujarat; RSS
    2019 election and, 3
    Assam and, 128, 249
    assassinations and, 72, 156
    capitalism and, 103–4, 151
    caste and, 146, 150, 198, 204
    Delhi pogroms and, 184
    demonetization and, 104
    fascism and, 144, 148–50, 151–52, 158
    Golwalkar on, 132
    Kashmir and, 62, 88, 113, 143
    language and, 2, 12, 21, 100
    Pakistan and, 101, 136, 149
    RSS and, 73, 94, 100–101, 139, 245
    slogans of, 41–42, 101, 136, 162–63, 177, 178
    terror networks of, 50–51
Hindus, 136, 218

2002 Gujarat massacre and, 23, 103, 223, 254
2020 Delhi massacre and, 4–5, 137, 184, 224–25
in Afghanistan, 179
Ahomiya, 118
Anandamath and, 42
Aryan identity and, 148, 158
in Assam, 118, 120, 121, 126, 128, 130
in Ayodhya, 106
in Bangladesh, 149, 179
CAA and, 130, 133
cremation grounds of, 239–40
Delhi pogroms and, 176, 184
Diwali celebrations of, 215
Hindi and, 2, 36
in Jammu and Kashmir, 87
in Kashmir, 88
Kumbh Mela and, 51
The Ministry and, 28, 30, 32, 152–55
NRC and, 178
in Pakistan, 149, 179
police violence and, 143
in Tripura, 129
UP ordinance and, 202–4
Urdu and, 33, 35
vigilante violence and, 60, 72, 94, 102, 106, 110–11, 152–54, 224, 233, 249
Hindustan Aeronautics Limited, 50

Hindustani language, 2, 40
Hindustan Times, 198
Hitler, Adolph, 73, 145
Hollywood, 19
Hong Kong, 97, 104
House Un-American Activities
    Committee, 65
Houston, 112, 117, 133
Hussein, Saddam, 25, 152
Hyderabad, 70, 86
Hyderabad House, 4

IG Farben, 133
Illegal Migrants (Determination by
    Tribunal) Act, 122–23
Imam, Sharjeel, 199
Independence, 30, 83, 93
Indian Air Force, 62
Indian Army, 59, 60, 63
    Kashmir and, 86–87, 157
    The Ministry and, 27
    RSS and, 102
Indian Constitution, 10, 20, 83,
    84, 93, 99, 108, 140, 199,
    221, 227
Indian Express, 47, 61, 198
Indian Meteorological Department,
    228
Indian Parliament, 5, 83–84, 86,
    95, 109, 112, 130, 139, 144,
    157, 183, 232, 234
Indian Supreme Court, 24, 61, 76,
    106, 123–24, 160, 229, 233,
    245
India Today, 198
Indigenous people, 204. *See
    also* Adivasis
    in Assam, 126
    displacement of, 24, 118
    diversity of, 100
    eastern and central India, 16
    Hinduism and, 34
    The Ministry and, 154, 155
    protests by, 97
    Singh on, 68
    in Tripura, 129
Instrument of Accession, 83–84,
    86–87, 108
Intelligence Bureau, 60
International Committee of the
    Red Cross, 64
In Which Annie Gives It Those Ones,
    19
Iran, 43, 67, 140
Iraq, 25, 66, 80–81, 97, 152, 228,
    231
Islam, 146, 152–53, 165, 167
    caste and, 34
    Dalits and, 153
    Hussain and, 25
    Kashmir and, 88
    Pakistan and, 12, 22
Islamic Republic of Pakistan, 12
Islamophobia, 201, 208

Israel, 85, 110, 133
Italy, 100

Jacques, Joseph, 212
Jafarabad, 177
Jafrabad, 221
Jahan, Ishrat, 53
Jaish-e-Mohammad, 58, 61
Jama Masjid, 167
Jamia Millia Islamia University, 140, 176
Jammu and Kashmir, 59–60, 87, 108, 114, 129, 227
    Article 370 and, 199–200
    assimilation and, 86
    siege of, 3, 83–84, 92, 99, 180
Jammu and Kashmir Police, 60–61, 91
Jammu and Kashmir Reorganization Act, 2019, 84, 112
Jammu city, 89
Jammu massacre, 87
Jawaharlal Nehru University, 51
Jews, 73, 100, 132, 167
Jharkhand, 110
Jindal, Savitri Devi, 197
Jones, Jamal, 210, 212

Kabul, 26
Kaithi, 35
Kalburgi, M. M., 72
Kali, 9

Kalita, Devangana, 199
Kappan, Siddique, 245
Karnataka, 50, 130
Kashmir, 9, 96–97, 199, 208. *See also* Domicile Law; Jammu and Kashmir; Pakistan Occupied Kashmir
    2019 election and, 3
    azadi and, 110, 140–42
    BJP and, 60, 117
    coronavirus and, 229
    ecology of, 84, 113
    fiction and, 79–80, 167
    Hindu nationalism and, 62, 88–89, 113, 143
    Hindus in, 88
    Indian Army in, 86–87, 157
    Indian migrant labor in, 91
    international law and, 64
    militarization of, 60, 89, 138
    The Ministry and, 26–27, 79, 137–38, 141–42, 151, 167–72
    misogyny and, 85
    Modi and, 57, 59, 62–63, 90–93, 228, 233–34
    Muslims in, 88–89
    nuclear war and, 57, 228
    Pakistan and, 57–58, 59, 64, 86–88, 92, 116, 234
    Pakistan Occupied, 228, 230
    protests in, 43, 141

siege of, 83–87, 91–94, 98–99, 108–9, 113–16, 139, 180, 227–34
silencing of, 85, 112–14, 138, 141, 228
State Subject Certificates and, 229
Kashmiri language, 26, 43
Kashmiri Pandit Sangharsh Samiti, 88–89
Kashmir Valley, 58, 87, 88, 108, 143, 169
Kathakali, 17
Kayasthas, 35
Kerala, 15, 16, 43
    The God of Small Things and, 21, 75–76, 151
Kevadia, 247–248
Khairlanji, 217
Khalid, Umar, 51, 199, 221
Khan, Imran, 64
Khan, Syed Ahmed, 36
Khan, Ustad Faiyaz, 40
Khari Boli, 33
Khattar, Manohar Lal, 85
Khetan, Ashish, 255
Kingdom of Jammu and Kashmir, 228
King, Martin Luther, Jr., 213
Kipling, Rudyard, 17
Kolkata, 7, 9, 15, 251
Kolse-Patil, Justice, 52, 53
Kottayam, 17

Krishen, Pradip, 19
Kumar, Kanhaiya, 142
Kurds, 231

Ladakh, 84, 129, 200, 227, 230, 232–33
Lalung, 118
Landless (film), 206
Lankesh, Gauri, 50, 72, 156
Laprea, Alejandra, 212
Latin, 15, 17, 26
Latin America, 8, 69
Lawrence, Sir Henry, 17–18
Lebanon, 97, 104
Lebensraum, 111
Libya, 66
London, 8, 129
Lord Ram, 96, 106, 109–10, 154–55
Loya, Justice Brijgopal Harkishan, 95, 177
Lucknow, 18, 187

MacDonnell, Sir Anthony, 36
Maddoke, Randeep, 206
Madhav, Ram, 94
Madhya Pradesh, 184, 203, 246
Madras, 74
Maharashtra, 47, 53, 147
Mahars, 193
Maithili, 37
Malayalam, 15, 17–18, 20–21, 23, 43

Malik, Satya Pal, 114
Mallya, Vijay, 49
Mander, Harsh, 243
Manipur, 86, 129
Maoists, 54, 71, 110
Marathi, 23
Marenbon, Dr. John, 136
Marx, Karl, 196
Meenachal River, 75
Meghalaya, 129, 178
Meghalaya Residents Safety and
    Security Act, 129
Mehta, Tushar, 244
Mexico, 72
Miller, Arthur, 65
The Ministry of Utmost Happiness
    2002 Gujarat massacre and,
        38–41, 161, 162
    Amrik Singh, 27, 170–72
    Anjum, 24, 28–30, 38, 41, 43, 45,
        81, 137, 152–53, 161–67
    Dr. Azad Bhartiya, 25, 28, 165
    Azadi and, 26, 141–42
    BJP and, 157
    Dalits and, 152, 154
    Dasgupta, Biplap. *See* Garson
        Hobart
    D.D. Gupta, 80
    Garson Hobart, 26, 40, 80,
        141–42, 170–73
    Gayatri Mantra and, 43–45
    God of Small Things and, 28, 79,
        81
    Hazrat Sarmad, 167
    Hindus and, 28, 30, 32, 154–55
    Indigenous people, 154–55
    Jahanara Begum, 30–31
    Kashmir and, 79, 137–38,
        141–42, 151, 167–72
    language and, 29–33, 37–38
    Language Map of, 29
    Lankesh and, 156
    Maryam Ipe, 27
    Miss Jebeen, 168, 170
    Mulaqat Ali, 30–33, 38
    Musa Yeswi, 26–27, 167–71
    Muslims and, 152, 154
    Nagaraj Hariharan, 27
    Pakistan and, 151
    Revathy, 28, 166
    Saddam Hussain, 24–25, 44–45,
        152–53, 164–66
    Tilotamma, 26–27
    translation and, 13–15, 29
    Ustad Kulsoom Bi, 161, 163
    Zainab, 24, 43–44, 161
    Zakir Mian, 38, 41, 43, 161–62
Ministry of Defense, 63
Mishing, 118
Mishra, Kapil, 177–78
Mittal, Lakshmi, 197
Miya language, 119, 128
Mizoram, 86
Modi, Narendra, 249
    2019 elections and, 3, 48,
        62–63, 66

Adityanath and, 143, 159
ascent of, 102–3
assassination charges and, 53, 72
cabinet of, 144
China and, 231–232
Congress Party and, 198
coronavirus and, 5, 185–89, 221, 235–37, 240–41, 246, 257
Dalits and, 153
Delhi pogroms and, 176
demonetization policy of, 48–49, 63, 103–4
"Father of the Nation" title and, 5
on graveyards, 159, 239
in Gujarat, 23, 103, 159–61, 164, 223, 254–55
"Howdy, Modi," 112, 117
Kashmir and, 57, 59, 62–63, 90–93, 228, 233–34
Kashmiris in India and, 61
lynchings and, 111
"Make in India" and, 49–50
masks of, 4
#ModiMustResign, 254
NRC and, 129–30
Pakistan and, 57, 61–62, 65, 90, 144
protests and, 143–44
RSS and, 94, 102–3, 105, 139, 145, 258
Sardar Sarovar Dam and, 97, 248
on secularism, 100

Trump and, 3–5, 112, 133, 248
Yogi Adityanath and, 216
Modi, Nirav, 49
Morrison, Toni, 136
Mother Teresa, 203
Mufti, Mehbooba, 91
Mughal Empire, 33, 167
Mumbai, 49, 53
Munda, Birsa, 155
Muralidhar, S., 177
Muslims, 96, 127, 142, 148–49, 195, 233
    2002 Gujarat massacre and, 23, 103, 159–60, 177, 223, 254
    2019 elections and, 63
    2020 Delhi massacre and, 219–20, 222, 224–25, 249
    Ahomiya, 118
    Anandamath and, 42
    in Assam, 118–23, 126, 128
    in Ayodhya, 106
    BJP and, 54, 60, 201, 217, 222
    CAA and, 4, 130–32, 140, 149, 155, 178, 183, 199, 220, 229, 237, 243
    coronavirus and, 185, 188–89
    Delhi pogroms and, 4–5, 137, 175–77, 184, 188
    Devangarai and, 35–36
    disenfranchisement of, 109–10
    Gandhi and, 147
    graveyards of, 29, 81, 136–37,

160, 219, 239–40
Indian state and, 9
in Jammu and Kashmir, 87
in Kashmir, 88–89
in Ladakh, 129
lynchings and, 20, 52, 60, 72,
    94, 137, 160
Mazaffarnagar massacre and, 103
media and, 197
The Ministry and, 28–30, 32,
    152, 154
in Naroda Patiya, 160
NRC and, 178, 199, 229, 237,
    243
Phule on, 203
police violence and, 143
protests and, 143, 199, 221
RSS and, 73, 100–1, 109,
    131–32, 139
segregation and, 137
UAPA and, 221
UP ordinance and, 201–4
Urdu and, 2, 33, 37–38
Mussolini, Benito, 73, 94, 145
Muzaffarnagar, 103
Myanmar, 250
My Seditious Heart, 79

Nagaland, 86, 129
Nagari Pracharini Sabhas, 35
Nagpur, 53, 106
Nariman, Justice Rohinton Fali, 123

Narmada River, 98, 112
Narmada Valley, 247–48
Naroda Patiya, 160, 177
Narwal, Natasha, 199
Natal Legislative Assembly, 148
National Anthem, 176, 200, 224
National Awards, 20
National Conference, 91
National Crime Records Bureau,
    107, 111
National Intelligence Agency, 60
National Population Register, 130,
    178, 220
National Register of Citizens, 51,
    98–99, 109, 117–18, 121–33,
    178, 233
    Domicile Law and, 229–30
    Muslims and, 237, 243
    protests against, 199, 220, 243
National Relief Fund, 188
National Rural Employment Guar-
    antee Act, 252
National Security Act, 245
NATO, 68, 212
Navlakha, Gautam, 52, 55
Naxalites, 54, 194, 220
Nazis, 101, 112, 230
Nehru, Jawaharlal, 87
Nellie massacre, 121–122
Nepal, 105, 188, 231
Neruda, Pablo, 45
New Delhi, 25, 62, 88, 89, 179, 249

Jammu and Kashmir and, 84, 92
New York, 66, 112, 114, 182
New York Times, 62, 114
North India, 33, 60, 62
North-Western Frontier Province, 87
North-Western Provinces, 36
nuclear weapons, 22, 57, 60, 63,
        64, 67, 77–78, 151, 228
Nuremberg Laws, 132, 139, 230

Old Delhi, 24, 30, 32, 81, 154,
        161, 167
Ootacamund, 16
"Operation Green Hunt", 69
Operation Vande Bharat, 237
O. P. Jindal Group, 197
Orissa, 19

Pakistan, 62, 105, 231–32
    CAA and, 130, 149
    East Bengal and, 120–22
    Hindu nationalism and, 101,
        136, 149
    Hindus in, 149
    Kashmir and, 57–59, 64, 86–88,
        92, 116, 228, 230, 234
    The Ministry and, 28, 151
    Modi and, 57, 61–62, 65, 90, 144
    nuclear tests and, 22, 77
    Partition and, 86, 149, 187
    RSS and, 101, 109

United States and, 120
Pakistan Army, 91, 120, 122
Palestine, 210
Pandits, 88–89
Pansare, Govind, 72
Partition, 32, 85–87, 120, 149, 187
Patel, Keshubhai, 23
Patel, Sardar Vallabhbhai, 247
PEN America, 65, 72
People's Democratic Party, 91
People's Tribunal and Congress,
        207–14
People's Union for Civil Liberties, 55
Persian language, 12, 30–31, 33,
        35–40, 43
Peshwa regime, 53, 193, 196
Phule, Jotiba and Savitribai, 147,
        155, 203, 206
PM Cares Fund, 248
Poona Pac, 206
Poonch, 87
Portugual, 8
Prasad, Chandra Bhan, 11
Prime Minister's National Relief
        Fund, 248
Prosser, Simon, 1
Public Safety Act, 139
Pulwama, 57–61
Pune, 47, 52–53, 110
Punjab, 18, 177, 223
Punjabi language, 23, 25, 28

The Quint, 111

Raees, Abdul, 153
Rai, Alok, 35
Ram Mandir, 200, 233, 234
Ramos DeBarros, Brittany, 211–12
Rao, Varavara, 52
Rashtriya Janata Dal, 107
Rashtriya Swayamsevak Sangh, 12,
    73–74, 94, 108–9, 145
  Assam and, 122
  BJP and, 139
  on coronavirus, 245
  Delhi pogrom and, 177
  Gandhi and, 147
  Ghar Wapsi and, 204
  Gujarat massacre and, 23
  on lynching, 111
  Modi and, 94, 102, 102–3, 105,
      145, 258
  Muslims ands, 100–1, 109, 131,
      132, 139
  NRC and, 131
  nuclear tests and, 77
  Pakistan and, 101, 109
Raut, Mahesh, 53
Ravan, 154–55
Ravidas, Sant, 147, 155
Rawat, Bipin, 114
Reliance Defence Limited, 50
Reliance Industries, 84, 197
Reporters Without Borders, 72

Republic Day, 183
Research and Analysis Wing, 60
Reserve Bank of India, 49
Reuters, 62, 103
Right to Information Act, 72
River Indus, 12
Robinson, Doria, 212
Rohingya refugees, 250
Roy, Mary, 15–17, 76

Saibaba, 55
Saifi, Khalid, 199
Salwa Judum, 54
Samajwadi Party, 107
Sanatan Sanstha, 50
Sanders, Bernie, 183
Sangh Parivar, 102, 148
Sanskrit, 12, 35–36, 43, 44–46
Sardar Sarovar Dam, 98, 112,
    247–48
Saudi Arabia, 133
Sawant, Justice, 52–53
Schalk, Dr. Sami, 211–12
Sen, Dr. Binayak, 54–55
Sen, Shoma, 53
Serum Institute of India, 251–52
Shah, Amit, 95, 114, 130, 144,
    178, 228, 250, 254
Shaheen Bagh, 140, 144, 199, 223
Shahjahanabad, 155
Shakespeare, William, 17, 29, 45,
    135, 165

Sharif, Lara, 212

Sheikh, Sohrabuddin, 53

Shillong, 15–16, 178

Shiva, 90

Siemens, 133

Sikhism, 146

Sikhs, 27–28, 34, 130, 204, 206

Singh, Bant, 206

Singh, Hari, 86–87

Singh, Manmohan, 68

Sinhala language, 12

Sonowal, Sarbananda, 123

Sontag, Susan, 12

South Africa, 119, 147–48, 205

South India, 16

South Vietnam, 88

Spain, 8

Sri Lanka, 12

Srinagar, 141, 180

Statue of Unity, 247

Su Han, 210, 212

Sultana, Rehna, 128–29

Syria, 66, 72, 231

Tablighi Jamaat, 189, 250

Taliban, 60, 66, 212

Tamil language, 12, 17

Tamil Nadu, 16–17, 153

Tanous, Osama, 212

Tehelka magazine, 160

Thakur, Anurag, 178

ThePrint, 241

Third Reich, 132, 139

Tibet, 85

TIME magazine, 223

Times of India, 198

translation, 12–13, 23–25, 28, 45,
    70

Travancore Christian Succession
    Act, 76

Trump, Donald, 3–5, 85, 112, 184,
    211, 220, 222, 248

Turkey, 66

Undercover (Khetan), 255

United Kingdom
    coronavirus in, 240, 252

United Nations, 180
    Framework Convention on
        Climate Change, 69
    Security Council, 69, 225

United Progressive Alliance, 50, 54

United States, 3–4, 52, 65–68, 102,
    111, 117, 133, 208–213, 231
    Afghanistan and, 66, 211–12
    Congress of, 112
    coronavirus in, 182–83, 188,
        190, 211, 235, 240
    January 6, 2020, Capitol attack
        in, 195
    The Ministry and, 26, 171
    Pakistan and, 120
    racism in, 73, 209–211
    South Vietnam and, 88

Taliban and, 60, 66
war on Iraq, 228
Unlawful Activities Prevention Act, 53, 95, 220–21
UP Prohibition of Unlawful Conversion of Religion Ordinance 2020, 201–3
Urdu, 2, 23
  Anjum and, 24
  Azadi in, 43
  Devangarai and, 35–38
  The Ministry and, 14, 25, 28, 30–33, 38–39
  Muslims and, 37–38
  Pakistan and, 12, 38
  partitioning of, 33
  poetry and, 32, 38–40
  slogans in, 43
Uri, Jammu and Kashmir, 59
Uttar Pradesh, 33, 38, 130, 178, 188, 215–16, 226, 245
  BJP in, 105, 107, 143–44, 159
  massacre in, 103
  Modi in, 239

Vaishyas, 197, 198
Vajpayee, Atal Bihari, 77
Varthaman, Abhinandan, 62, 64
Vasquez, John, 209, 212
Vemula, Rohit, 193, 205
Verma, Parvesh, 178

Vietnam, 231
Vishwa Hindu Parishad, 106, 200, 204

War on Terror, 211, 212
Washington Post, 114, 240
Welsh language, 16
We or Our Nationhood Defined (Golwalkar), 131
West Bengal, 131, 144, 250–251
What the Fields Remember (film), 122
Wilson, Rona, 53, 55
women's activism, 4, 43, 102, 140, 144, 178, 199, 221, 223
World Economic Forum, 240
World Health Organization, 185

Yemen, 72

Zafar, Bahadur Shah, 34

About Haymarket Books

Haymarket Books is a radical, independent, nonprofit book publisher based in Chicago. Our mission is to publish books that contribute to struggles for social and economic justice. We strive to make our books a vibrant and organic part of social movements and the education and development of a critical, engaged, international left.

We take inspiration and courage from our namesakes, the Haymarket martyrs, who gave their lives fighting for a better world. Their 1886 struggle for the eight-hour day—which gave us May Day, the international workers' holiday—reminds workers around the world that ordinary people can organize and struggle for their own liberation. These struggles continue today across the globe—struggles against oppression, exploitation, poverty, and war.

Since our founding in 2001, Haymarket Books has published more than five hundred titles. Radically independent, we seek to drive a wedge into the risk-averse world of corporate book publishing. Our authors include Noam Chomsky, Arundhati Roy, Rebecca Solnit, Angela Y. Davis, Howard Zinn, Amy Goodman, Wallace Shawn, Mike Davis, Winona LaDuke, Ilan Pappé, Richard Wolff, Dave Zirin, Keeanga-Yamahtta Taylor, Nick Turse, Dahr Jamail, David Barsamian, Elizabeth Laird, Amira Hass, Mark Steel, Avi Lewis, Naomi Klein, and Neil Davidson. We are also the trade publishers of the acclaimed Historical Materialism Book Series and of Dispatch Books.

Also Available from Haymarket Books

BY ARUNDHATI ROY

The Doctor and the Saint: Caste, Race, and Annihilation of Caste, the Debate Between B.R. Ambedkar and M.K. Gandhi

The End of Imagination

Field Notes on Democracy: Listening to Grasshoppers

Capitalism: A Ghost Story

My Seditious Heart: Collected Nonfiction

Things That Can and Cannot Be Said: Essays and Conversations with John Cusack

AND

Freedom Is a Constant Struggle
Ferguson, Palestine, and the Foundations of a Movement
Angela Y. Davis, edited by Frank Barat, preface by Cornel West

Until My Freedom Has Come: The New Intifada in Kashmir
Sanjay Kak

About the Author

Mayank Austen Soofi

Arundhati Roy is the author of *The God of Small Things*, which won the Booker Prize in 1997, and *The Ministry of Utmost Happiness*, which was longlisted for the Man Booker Prize in 2017. Both novels have been translated into more than forty languages. *My Seditious Heart* collects her nonfiction work written over twenty years. She lives in Delhi.